武大国际法讲演集

第一卷

主　编　曾令良　肖永平
副主编　左海聪　黄志雄

WUHAN UNIVERSITY PRESS
武汉大学出版社

图书在版编目(CIP)数据

武大国际法讲演集．第一卷/曾令良，肖永平主编；左海聪，黄志雄副主编．—武汉：武汉大学出版社，2006.3
ISBN 7-307-04831-0

Ⅰ.武…　Ⅱ.①曾…　②肖…　③左…　④黄…　Ⅲ.国际法—演讲—文集　Ⅳ.D99-53

中国版本图书馆 CIP 数据核字(2005)第 134796 号

责任编辑：钱　静　　　责任校对：黄添生　　　版式设计：支　笛

出版发行：**武汉大学出版社**　(430072　武昌　珞珈山)
(电子邮件：wdp4@whu.edu.cn　网址：www.wdp.whu.edu.cn)
印刷：武汉中远印务有限公司
开本：787×980　1/16　　印张：11.25　　字数：206 千字
版次：2006 年 3 月第 1 版　　　2006 年 3 月第 1 次印刷
ISBN 7-307-04831-0/D·655　　　定价：20.00 元

卷首语

21 世纪仍然是一个以和平和发展为主要潮流的时代，各种多边、区域和双边协定和机制仍然是国际合作的主要法律形式。随着全球化趋势的日益加深和加快，和平发展中的中国，必将在国际政治、经济和法律秩序中发挥越来越重要的作用；中国在推进依法治国和构建和谐社会的过程中也必须重视国际法的地位与影响。

为了推动国际法的发展，提升中国国际法学的水平，传播中国国际法学界的研究成果和理论主张，教育部人文社会科学重点研究基地武汉大学国际法研究所决定启动“武汉大学国际法讲演项目”。该项目同时也是武汉大学国家“211 工程”第二期建设项目“当代国际法与法制现代化”的组成部分。根据这一项目，我们计划每年邀请一些国内外著名的国际法学家及国际公法、国际私法和国际经济法领域的知名中青年学者来武汉大学国际法研究所，就重大的国际法理论与实践的前沿问题发表讲演；讲演稿，经讲演者整理或修改后，将结集出版，定名为《武大国际法讲演集》。

一年多来，我们先后特邀了二十多位国内外的国际法专家来到珞珈山作专题讲演，从中选择了七位讲演者的讲稿编辑为《武大国际法讲演集》的第一卷。这七篇讲稿的选题都是近几年国际法理论与实践的前沿或热点问题，每位作者以其独特的视角和研究方法，就其讲演的主题发表了自己的见解，以飨读者。

2003 年的伊拉克战争，给国际法律秩序带来了巨大的冲击。为此，武汉大学国际法研究所的梁西先生特别作了题为《国际法的危机》的讲演。该文选取当今世界的经济全球化、国际无政府状态、伊拉克战争、联合国困境等几个同国际法律秩序密切相关的问题加以深邃剖析后，进而指出：人类社会在进入 21 世纪后，一方面，随着国家间互赖性的增强，“人类共同利益与价值”日益突出，从而加深了国际社会的凝聚力；另一方面，由于国际无政府状态的加剧，国际社会仍然动荡不安，从战争废墟上建立起来的联合国已无力制止战争，国际秩序处于风雨飘摇之中。文章针对改进和加强似已危机四伏的国际法律秩序和联合国的现有机制提出了若干独到见解，特别是针对美国的“先发制人”战略，提出了有关“国家自卫权制度”的“三驾马车”理论，将《联合国宪章》第2、39、51条等条款联系起来进行系统解释，具有重要的理论与现实意义。

美国政府于2002年9月发布了新的《国家安全战略》，其中贯穿的“先发制人”战略思想被后来一些美国政治家和国际法学者阐释为“先发自卫”、“提早自卫”或“预防自卫”学说，以此作为美英发动对伊战争的国际法理论依据。波士顿大学的Daniel G. Partan教授在其演讲和论文中深刻揭示了美国的新《国家安全战略》对国际法产生的影响。他首先直接指出了该文件的出台给国际法上的自卫概念所带来的表述上的混乱，接着从习惯法和条约法的双重角度阐释了国际法上自卫规则的形成和发展，然后剖析了《国家安全战略》的实质就是采用“先发制人”的行动以对付美国所认定的“无赖国家”和恐怖主义者。作者注意到，《国家安全战略》的预防打击理论没有提及联合国、安理会和《联合国宪章》在采取行动维持国际和平与安全中的作用。作者认为，美国新国家战略给国际法上自卫权的行使产生了直接的影响，一个国家可以运用三种不同的理论来行使武力自卫权：（1）《联合国宪章》第51条意义上的自卫权，即对实际或继续的武力攻击的武力自卫；（2）习惯国际法确认的自卫权，即运用“提早”或“先发”武力应对一种被证明为迫在眉睫的武力攻击威胁；（3）新国家安全战略宣称的自卫权，即运用“预防”武力打击一种被意识到会潜在使用大规模杀伤性武器的未来攻击的威胁。作者一针见血地指出，美国新国家安全战略表达的这种自卫权给国际社会带来的一个核心问题是，到底什么样的国际法规范最适合世界和平与安全利益？

国际法院对国际法的发展发挥着独特而重要的作用，这一点已经为人们所普遍承认。长期担任国际法院首席法律秘书的英国学者Hugh Thirlway教授，在其讲演《国际法院对国际法发展的贡献》中并没有停留在对这一命题本身的阐释，而是对“法律的发展”的内涵以及依赖国际法院来发展国际法是否合适进行了深入探究。作者首先区分了三种不同形式的“法律的发展”：通过对法律的解释或扩大适用来弥补法律的空白；在现有法律规则适用于特定案件中会导致非正义的结果时，根据公平原则对有关规则加以限制或修改；在法律因技术和社会的发展而与社会脱节时，可能需要对其作出“政治导向的发展”。基于对有关案例的分析，作者认为法院在通过扩大适用带来国际法的发展方面发挥了有益的作用，同时又十分明智地避免了后两种方式对国际法加以“发展”，因为这会危及法院的信誉。文章还对国际法院与联合国国际法委员会在国际法的发展方面开展合作进行了评析。

中国与东盟之间的战略伙伴关系迅猛发展，举世瞩目。然而，从国际法的角度对中国—东盟关系进行的理论研究则显得相对滞后。武汉大学国际法研究所曾令良教授的这篇演讲稿对中国—东盟关系的国际法层面进行了颇为系统的考量。首先，作者从国际法的角度巡视中国—东盟关系业已形成的框架，梳理出中国与东盟从对话伙伴关系发展到战略伙伴关系的法律轨迹。接着，作者通过研读中国—东盟关系中的一系列法律文件，得出两项基本认识：（1）这些文件明示地确立《联合国宪章》、《东南亚友好合作条约》所规定的原则、和平共处五项原则和其他公认的国际法基本原则在中国—东盟关系中的支配地位；（2）旨在以建立自由贸易区为核心的中国—东盟经贸合作关系的法律文件与 WTO 的原则、规则、规章和制度保持着高度的一致性。作者同时指出中国—东盟关系在法律层面上存在着发展不平衡、硬性规范偏少、可操作性的制度不多等缺陷，并得出结论：中国—东盟关系的法治水平整体上处于初级阶段。作者提出建议，双方应在现行法律框架下，建立一个稳定的、系统的和操作性强的法律机制，使中国—东盟战略伙伴关系朝着全面法治的方向发展。

随着经济全球化和中国对外开放的不断发展，特别是中国加入 WTO 以后，国际条约在我国法律体系中的作用越来越强。近些年来，中国法学界对国际条约在我国的适用问题进行了很多探讨，对我国的理论、立法和司法实践产生了有益的影响。但多数学者对国际条约的适用只是进行笼统的研究，没有根据不同条约的性质和特点分析它们不同的适用规则。武汉大学国际法研究所肖永平教授在题为《国际私法条约规则在我国的适用》的讲演中，首次提出区分国际公法条约、国际私法条约和 WTO 协议，主张对这三类条约在国内的适用采取不同的规则。以此为基础，他进一步归纳和总结了国际私法中国际统一实体法条约、国际统一程序法条约、国际统一冲突法条约以及 WTO 协议在我国适用的规则，并评析了我国现有立法的不足和缺陷，对我国国际私法立法中如何规定国际私法条约的适用规则提出了具体的立法建议。

在现代科学的发展过程中，学科交叉是一个必然要求和普遍现象，因为对一个学科基本规律和基本秩序的认识，往往需要借助其他学科的理论解说和研究方法。厦门大学国际经济法研究所徐崇利教授在《国际关系理论与国际经济法律秩序的构建》的讲演中利用国际关系理论的知识和研究方法解释国际经济法律秩序。他认为，在“无政府状态”下的国际社会，国际经济法律制度的创制和变迁不易，其实施（维持）效果可能也不及国内法；但是，国际经济关系的法制化进程蕴涵着自身的规律。

武汉大学国际法研究所左海聪教授的讲演，首先分析国际商法的产生，进而从宏观的角度检视国际商法在 20 世纪的发展，最后探讨国际商法在 21 世纪的发展趋势和我国的相应对策。左教授认为，国际商法，作为一个独立的法律部门，产生于19世纪末和20世纪初，其标志为1919年国际商会的成立；国际商法在20世纪获得了巨大的发展，已经初步形成了体系。左教授对国际商法在21世纪的发展作了全面展望，总结出七大趋势。左教授建议，我国政府和企业进一步重视和加强对国际商事立法活动的参与，积极加入国际公约和采纳国际惯例；我国法学界尽快确认国际商法的独立学科地位，实现与国际学术界的接轨。

需要指出的是，我们对于外国学者的讲稿没有翻译成中文，而是保留原作的语言文字，以便读者能够鉴赏作者原有的讲演风格，犹如身临其境。我们衷心希望这个讲演集项目对广大的国际法律共同体成员有所裨益。我们也热情欢迎国内外的国际法学者和国际法律工作者积极参与这个项目，亲临珞珈山作讲演，并为讲演集提供您的佳作。我们也热忱地期待国际法学界同仁不断地引荐国内外、境内外的演讲者。我们坚信，在国际法学界新朋老友一如既往的支持下，《武大国际法讲演集》这一项目一定会越办越好！

编　者

2005年10月

目　录

作者简介

梁 西

梁西，别名梁宋云，1924 年生，湖南安化人。1953～1982 年执教于北京大学法律系。从 1983 年起执教于武汉大学，任国际法教授，1986 年经国务院学位委员会评选批准为博士生导师。曾先后兼任中国国际法学会理事、顾问，中国海事仲裁委员会委员，国家邮电部法律顾问，湖北省人大常务委员会法律顾问等职。

主要著作有《国际法》修订第 2 版（2000）、《现代国际组织》（1984）、《国际组织法》修订第 5 版（2001）等。主要译著有《联合国与裁军》（1972）、《希思外交报告：旧世界新前景》（1973）、《吉米·卡特》（1978）等。主要代表性论文有《论国际法的发展》（1990）、《论现代国际法中的集体安全制度》（1988）、《国际困境：联合国安理会的改革问题》（2005）、《论国际社会组织化及其对国际法的影响》（1997）、《联合国：奔向 21 世纪》（1995）等。主要译文有《非洲国家与国际法的渊源》（1980）、《从国际司法角度看联合国的各项原则》（1979）等。其《国际组织法》（专著）和《国际法》（主编）两书，均以繁体字在中国台湾（志一出版社）出版，具有学术影响。

国际法的危机*

梁 西

目 次:

同学们:

在五十多年前，我上大学的时候，曾经听过周鲠生校长和胡适先生一次有趣的讨论式讲演。主题大意好像是：历史的发展，是“圆圈式”的还是“螺旋式”的？进入21世纪之后，在伊拉克战争发生时，我又听到不少学法律的学生在问：国际法律秩序将如何发展？关于国际法的发展方向问题，不是一两个小时能够说得清楚的。它涉及社会生活和国际关系的方方面面，今天，只能选择几个同国际法律秩序相关的问题来讲一讲，请大家指正。

一、经济全球化与国际社会的无政府状态

最近二三十年来，人类社会进步特别快，科技、经济、文教卫生等各方面，都在以物理学上的“加速度”向前发展，日新月异！这些发展与变化，为人类社会创造了巨额的财富和无比的活力，使人们欢欣不已！

冷战结束后，大家热切地期盼着：一个远比过去和平与安全的世界和一个远比过去公正平等的国际法律秩序，一定很快就会到来。但是，历史的巨轮并未驶入这个方向，我们所面临的是又一段坎坷不平的路程。

当前，国际社会具有两大特征：一是经济上的全球化，二是政治上的无政府状态。

---

* 本文内容，原系作者分别于2003年11月11日为武汉大学研究生会主办的讲座和11月16日为深圳大学法学院主办的广东法学研究生论坛所作的学术报告的“提纲”。这次发表时，作者对原文进行了一些修改。

随着国家间互赖性的加强和“无远弗届”的信息技术的进步，地球变得愈来愈小了。世界商品、资金、服务和人力资源的流通获得了高度自由，工业生产大幅增加，消费市场迅速扩大，社会发展加快，跨国公司已成庞然大物，国际贸易蓬勃发展，迎来了经济的全球化。其实，全球化并不止于经济，正在向各方面渗透，也渗透到了人们的思想深处。现在，人们对“地球村”（earth village）这个词，算是有真正的体会了：如果此村的一端刮起一阵旋风，就很有可能削平另一端的高楼大厦！如今的国界，正日益淡化，对于金融风暴、导弹袭击、跨国洗钱、毒品走私、艾滋病、SARS 等来说，似乎已形同虚设。2001 年 9 月 11 日纽约双子楼的倒塌，已逼真地说明了这一点。日益加深的全球化运动，给国际生活打下了深刻的烙印，产生了巨大的影响。这是我们研究和探讨国际法律秩序的重要社会背景之一。

现今国际社会的另一特征，是“无政府状态”进一步加剧。① 尽管全球化进一步促进了国家间的互赖性，然而从政治角度来观察，世界似乎比以往更加无政府（分裂）了。美苏两极对抗消失之后，过去深藏在冷战背后的尖锐矛盾，又重新暴露出来。国家和地区性的争端及冲突，以及民族、宗教、边界等纠纷，层出不穷。国际生活“武力化”的苗头，十分值得注意。我们虽然已经进入一个高度文明与发展的时代，但世界各地仍有三十多场大大小小的流血冲突，正在继续大量吞噬着人类的生命和财产。2002 年 7 月 24 日在菲律宾公布的《联合国开发计划署 2002 年人类发展报告》认为：“9·11”事件后，“人们有理由担心出现更加严重的全球分裂现象”。事实上，发展中国家因不公平待遇而产生的失望情绪，从来没有现在这样强烈；中东地区的暴力活动，在日益升级；武装冲突易发区的数目，达到了令人吃惊的地步；国际体系中的超强国家，在国际安全问题的解决上不顾一切地崇尚单边主义，并表明了摆脱国际法约束的明显倾向。综观全局，人们竟惊讶地发现：经过两次世界大战，以八千万人的生命为代价而勉强建立起来的国际协作体系与国际法律秩序，已大大滞后于国际社会的快速演变，并已濒临崩溃的边缘。

主要由国家组成的国际社会，是国际法律秩序最重要的“社会基础”。国际法的形成、实施和实际运作，无不与国际社会的状况密切相联。上述有关国际社会发展变化的特征，对国际法律秩序的现在和未来，无疑将产生重大影响。

---

① 从构词学上分析：把“inter（中间）”这个拉丁字头作为前缀（prefix），缀在 national 之前，就从根本上说明了“国际”社会的原义，本来就是无政府性质的。

二、伊拉克战争会打开“潘多拉盒子”吗？

当我们讨论国际法律秩序时，在世界历史的长河中，有三场战争特别值得注意：

第一场战争，是17世纪上半叶发生的“三十年战争”。这是一场因宗教意识形态分歧引起的欧洲列强你争我夺的战争。1648年为结束这场战争而召开的威斯特伐利亚和会及其所缔结的和约，是国际法漫长发展过程中一块重要的里程碑。它不仅标志着一个由众多主权国家组成的实际的国际社会的存在，而且标志着一种对国际行为产生直接约束力的国际法的产生。

第二场战争，是在20世纪初期进行的“第一次世界大战”。1919年，为了结束这场扩张势力范围的战争，在巴黎召开和会，并缔结了包括《国际联盟盟约》在内的凡尔赛和约。盟约首次规定了国际“集体安全制度”的基本条款，对此后的国际法律制度具有重要意义。

第三场战争，是20世纪中叶爆发的“第二次世界大战”。在战争即将结束之际，参加（反法西斯的）《联合国家宣言》的各国，于1945年在旧金山举行“联合国家关于国际组织的会议”，制定了《联合国宪章》并成立了联合国。《联合国宪章》是国际法和国际关系史上一部划时代的辉煌文献。它勾画出了战后维持世界和平与安全的蓝图，是世界各国争取和平与反对侵略的伟大旗帜。它所确立的（“维持国际和平与安全”、“促进国际合作”等）四项宗旨和（“各国主权平等”、“禁止侵略”、“不干涉内政”、“和平解决国际争端”等）七项原则，其精神符合人类生存的愿望，是全世界公认的指导一切国际关系的基本准则，是人类现代文明社会的最高精神标志和国际法律秩序的最高理念。《联合国宪章》进一步充实完善了“集体安全制度”，比19世纪及此前在国际法律制度中所形成的“国家等级格式”有了重大进步。它为现代国际法奠定了坚实的基础，是国际法中具有最高约束力的权威文献。

进入21世纪之后，另一场战争引起了全世界的普遍关注，这就是2003年的“美英伊拉克战争”。今天去评估伊拉克战争对现代国际法律秩序的影响，肯定还为时过早，不过若干已显露出来的事态及苗头，却很有引人深思的启发性。

伊拉克所在的中东地区，历来是一个“战争多发区”。为什么？这里，大多数是以阿拉伯民族为主的信奉伊斯兰教的阿拉伯国家。从地缘政治角度来看，它是欧亚非三大洲的连接地带，自古以来为东西交通的必经之地，战略地位十分重要。1869年苏伊士运河开航后，又把地中海与红海连接起来，沟通了大西洋与印度洋，从而使之成为海上交通和远航运输的咽喉。中东还拥有极其丰富的石油资源，西欧、日本、美国等工业发达国家所需石油的绝大部分，都是靠这里供应的。而伊拉克石油的储量，据估计则在100亿吨以上，在阿拉伯国家中仅次于沙特（也有专家估计与沙特相等）。正因为中东是一个战略要地和交通枢纽，是一块宝地，所以历来成为列强角逐之所。远的不说，仅从最近两百多年来考察：1798年，拿破仑曾长驱直入，将其军队开进开罗；1801年法国人被迫离开埃及后，英国接着于1882年又入侵埃及，并掌握了苏伊士运河这一海上要道。此后，英国部队又于1914年攻进了现在的伊拉克。国联成立后，伊拉克成为英国的“委任统治地”。在英国对伊拉克统治结束后不久，英国和法国又于1956年占领了苏伊士运河区域。之后，在美国的干预下，苏伊士运河才得以物归原主。此外，在（欧美列强）外力的影响或捉弄下，中东内部各国间也发生过不少战争，如巴以战争、阿以战争、以黎战争、两伊战争、伊拉克侵占科威特的战争等。这次，美英为何发动伊拉克战争？值得深思。

据以上多种角度分析，似乎可以看出：这次的伊拉克战争“正好发生在新世纪之初”和“进行战争的种种理由”，以及“由谁来打”，等等，虽然都具有几分偶然性，但是，伊拉克战争本身迟早会到来这一点，却几乎是历史的必然。

关于伊拉克战争的性质问题，众说纷纭，一时还很难作出一个简单明确的结论。不过从表象来看，至少有下列几个特点值得考虑：第一，它是一场高科技战争。这主要表现在美英联军方面，因此它是一次典型的“不对称战争”。第二，它在名义上是一场反恐战争。其开战理由据（美英）说是伊拉克藏有大规模杀伤性武器（WMD，Weapons of Mass Destruction）① 并与“基地组织”有联系。第三，它是一场“预防性”战争。其战略根据是“先发制人”。第四，它是一场经过安理会漫长讨论而未能获得安理会授权或批准的战争。安理会15个理事国因此出现了多极分化，欧美之间产生了严重裂痕，国际社会也对此作出了强烈反应。伊拉克战争是21世纪的战争，以上四点概括，对进一步分析和评估21世纪的国际法律秩序，具有重要的参考价值。

早在2003年3月20日伊拉克战争爆发的半年之前，美国国会已于2002年10月11日通过了授权对伊拉克动武的决议。并且在此前20天，美国总统（布什）还于2002年9月20日正式公布过一份《国家安全战略》报告。此项

---

① 如译为“大规模毁灭性武器”，其包容性似乎更全面一些。

报告旨在阐明外交与军事方面的广泛原则,① 它标志着美国的国家安全战略发生了重大转变。报告把“预防性”攻击作为一种“自卫”形式,列为国家安全保障战略的核心。这份国家安全文件,被认为是“美国外交政策的一个分水岭”,其地位“与上世纪中叶确立杜鲁门主义的 NSC68 号文件②相当”。(上句是英国《金融时报》2002 年 9 月 20 日文章的用语。)报告认为,世界直接面对的最大威胁是企图拥有大规模杀伤性武器的组织及国家,因此过去的“遏制战略”已经无济于事,美国有权甚至有责任对这样的国家采取“先发制人”③ 的进攻。

上述文件所阐述的“预防性”攻击及“先发制人”战略,是否真的符合现代国际法关于“自卫”的规定,这是一个很值得研究的问题。

自卫权,是国家主权的应有之义,是伴主权而存在的一种“自然权利”(inherent right)。早期(国际习惯上)的自卫权,运用甚为广泛(甚至被强者作为借口而发动侵略战争)。但随着时代进步和对战争残酷性的认识,国际社会对国家战争权(包括武力自卫权)的限制日渐加强。从而,使自卫(作为合法使用武力的根据或理由)成了现代国际法上一项非常严格的成文法制度。

在进一步分析自卫权制度之前,需要先对《联合国宪章》第 2 条作些说明。④ 该条第 4 项规定:各会员国在其国际关系中,不得以武力相威胁或使用武力来侵害任何国家之领土完整或政治独立,亦不得以任何其他同联合国宗旨不符之方式以武力相威胁或使用武力。这项(禁止以武力相威胁或使用武力)原则,是适用宪章第 7 章(对于和平之威胁、和平之破坏及侵略行为之应付办法)各条款的基础,一般来说,除下述两种“例外”情况之外,具有普遍适用的效力。例外之一,是联合国根据宪章所采取的或授权采取的行动;例外

---

① 这份长达 30 余页的国家安全文件(The National Security Strategy of the United States of America),包括国际战略、人权、反恐、地区冲突、大规模毁灭性武器、全球经济增长、民主及社会发展、全球合作、国家安全机构等问题,共九大部分。

② 该文件英文全称是 NSC68:United States Objectives and Programs for National Security (April 14, 1950), A Report to the President Pursuant to the President's Directive of January 31, 1950.

③ …… “destroying the threat before it reaches our borders”. “to exercise our right of self-defense by acting preemptively ……”. See The National Security Strategy of the U. S. A, p. 6. 汉译“先发制人”一语,出自《汉书·项籍传》,谓敌对中的双方,先发起进攻者,可制服他方,即俗语“先下手为强”的意思。《史记·项羽本纪》亦云:“吾闻先即制人,后则为人所制。”

④ 在《国际法原则宣言》及不少条约中均有关于此条内容的规定。

之二，就是作为一种救急手段的“自卫”。

宪章第7章第51条规定：任何国家受武力攻击（armed attack）时，在安理会采取必要办法以维持国际和平及安全以前，本宪章不得认为禁止行使单独或集体自卫之自然权利。……条文规定“受武力攻击时”，这意味着：必须有武力攻击之客观事实存在，方能使用相应之武力进行反击（自卫）。换一个角度说：谁首先使用武力攻击他国，谁就构成对他国领土完整及政治独立的侵害，这正好是被侵害国可以使用相应武力进行自卫（反击）的合法根据。所以，任何国家都不可能享有为预防紧迫的“可疑事实”而进行“事先自卫”（先发制人的预防性攻击）的权利。除此之外，对宪章第51条的任何扩大解释都是没有法律根据的。因为如前所述，第51条是宪章第2条第4项关于禁止使用武力的例外条款，而根据“法律解释”的基本规则，对原则的例外规定，只能作限制性解释。不然，扩大解释就会破坏“禁止使用武力原则”与“自卫权制度”之间的平衡与协调，原则本身的核心部分就有被抵消的可能。如果由于滥用例外条款而使原则本身的核心内容受损，那当然不是立法者设立例外条款的意旨。（尤其在武器杀伤力巨大的时代，对第51条之解释更应严格行事。这最适合世界和平与安全的利益。）

如上所述，武力攻击事实之客观存在是行使自卫权的前提（首要条件），但这一前提究竟存在与否，其最终判断（determine）权（或督察权）属于谁？宪章第39条规定：安理会应断定任何和平之威胁、和平之破坏或侵略行为之是否存在……。因此，从集体安全制度整体来分析，就第51条的实施过程及效果而言，第39条是一个关联性条款。并且宪章第51条之后半段还规定：（受武力攻击之）国家因行使此项自卫权而采取之办法，应立即向安理会报告，此项办法之任何方面不得影响该会按照宪章随时采取其所认为必要行动之权责，以维持或恢复国际和平与安全。

根据对上述各条的分析，可见宪章所确认的自卫权制度，无论在立法意旨、内容解释、事实判断及实施程序上，都是非常严格的。宪章第51条是自卫权制度的主干条款；第2条第4项是主干的前提条款；第39条是主干的断定（督察）条款。这三个条文很像是一组拉动自卫权制度的“三驾马车”，缺一不可，否则，自卫权制度即会瘫痪。因此，我们应将这一组条文联系起来研究，才能理解自卫权制度的真谛。只有这样解释，才能进一步体现宪章“维持国际和平与安全”这一宗旨的重要精神。

综上所述，“预防性”攻击与“先发制人”战略（做法），只是强者的逻辑，并不符合“自卫”条款的有关规定，因此是违反国际法的。如果这一做法被国际社会仿效（甚至作为自卫的一种形式而接受），那不仅是对现代国际法上自卫权制度的破坏，而且是对自《威斯特伐利亚和约》三百五十多年以来所逐步形成和发展起来的现代国际法体系的一次严重冲击和倒退，也是对以联合国为主导的国际法律体制的一种践踏。美国《洛杉矶时报》在美国国会授权对伊动武的当天，以《错误的决议》为题发表文章说："对伊拉克发动一次先发制人的打击，可能突然打开一个侵略的潘多拉盒子（pandora's box）。俄罗斯可以以它为例来镇压在格鲁吉亚的叛乱分子，印度可以利用它来证明对巴基斯坦发动一场核打击是有道理的，因为它可以预防对方发动这样一次攻击。"该报在最后指出："9·11 事件以来，世界确实已经变了。但是，尽管出现了新的恐怖主义威胁，它也不应该使美国恐慌到放弃指导原则。"联合国秘书长（安南）于 2003 年 3 月 12 日在俄罗斯《生意人报》上发表文章，就对伊动武问题明确表示："如果一些国家在没有安理会批准的情况下开始行动，那么合法性就无从谈起，它们将得不到政治上的支持。"后来他又于 9 月 23 日严肃指出：先发制人的军事干预原则所引起的危机，将联合国带到了一个具有决定性的"岔路口"；并且担心这可能开创先例，导致"非法使用武力"的现象会进一步泛滥起来。

这个装满人类"苦难"的潘多拉盒子会不会打开呢？这还要看国际社会有没有足够的智慧来化解潘多拉这位"下凡仙女"的作为。我们希望这个盒子永远也不会打开。

三、联合国已走到"三岔路口"

我在 1998 年，将有关解释国际组织发展规律的一个观点初步写入了《国际组织法》一书的第 4 版。到第 5 版时，我就这一问题所给出的核心论点是：国际组织的产生是国际社会两种潮流（力量）的汇合。一种潮流是，各主权国家基于各自的文化传统与民族利益，热衷于追求己国的独立。在各种国际竞争因素的影响下，国家利益的冲突、权力配置的矛盾和意识形态的分歧，时隐时现，没有最终消失的时候。所以国际社会无法将众多分散的国家权力完全融合为一个整体，因为这里存在的是一种"分力"（离心倾向）。另一种潮流是，由于各种国际关系和科学技术的发展，国家间联系日益增多，国内管辖事项往往溢出国外，因此需要国际互助，不如此，国家就难以实现其相关的管辖任务。所以各国都希望找到一种合作的方式。这里存在的是一种"合力"（向心倾向）。国际组织的产生，正是上述这两种力量和愿望的调和与平衡。国际组织的形成与发展，既符合国家离心倾向的要求，也符合国家向心倾向的要求。这是现代国家"既彼此独立又相互依存"的必然结果，是国际社会进入上世纪以后一种结构性的新现象。以上论点，我将之概括为"结构平衡论"。说开来，社会现象也有类似自然现象之处，它们都受平衡规律的支配。我们的地球，日月星辰，包括整个宇宙，都只有在反复和不断保持平衡的条件下，才能正常运行。一旦失去平衡，就不可能再有现在的秩序；需要重新建立新的平衡，才可能有新的秩序。国际组织，作为现代国际社会的一种结构形态，显然是国家间诸种愿望和力量的平衡结果。①

联合国的情况怎么样？

从联合国的诞生，特别是从以联合国为中心的国际组织网的形成与发展来看，上述平衡理论同国际实践情况是颇为接近的。联合国，是第二次世界大战行将结束时，本着联合起来反对法西斯的合作精神，由战胜国在战争废墟上建成的一个维持国际和平与安全的综合性国际组织。《联合国宪章》在第 1 条，明确规定“促成国际合作，以解决国际间属于经济、社会、文化及人类福利性质之国际问题”，并以之作为其主要宗旨之一。在第 2 条，又将“各会员国主权平等”作为原则，并置于联合国及其会员国应遵行的各项原则之首项。半个多世纪以来，联合国在国际和平、社会经济发展、反殖民化、国际法律秩序等方面，作了许多有益的工作。对其功过是非，虽然众说纷纭，但它所取得的种种成就，是不容忽视的。20 世纪，是人类历史上最血腥的一个世纪，但是在联合国的体制下，毕竟没有发生第三次世界大战。从这个角度讲，联合国至少给人类带来了超过半个世纪的和平。虽然幸免于大战的原因是多方面的，但是联合国功不可没。联合国过去之所以能够取得成就，并能避免国际联盟夭亡之命运，与它能在继续维护国际合作关系的同时并能保持国家平等独立原则，是分不开的。

我们还可以从反面来分析这个问题。由于国家在国际社会具有双重倾向，所以，如果一个国际组织的合作功能愈来愈削弱，而且（或者）不能使其成员国获得和平与安全并可能使之丧失平等独立的地位，这个国际组织就必然走向衰落。这是因为：它在国际结构上已经失去平衡。它既不能适应国家的向心倾向，也不能适应国家的离心倾向。只有恢复新的平衡，它才能建立新的秩序。因此在这里，还有必要从这一角度来考察一下联合国的实际运作情况。

联合国成立之初，在头几年里，其六大机关（及各会员国），承继反法西斯的联盟精神，步调比较一致，运行比较平衡和协调。在处理战后遗留问题、调整机构、健全体制、建立国际法律秩序、开展经济及社会工作等方面，均显得颇具生气。特别是在刚开始的国际维和行动中，出手不凡，引人注目。但

---

① 参见梁西：《国际组织法》（总论），武汉大学出版社 2001 年修订第 5 版，第 327 ~ 330页。

是，由于第二次世界大战的胜利并未使一切矛盾终结，因此，战后不久，冷战气氛即乘隙而来，并有愈演愈烈之势。在以美苏为首的两极对抗的冷战格局下，联合国各机关（特别是安理会），在其机制运作中，举步维艰，经历了严峻的考验。其合作机制，岌岌可危！这一点，只要分析一下安理会的决策情况，即可略知一二。

《联合国宪章》第 27 条规定：关于程序事项以外的一切事项的决议，应以九个理事国的可决票决定之，其中应包括全体常任理事国的同意票在内。即五个常任理事国对一切实质性事项享有“否决权”。也就是说，对此类事项，即使 15 个理事国中有 14 个投赞成票，如果有一个常任理事国投反对票，其决议也不能通过。这真像孙悟空的“金箍棒”，天下无敌！安理会的决策程序，是以战后所形成的力量对比及特殊协作关系为基础的。当时的英美，力图凭其优势建立一个能由其控制的联合国，因此一个便于其驾驭的有限度的否决权，是符合其愿望的。当时的苏联，鉴于西方国家在联合国处于多数地位，因此希望有一个可作为其抗衡工具的广泛的否决权。而此时的广大中小国家，则发现一个没有否决权的联合国根本不可能为各大国所接受。可见，几经周折和妥协，最后稍加折中的否决权条款的确立，是战后东西方既矛盾又合作的平衡产物。

在联合国头 10～20 年中，英美一极的国家掌握着联合国的表决机器。因此，冷战开始以后，苏联动辄使用否决权，使很多决议都无法通过。苏联是这一时期行使否决权占总数绝大多数的国家，仅在 1955 年 12 月 13 日这一天，它就连续投了 15 次否决票。有人讥称当时苏联驻联合国的代表葛罗米柯为“Mr. No”。在联合国的第三个十年中，新会员国激增，发展中国家在联合国占了多数，美国已感到难以控制，因此转而成了使用否决权最多的国家。在此期间内，共行使过 31 次否决权，美国占了其中的 12 次，英国 8 次，苏联 7 次，中国与法国各两次。值得注意的是，到联合国的第五个十年时，否决权的使用情况发生了戏剧性的变化，次数急剧下降。特别是从 1990 年 8 月 2 日伊拉克入侵和吞并科威特后截至 1990 年 11 月 29 日，安理会针对海湾危机陆续通过了 12 项决议，在此过程中，五个常任理事国没有行使过一次否决权。这在安理会的表决史上是空前的。这也反映了在经历长期的冷战折磨后，此时的世界格局与国际力量对比已经发生了巨大的变化。

在冷战逐渐消失的过程中，联合国从美苏对抗的夹缝里逐渐解脱出来。在开始进入 20 世纪 90 年代的前后几年中，联合国利用已出现的缓和形势，曾一度充满活力并积极开展工作。在阿富汗、尼加拉瓜、柬埔寨等问题上和第一次海湾危机中，它作为国际上一个必不可少的和平维护者，发挥了非常重要的作用。然而，历史的发展，有其自身的规律，联合国在跨过冷战鸿沟之后，谁知好景不长，没有多久，竟又走到了另一个“三岔路口”。

联合国在前述两大国际潮流（倾向）中，会失去平衡吗？

早在伊拉克战争爆发之前，在联合国范围内即已开始磋商（争论）是“对伊动武”还是“继续对伊核查”的议题。关于这个问题的激烈讨价还价，实际上已席卷了欧美、中东和亚非拉各国的首都，并对安理会的决策进程产生了重大影响。这次，与第一次海湾危机时截然不同，安理会的15个理事国，对议案存在着严重分歧。而且，一反常态，这次的分歧不是以欧美对亚非拉作分界线，也不是以东方对西方或者南方对北方区分，更不是以不同的价值观或意识形态为标志，而是呈现出一种尤为错综复杂的局面。根据世界各媒体有关内情的报道，安理会实际上已因此逐步形成了两种泾渭分明的主张（或者说三种不同的倾向）。联合国秘书处人士将其描述为“4·5·6格局”。它们分别指：主张动武的美国、英国、西班牙、保加利亚；主张继续核查的法国、德国、中国、俄罗斯、叙利亚；以及倾向比较模糊的墨西哥、智利、喀麦隆、安哥拉、几内亚、巴基斯坦（以上分类名单引自日本《朝日新闻》2003年2月26日的报道）。如果说，在第一次海湾危机时安理会是用一个声音说话的话，那么，此时的15个理事国可以说已是分崩离析了。这次分裂或许是一时现象，但给联合国留下的烙印和影响则是十分深远的。

这次决策危机与安理会过去的历次碰撞（包括冷战中的长期对抗）相比，后者只是因使用否决权而常常使议案无法通过并形成僵局，但是，前者却是在决策程序尚未完成之前（核查尚在进行之中）即开始了宪章所禁止的武力行动。这表明，安理会纸面（宪章）上的权威，在强大成员国势力面前是多么的脆弱！它在国际社会危难的时刻已经身手乏力了。

联合国虽然遭到了重大挫折，但悲观失望是毫无根据的。国际社会漫长和曲折的历史，曾以无数事实昭示人们：社会总是退一步进两步并“螺旋式”地向前发展的。尽管联合国存在不可否认的弱点，急需改革，但它仍然是世界上迄今最重要的与代表性最广泛的国际组织，同单边主义相比，通过联合国的多边外交来解决国际争端，具有更大的合理性。尽管宪章的若干过时条款需要修正，但宪章所载的宗旨及原则，则是世界一致公认的不可损抑并具有普遍效力的国际法最基本的原则。各国务实的领导人，以其卓识远见，审时度势，必能就联合国的改造及国际法律秩序等问题达成妥协，从而使坚冰化解，使联合国重新恢复活力和平衡，并为改善和加强国际法律秩序发挥其无可替代的作用。能否使危机峰回路转，这将是对联合国和人类意志的一次严峻的考验。人们对此抱有无限希望！

如前所述，全球化浪潮和世界无政府状态的加剧，向国际社会提出了严重挑战。在严峻的国际情势下，联合国也危机四伏！20世纪诞生的联合国，要使之能适应21世纪的新局面，改造是必经之路。联合国经过半个多世纪的风云变幻，已经“大腹便便”，运转欠灵；预算急剧膨胀，财政紧缺；机构十分臃肿，亟待精简；有的机制过时，必须改进。近二十多年来，来自会员国的改革呼声日渐增多。从第五任至现任秘书长，在内部行政改革上已取得若干成就。特别是秘书长安南于1997年7月16日在纽约总部公布《联合国改革初步方案》之后，在行政管理、财政经费、会议程序等方面，有了不少改进，颇受舆论欢迎。但是，在体制结构方面，其改革成效则十分有限。

人类的发展是川流不已的，历史不会回头走，为了与时俱进，国际社会必须继续改进和加强似已摇摇欲坠的国际法律秩序和联合国的现有机制。下面，提出几点粗浅的想法及思路，系“书生”之见，谨供各位作进一步研究的参考。

第一，联合国，是191个主权独立国家在宪章所载宗旨与原则基础上进行广泛国际合作的一种最高形式，但它并不是一个世界政府。它没有自己的领土，对于世界事务的管辖权、可供其使用的资金、人员、机构、兵源等，都是很有限的。它只有可能根据宪章规定做它力所能及的工作。有些事，它可不管；有些事，它不可管；有些事，它无能管。21世纪的联合国，应从某种理想主义步入一条更加现实与创新的道路。人们也不能对其抱有超越现实条件的过高的期望（有不少对联合国的抱怨，都是由此而引起的）。

第二，安理会是联合国的权力核心和执行机关，其组成应根据国际社会五十多年来的发展予以扩大。一个由包括7~9个常任理事国在内的21~27个理事国组成的安理会，估计是有可能为国际社会所接受的。常任理事国及理事国的名额，应适当注意地域分配上的公允。如常任理事国增至或者超过7名，除原来已有否决权的常任理事国外，其余则可为无否决权但任期较长并可连选连任的（半）常任理事国。

第三，为了缓和对安理会否决权制度的不满，为了扩大国际民主，可以考虑将常任理事国的“1票否决制”改进为“2~3票（缀连）否决制”。

第四，应在安理会权力之下，由根据宪章第47条建立之军事参谋团协助，加强传统意义上的维持和平行动，并建立或授权若干中小国家（会员国）建立可供安理会使用的中立性常备部队，以备维持和平行动的紧急需要，遏制地区突发性事件的发生或进一步恶化。在裁军、防止核扩散及反恐等方面，建立有效机制。

第五，联合国应该加大在“发展”领域的投入，认真推动落实在2000年通过的“千年发展目标”。应该加强联合国人道主义援助机构，尽力解决其捉襟见肘的财政困难。使之在紧急危难关头，能够及时履行救援职责。

第六，进一步精简机构，简化办事及公文等程序，提高工作效率，加强对联合国预算及其下属机构经费开支的监督，以缓和多年来的财政危机，并防止腐败滋生。①

第七，联合国的改革（特别是在体制结构方面的重大改革），均将涉及宪章若干条款相应部分的修正问题。例如，继 1990 年 3 月 21 日纳米比亚这块非洲大陆的最后殖民地正式宣告独立后，北太平洋岛国贝劳（Palau）于 1994 年 12 月 15 日独立。于是，作为联合国六大机关之一的托管理事会已经基本上胜利完成其历史任务。因此，其建制应予撤销，宪章第 13 章的全部条文应按宪章修正程序予以删除。宪章第 17 章的“敌国条款”已经失效，亦应删除。此外，对现有的集体安全制度、自卫权制度、宪章修正程序（第 18 章）等需要改进、补充、完善的部分及相关条款，亦应根据宪章宗旨原则的精神，加强调查研究工作，予以改善和修正，使之能适应新世纪国际关系的需要。

第八，在缺乏最高统一立法机关的国际社会里，为了加速国际法律秩序的改进与建设，需要进一步发挥国际法委员会编纂工作的创造性功能。国际法委员会在过去的半个多世纪中，曾经起草过三十多项重要的法律草案，其中一部分已经过国际会议缔结为正式公约，成绩显著。但是，在国际法律秩序还严重落后于时代发展的情况下，国际法委员会应迅速克服其先天性缺陷，健全工作机制，改进编纂程序，以提高其促进国际法制的效能。例如，对于高度信息化和因特网所带来的法律问题、恐怖犯罪问题、以人工诱导无性繁殖方式克隆（clone）人的问题、全球化过程中滋生的种种法律问题等，国际法委员会应具有时代精神，从全人类的根本利益出发，加强调查研究工作，提出（建议性的）研究报告，以加快造法（起草）步伐，促进国际法律秩序的改进与发展。

四、简短的结语

现在时间已到，让我用下面一段话来结束我们今天的讲座：

在经过上一个 100 年以来国际关系的许多重大转折之后，世界进入了 21 世纪。一方面，随着世界组织化加深和全球化的影响，国家间的互赖性进一步增强，“人类的共同利益与价值”日益突出，从而加深了国际社会的凝聚力；另一方面，由于国际社会无政府状态加剧，国际社会仍然动荡不安，从战争废

① 据新闻报道，联合国曾每年花费 15 万美元租借一条用以检查爆炸物的警犬，这笔经费大致相当于一位联合国副秘书长一年的薪金。可见这方面还大有可改之处。

墟上建立起来的联合国，已无力制止战争，国际秩序处于风雨飘摇之中。但是，我们深信：人类以其特有的智慧，必能绕过危机，排山倒海，走出困境；各国有胆识的政治家及外交家，在维护全人类共同与根本利益的崇高目标下，必能为新世纪开创一个崭新的国际局面。上世纪的惨痛教训再三启示人们：在国际关系中，不可恃强凌弱；弱肉强食的逻辑，并未能把强大无比的古罗马帝国延续下来。国家是国际法律秩序最重要的支柱。各国不仅通过协作形成国际法，而且通过协作实现国际法。同时，国际法律秩序也是国家赖以正常行使职能必不可少的法律环境。因此，各国惟有“同舟共济”，国际社会才有可能共渡难关，共同进步，才有可能获得物质文明和精神道德的至高成就，才有可能迎来一个更加安全的世界与持久和平的国际法律秩序。

作者简介

Daniel G. Partan

Daniel G. Partan is the R. Gordon Butler Scholar-in-Law and a professor at the Boston University School of Law (BUSL). He also serves on the WTO dispute settlement roster and binational panels appointed to review dumping and subsidy cases under North American Free Trade Agreement(NAFTA).

Professor Partan's academic interests include international lawmaking methodology, dispute resolution, and trade regulation. As a senior member of the BUSL faculty, Partan teaches International Trade Regulation and the two-part introductory International Law Process course.

In addition to his BUSL teaching, Professor Partan enjoys teaching abroad, most recently at BUSL's summer institute in London and as a Fulbright professor at Beijing's Tsinghua University Law School (2003) and visiting professor at Beijing University's School of International Studies (2001 and 2005).

Professor Partan's extensive publications include his *International Law Process* coursebook, books and articles on contemporary international issues and NAFTA binational panel decisions. He has been a visiting scholar at Cambridge University (England) and Harvard Law School, and consultant to the ABA, the American Academy of Arts & Sciences, the U. S. State Department, the U. N. Development Programme and the U. N. Fund for Population Activities. Partan is an elected member of the American Law Institute, and has served as chairman or rapporteur for studies or programs undertaken by ABA, the American Society of International Law, the International Law Association (American Branch), the Commission to Study the Organization of Peace and the Academic Council on the U. N. System.

The New "National Security Strategy" of the United States: Implications for International Law

Daniel G. Partan

Main Contents:

Ⅰ. Poverty of Language

Ⅱ. The Customary and Conventional Law of Self-Defense

Ⅲ. The Bush Administration's "National Security Strategy" (September 2002)

Ⅳ. Implications of the NSS for International Law Norms on Use of Defensive Force

Ⅴ. The Hegemonic Role of the United States

Ⅵ. The Way Forward

It would be comforting to believe that in the sweep of time international law moves inexorably towards order out of chaos and towards peace and justice in the world at large. In some sense I suppose this can be true. To take one example, international human rights law, virtually unknown a century ago, is now a centerpiece of international law doctrine. Although governments may differ sharply as to the role and scope of human rights law, today no government would deny its existence, and all governments would accept that human rights law applies to all persons subject to their jurisdiction. That, certainly, is a step forward. Yet, looking more closely, one finds today's governments rather adept at blocking effective application of human rights law, and self-righteously so. To say the least, this recognition tempers enthusiasm about the inevitability of progress, or even of stability in the gains made by international law. But, is this situation cause for despair?

One answer may lie in the structure of the international community and the procedures of international law. How is it that governments can successfully join in paper progress towards the rule of law, but cover over their true unwillingness to accept the constraints of law? Is it, at least in part, because there is no authority, either national or international, which is capable of holding governments accountable?

These questions are urgently presented by the " self-defense " theory that underlies the new United States " National Security Strategy " issued by the Bush administration in September of 2002. ① Before examining that document in any detail, however, it is useful, first, to distinguish between the terms " anticipatory ", " pre-emptive ", " preventive " self-defense, and, second, to describe the general contours of existing international law on the use of force in self-defense.

I . Poverty of Language

Regrettably there is no uniform or settled usage of the terms " anticipatory ", " pre-emptive " or " preventive " self-defense, either in government statements or in current literature on the use of force in self-defense. But, as will be seen below, there is now an important distinction in concepts, a distinction that needs to be embodied in the use of different terms to express different ideas.

The crucial distinction is between the use of force to forestall a credible threat of imminent attack and the use of force to eliminate a perceived threat of future attack. Although the term " preventive " could be used to describe a defensive response in both situations —— that is, against both a credible threat of imminent attack and a perceived threat of attack in the more distant future —— in this paper I will distinguish between the two situations by using the terms " anticipatory " and " pre-emptive " interchangeably to mean the use of force to forestall a credible threat of imminent attack, and the term " preventive " to mean the use of force to eliminate a perceived threat of future attack.

By " credible threat " I mean that an objective observer would agree that a state's adversary is preparing to launch —— or to continue —— an attack against the defending state. By " perceived threat " I mean that a state that believes itself to be an intended victim of an attack believes both that its adversary intends to attack at some unspecified future time, and that the adversary is currently developing the capacity to mount the intended attack.

---

① See http:// www. whitehouse. gov/nsc/nss. html for the full text of the National Security Strategy document.

My use of the term "preventive" thus represents only a limited meaning of the English verb "to prevent". I use "preventive" to mean to meet, or to deal with, a threat that is perceived, but has not yet materialized, or has yet to be expressed, or otherwise to be made objectively evident. ①

Note that, in the sense in which I use the term, "preventive" defensive actions are actions that respond to risks of future attack that cannot be objectively established. As contrasted with "anticipatory" or "pre-emptive" defensive responses, which require evidence of an impending attack that would satisfy an objective observer, the state mounting a "preventive" defensive response cannot expect objective observers to agree with its judgment that it must expect in future to be the victim of attack. As we shall see, this distinction lies at the heart of the change in the law advanced by the Bush administration's National Security Strategy.

Ⅱ. The Customary and Conventional Law of Self-Defense

In the international system of law that typically lacks courts and legislatures, authoritative expressions of governing law often comes from pronouncements by prominent participants in events that have shaped the law. Such pronouncements gain their authority through their general acceptance both by the participants and by others in the international community of states. This has been true of the customary international law of self-defense, which was given cogent expression in diplomatic correspondence between the United States and the United Kingdom in the so-called *Caroline* incident of 1837-1842.

When in 1837 British forces acted in U. S. waters to seize and destroy a U. S.-flag vessel, the *Caroline*, that had been aiding insurgents in Canada, the British government defended its action as necessary for self-defense in light of the failure of the U. S. government to prevent armed assistance flowing to the rebels from U. S. territory. Diplomatic exchanges over the following four years featured disagreement as to the necessity of the British action, but resulted in agreement on the legal standard that both sides believed it is necessary to govern resort to force in self-defense. As framed by Daniel Webster, then the U. S. Secretary of State, the British might lawfully use force on U. S. territory to prevent attacks on Canadian territory where the need to act was "instant, overwhelming, leaving no choice of means and no moment

① See Concise Oxford English Dictionary, p. 814 (7th ed. 1982).

for deliberation."

In its context, the *Caroline* formulation was founded on the history of actual use of force from U. S. territory against the authorities in Canadian territory: the *Caroline* had been used to ferry men and weapons across the Niagara River from U. S. to Canada to aid the revolt against Canadian authorities then underway in Canada. Although the facts thus show that the British attack was plainly conducted to interrupt and to put an end to the use of the *Caroline* to assist rebels in their ongoing attacks against the Canadian authorities, the *Caroline* precedent is sometimes cited as authority for a broader meaning of "anticipatory" or "pre-emptive" use of force. Properly construed, however, the *Caroline* precedent meets the definition used in the present essay of "anticipatory" or "pre-emptive" use of force: the British forces acted to forestall a credible threat of imminent attack by way of continuation of the *Caroline*'s assistance to the armed insurrection that had already begun in Canada.

The distinction between using force to end existing attacks and using force to forestall threatened future attacks became of central importance in drafting the Charter of the United Nations a century after the *Caroline* incident. Three provisions of the U. N. Charter are central to this inquiry. The Preamble to the Charter states that "armed force shall not be used, save in the common interest", through what was known as the U. N. Charter's collective security system. Second, Charter Article 2(4) provides that states shall not threaten or use force "against the territorial integrity or political independence of any state, or in any other manner inconsistent with the Purposes of the United Nations", which are stated in Article 1(1) to include maintaining international peace and security. Third, Charter Article 51 provides that states nevertheless have "the inherent right of individual or collective self-defence if an armed attack occurs ... until the Security Council has taken measures necessary to maintain international peace and security."

In the years since the drafting of these provisions at the San Francisco conference, scholarly debate has failed to clarify the somewhat perplexing terms of Article 51. Since the Charter acknowledges that self-defense (including "collective" self-defense) is an "inherent right", the question is what source of law defines the circumstances and extent of the right to use force in self-defense? Should the contours of the right of self-defense be determined by reference to the "natural law" embodied in the sovereign state system? Or, instead, should the reference be to customary international law, which will be shaped by "state practice" engaged in out of the somewhat mystical "sense of legal obligation"? Or, indeed, since under Charter Article 24(1) the Security Council has "primary responsibility for the maintenance of international peace and security", should the reference in Article 51 the right to use defensive force be to the practice of the United Nations, which for this purpose would chiefly be the practice of the Security Council?

Although it would be fascinating and perhaps instructive to do so, this is not the place to explore competing ideas as to the sources and range of possible meanings of the several central terms used in Article 51, that is, the terms "inherent right", "collective self-defense", "armed attack", "occurs" and "measures necessary to maintain international peace and security". Suffice it to say here only that most informed opinion falls somewhere on the spectrum that begins with the textual conservative view that "armed attack" is an objective standard intended to limit resort to self-defensive force to a response to an actual attack that has occurred. At the more radical end of the spectrum, the "inherent right" to use defensive force would include a response to attacks that demonstrably are about to occur, that is, as authorizing "anticipatory" or "pre-emptive" defensive action in the sense used in the present paper: the use of defensive force to forestall a credible threat of imminent attack.

In so far as authoritative sources of law are concerned, although the International Court of Justice has not been called upon to directly decide such issues in any contentious case, the Court's pronouncements fall at the conservative end of the spectrum described above.

In its opinion on the Merits in *Military and Paramilitary Activities in and against Nicaragua*(Nicaragua v. United States, 1986), in which the Court addressed the concept of self-defense in customary international law, the Court stated that "the exercise [of the right of self-defense] is subject to the State concerned having been the victim of an armed attack". In making this statement, the Court drew upon the "Definition of Aggression" adopted by the General Assembly in 1974. ① As endorsed by the Court, the Assembly concluded that, under the customary international law of self-defense, "armed attack" includes both an "action by regular armed forces across an international border" and also "the sending ... of armed bands ... which carry out acts of armed force ..." equivalent to an armed attack by regular forces. Note

① Resolution 3314 (XXIX) (1974).

that this concept of "armed attack" would require the defending state to make an objective showing that the conditions for resort to self-defense had been satisfied.

In its most recent opinion in the *Case Concerning Oil Platforms* (Iran v. United States, 2003), the Court addressed the issue of self-defense in the context of the United States argument that its self-defensive actions had been "necessary to protect its essential security interests" within the meaning of Article XX(1)(d) of the 1955 "Treaty of Amity" between Iran and the United States. The Court stated (in ¶ 51) that "in order to establish that it was legally justified in attacking the Iranian platforms in exercise of the right of individual self-defense, the United States has to show that attacks had been made upon it ... and that those attacks were of such a nature as to be qualified as 'armed attacks' within the meaning of that expression in Article 51 of the United Nations Charter, and as understood in customary law on the use of force." Although the Court's opinion was criticized by some judges who believed that the decision in the case did not require the Court to address the requirements for self-defense, none objected to the substance of the Court's declaration about the customary law of self-defense.

Ⅲ. The Bush Administration's "National Security Strategy" (September 2002)

The Bush administration's "National Security Strategy" document① seeks to bring about a fundamental change in the traditional dimension of the state's "inherent right" to use defensive force.

In his introduction to the NSS, President Bush asserted that avowed enemies of the United States "have openly declared that they are seeking weapons of mass destruction" and that the U.S. "will not allow these efforts to succeed." The generic term "weapons of mass destruction" includes chemical weapons, biological weapons, and nuclear weapons. Interestingly, the NSS doctrine does not distinguish between the three types of "weapons of mass destruction" although nuclear weapons are potentially the most destructive and only a few governments would have the technical capacity to develop nuclear weapons, whereas both chemical and biological weapons could much more readily be present in national arsenals.

---

① cited as the NSS and available online at http://www.whitehouse.gov/nsc/nss.html.

The NSS document asserts that "rogue states" and terrorists "reject basic human values and hate the United States and everything for which it stands". ① Given the goals of rogue states and terrorists, the United States can no longer solely rely on a reactive posture as we have in the past. The inability to deter a potential attacker, the immediacy of today's threats, and the magnitude of potential harm that could be caused by our adversaries' choice of weapons, do not permit that option. We cannot let our enemies strike first.

Traditional concepts of deterrence will not work against a terrorist enemy whose avowed tactics are wanton destruction and the targeting of innocents; whose so-called soldiers seek martyrdom in death and whose most potent protection is statelessness. The overlap between states that sponsor terror and those that pursue WMD compels us to action. ②

For these reasons, the NSS states that the United States will "act pre-emptively" against any "rogue state" that "attempts to gain or use weapons of mass destruction (WMD)"—— so as to "destroy the threat" before it reaches the United States. ③ As put by President Bush in his introduction to the NSS, "as a matter of common sense and self-defense, America will act against such emerging threats before they are fully formed." Again, this policy apparently applies to all three forms of weapons of mass destruction.

Note that the NSS reference to "act [ing] pre-emptively" confuses "pre-emption" with "prevention" as those terms are used here. The NSS action against "emerging threats before they are fully formed" plainly contemplates action against a perceived threat of future attack rather than against a credible threat of imminent attack. Note also that, in common with preventive defensive force generally, the perception of the risks of future attack is in the eye of the defender; there can be no expectation that others will agree that the threat is real enough and serious enough to warrant resort to preventive force.

The Bush NSS doctrine forthrightly calls for a dramatic shift in international law doctrine on the conditions for resort to defensive force.

For centuries, international law recognized that nations need not suffer an attack

---

① NSS p. 14.

② NSS p. 15.

③ NSS p. 6.

before they can lawfully take action to defend themselves against forces that present an imminent danger of attack. Legal scholars and international jurists often conditioned the legitimacy of pre-emption on the existence of an imminent threat—most often a visible mobilization of armies, navies, and air forces preparing to attack.

We must adapt the concept of imminent threat to the capabilities and objectives of today's adversaries. Rogue states and terrorists do not seek to attack us using conventional means. They know such attacks would fail. Instead, they rely on acts of terror and, potentially, the use of weapons of mass destruction——weapons that can be easily concealed, delivered covertly, and used without warning ... To forestall or prevent such hostile acts by our adversaries, the United States will, if necessary, act pre-emptively. ①

Note the use of the term "potentially": rogue states and terrorists rely "potentially, [on] the use of weapons of mass destruction." This term makes clear that the Bush NSS doctrine invokes what I have called "preventive" force. In "adapt [ing] the concept of imminent threat to the capabilities and objectives" of rogue states, the Bush NSS doctrine announces the intention of the United States to use defensive force without establishing that its perception of future attack is sound and should be accepted by objective observers. According to the NSS, "We cannot let our enemies strike first."②

Evidently anticipating the possibility that other countries may mimic the U. S. National Security Strategy, the Bush doctrine asserts that the U. S. "will not use force in all cases to pre-empt emerging threats" and other nations should not "use pre-emption as a pretext for aggression". Note that this statement apparently assumes that, in addition to the United States, other nations will similarly be entitled to resort to "preventive" uses of defensive force, so long as such action is not a "pretext for aggression". As with the decision to use "preventive" force, a "pretext for aggression" lacks an objective standard and exists only in the eye of the beholder.

For its part, without addressing when preventive action will be taken and when not, the NSS doctrine asserts that U. S. actions will always be directed at a "specific threat to the U. S. or our allies and friends. The reasons for U. S. actions will be

---

① NSS p. 15.

② NSS p. 15.

clear, the force measured, and the cause just." ①

Note that the NSS preventive force doctrine makes no mention of the United Nations and does not refer to the U. N. Charter role of the Security Council in taking action to maintain international peace and security. In particular, the doctrine ignores the Chapter VII role of the Security Council in determining the existence of threats to the peace, breaches of the peace, and acts of aggression (See U. N. Charter Article 39).

Ⅳ. Implications of the NSS for International Law Norms on Use of Defensive Force

Following from the goals and provisions stated in the new U. S. National Security Strategy doctrine, there are now three fairly distinct theories that a state might seek to invoke to justify resort to force in self-defense:

a. The traditional strict or conservative textual reading of U. N. Charter Article 51, which would require justification of defensive force as a response to an actual (or continuing) "armed attack";

b. An asserted customary international law standard of using "anticipatory" or "pre-emptive" force against a credible threat of imminent armed attack;

c. The Bush NSS doctrine of resorting to "preventive" force against a perceived threat of future attack that would potentially use weapons of mass destruction.

The central question presented by the NSS doctrine for the world at large is: which international law norm would best serve the interests of world peace and security?

Speaking to the General Assembly on September 23, 2003, one year after the release of the Bush National Security Strategy, comments by U. N. Secretary-General Kofi Annan suggest the complexity of the issues involved. ②

The Secretary-General observed that "if attacked" states have the inherent right of self-defense, but that, if they "use force to deal with broader threats", they need the "unique legitimacy" provided by the United Nations. In his view, resort to force in response to perceived threats would pose a "fundamental challenge" to principles of world peace and stability —— and, when undertaken without U. N. authorization,

① NSS pp. 15 & 16.

② U. N. Press Release SG/SM/8891, GA/10157 (2003).

such a use of force would be "unilateral and lawless".

Underlying the Secretary-General's observations is a most significant issue: can the United Nations effectively control resort to "preventive" uses of force against perceived future threats by states that seek to develop or to acquire weapons of mass destruction? Charter Article 24(1) gives the Security Council "primary responsibility" for maintaining peace and security, but such Security Council action would be subject to the "permanent member" veto. And, to date, the Security Council has only rarely acted with the unanimity needed to provide collective security against either threats to the peace or breaches of peace.

Two central factors make it clear that a more effective collective security system would be needed before the United States could or would place their trust in multilateral United Nations measures as an alternative to unilateral "preventive" use of force against a perceived future threat of attack using weapons of mass destruction. First, the proliferation of weapons of mass destruction, including nuclear weapons, magnifies the risk that such weapons may fall into the hands of what the NSS terms "rogue states and terrorists". Second, the September 11 attacks on civilian targets in the United States raised broad and sustained fears of future attacks against which there can be no effective defense. It is perhaps to be expected that governments that depend for their authority on the support of the people will embrace "preventive" measures both as a means of reducing the risk and of assuring the electorate that every feasible step is taken.

Can a more effective collective security system be devised? In his address to the General Assembly, the Secretary-General called for "a hard look at fundamental policy issues, and the structural changes that may be needed", mentioning specifically the composition of the Security Council and the "urgent need for the Council to regain the confidence of States ... by demonstrating its ability to deal effectively with the most difficult issues". On the issue of self-defense, the Secretary-General called upon the Security Council to consider "how it will deal with the possibility that individual States may use force pre-emptively [in my terms 'preventively'] against perceived threats" and to develop "criteria for an early authorization of coercive measures to address ... terrorist groups armed with weapons of mass destruction."

The Secretary-General also announced that he would appoint a "High-Level Panel of eminent personalities" charged with examining "current challenges to peace and security" and "the contribution which collective action can make in addressing these challenges." He asked that the High-Level Panel submit its report in time for consideration at the fall 2004 session of the General Assembly.

In view of the challenge presented by the new U. S. National Security Strategy doctrine, at least two decisive steps may be required in the quest for a more effective collective security system. The initial step would surely be to revise the composition of the Security Council so as to be more broadly representative of the international community. Perhaps in this way states can come to believe that the Council will act in the long-range interests of the international community of states, rather than, at times, in the short-range interests of a shifting coalition of "like-minded" states, some of which are virtually client-states of the Council's most powerful members.

Revision of the composition of the Security Council has been under discussion for many years with many different formulae suggested. While reaching agreement would necessarily be difficult, the Secretary-General's remarks suggest that such an agreement may no longer be seen as impossible to attain. However, in my view, while such a change would respond to concerns of small and medium powers, it would likely do little to assure the United States that U. S. security concerns can be effectively addressed through the Security Council.

This brings me to the second and most difficult issue, the permanent member veto. As I see it, the crucial step in restoring confidence in the Security Council would be to revise the Council's voting structure so that effective action to maintain international peace and security cannot be blocked by a single state's veto. Only then might governments generally expect the Security Council to act with any consistency in the long-range general interest of maintaining international peace and security.

While the permanent member veto was seen as essential to satisfy the security concerns of the five permanent members in 1945 (China, France, Russia, the United Kingdom, and the United States), it may be that the veto has outlived its usefulness. It was known that the Council was unable to take effective action in the case of Iraq. Of course opinions differ as to why this was so. The United States has condemned the unwillingness of the Britain, France, and Russia to join in the U. S. initiative to topple Saddam Hussein. Others would say that the refusal of the United States to consider non-force measures of attaining Security Council ends lay at the heart of the Council's failure. Whichever explanation is the more persuasive, would it have been helpful for the Council's voting rules to have permitted Council action to override the wishes of permanent members on either side of the issue?

Herein lies the basic problem for reconstituting collective security: Would each of the five permanent members agree that their security interests would be best served by changing the Council's voting rules to make Security Council responses to threats or uses of force "veto proof"?

The veto question is surely important for each of the five permanent members. But, although differing considerations may apply in respect of each permanent member, in view of the claims made by the United States in the NSS doctrine, it seems to me that each of the other four permanent members may see it in their interest to modify the veto power so that no single state can prevent Security Council action. If so, the attitude of the United States would be the most significant factor.

V. The Hegemonic Role of the United States

The Bush National Security Strategy doctrine implicitly asserts a dominant and unilateral role for the United States as the world's hegemonic power. The NSS makes no mention of the role of the Security Council or of the United Nations, and, while it asserts that the U. S. "will respect the values, judgment, and interests of our friends and partners", the NSS asserts that the U. S. will always "be prepared to act apart when our interests and unique responsibilities require."①

The Bush NSS doctrine asserts that U. S. armed forces must "build and maintain our defenses beyond challenge."② The U. S. goal will be to "dissuade future military competition" and thereby to "deter threats against U. S. interests, allies, and friends".③ To this end, the NSS doctrine declares that U. S. military forces must be strong enough so that potential adversaries cannot hope to surpass, or even to equal, U. S. military power.④

The United States may already have attained an unchallengeable position as the single overwhelming superpower. It is said that currently the U. S. military budget exceeds the combined military expenditures of the next twenty largest states. In such a posture, there seems no role for multilateral cooperation either through the United

---

① NSS p. 30.

② NSS p. 28.

③ NSS p. 28.

④ NSS p. 29.

Nations or even through the Security Council.

The central question for the United States, however, is whether such overwhelming military force ensures U. S. security. It is just this question that was placed in doubt by the September 11 attacks, which have led to formulation of the preventive war doctrine of the National Security Strategy. The problem is that the NSS answer may be found inadequate in several dimensions.

First, without Security Council action against putative imitators, the preventive war doctrine cannot be confined to the United States. Other militarily significant powers may see it in their interest similarly to act against perceived future threats to their security, and the resulting instability may pose fundamental dangers to U. S. interests around the world. Second, at some level U. S. authorities would agree that potential terrorist threats often cannot be successfully prevented or contained by unilateral military action. The overwhelming force possessed by the United States may be ineffective against such threats unless backed by active cooperation from many other governments. Next, as the U. S. has found in Iraq, another factor will be the cost both of the preventive war measures and of post-war administration of defeated countries. Combined, such factors should lead to reexamination of the effectiveness of the preventive force strategy.

Ⅵ. The Way Forward

At the outset it is important to note that, at this writing (December 2003), the United States has not yet squarely taken self-defensive measures founded upon the new National Security Strategy doctrine.

With respect to the war in Iraq, on March 20, 2003, the United Kingdom informed the Security Council that the U. S. -U. K. military action in Iraq was being undertaken under the authority of previous Security Council resolutions, namely resolutions 678 (1990) and 687 (1991), together with the Council's statement in resolution 1441 (2002) that Iraq "is in material breach of the conditions for the ceasefire at the end of hostilities in 1991 laid down by the Council in its resolution 687 (1991)." ①No mention is made in the U. K. formal statement of self-defense.

While the parallel notification by United States did state that coalition actions in Iraq "are necessary steps to defend the United States and the international community

① Security Council document S/2003/350 (2003).

from the threat posed by Iraq", the self-defense rationale was mentioned only at the end and without elaboration. The U. S. notification asserted both at the outset and in detail that the U. S. -U. K. military actions "are authorized under existing Council resolutions, including resolutions 678 (1990) and 687 (1991)." The U. S. notification also asserted that: "It has been long recognized and understood that a material breach" of Iraq's obligations under the cited resolutions "removes the basis of the ceasefire and revives the authority to use force under resolution 678 (1990)."①

In view of the British and U. S. specific and detailed reliance on authorization to use force under existing Security Council resolutions, the penultimate U. S. reference to a need "to defend the United States and the international community from the threat posed by Iraq" falls short of a claim to the legitimacy of unilateral resort to force to prevent Iraq from acquiring or using weapons of mass destruction. This observation is of central importance considering the role played in customary international lawmaking methodology by claims to legitimacy of state action, and of responses to such claims.

Had the United States forthrightly and consistently claimed to have used defensive force in Iraq on the basis of the expanded preventive force theory of self-defense proclaimed in the National Security Strategy doctrine, all other states would be challenged to respond to that claim to avoid embedding the NSS doctrine in customary international law as a legitimate exercise of the right to use force in self-defense. As matters now stand, however, states may and should make clear their belief that, rightly or wrongly, both the United States and the United Kingdom had rested their claim to use force in Iraq on continuing authorization under existing Security Council resolutions. In this way it would become clear that, notwithstanding the summary U. S. reference to defense of the U. S. and the international community, their claim to a legal basis for the U. S. -U. K. action has been Security Council authorization and not an expansion of the customary law of self-defense to include resort to preventive force against perceived future threats.

In this connection, it is of interest to note that the U. S. "Proliferation Security Initiative" made public in September 2003 also does not rely on self-defense. The Proliferation Security Initiative relies wholly on the existing international law

① Security Council document S/2003/351 (2003).

jurisdiction of each cooperating state to control activities that take place within its territories, or within its territorial seas or contiguous zones, or are engaged in by its nationals or by ships or aircraft registered under its authority. The Proliferation Security Initiative is intended to prevent proliferation of weapons of mass destruction. Participating states undertake to "support . . . interdiction efforts regarding cargoes of WMD . . . consistent with their obligations under international law". Consistent with this characterization, each of the six specific interdiction measures listed in the Department of State "Fact Sheet" on the Proliferation Security Initiative rest clearly on the participating state's existing international law authority over its nationals, its territory, or its ships or aircraft. There is no mention of any broader authority based upon the NSS doctrine of self-defense against perceived future threats from the development or possession of weapons of mass destruction.

Even though the United States has yet to act upon the claims made in the National Security Strategy document, the foregoing review of the new United States NSS doctrine does show that progress towards an effective multilateral security system cannot be accomplished without the agreement of the United States. The review also implies that such an agreement cannot be expected unless the leaders of the United States come to believe that true national and international security cannot be achieved without broadening the "coalitions of the willing" to include most if not all militarily significant states.

Therein lies some basis for hope. If two conditions are satisfied, it may be possible for the United States to come to believe that the risks of using unilateral self-defensive force against perceived future threats of the use of weapons of mass destruction outweigh the risks of giving up its current control over decisions of the Security Council. First, the militarily significant states, including the four other permanent members of the Security Council, must join together in an effort to convince the United States that they will cooperate in effective collective security measures. Second, the decision-making structure of the Security Council must be changed to provide practical assurance that such cooperation can be achieved. To achieve this result, each of the five permanent members of the Security Council will need to accept reduced control over Security Council actions, but such a step is essential to achieve effective collective security decision-making.

作者简介 —— Hugh Thirlway

Hugh Thirlway was born in London on 14 June 1937 and is a British national. He studied at Bradfield College, UK (1950-1955), St. John's College, Cambridge (1955-1959) and Université de Nancy, France (1965-1966), and was awarded B. A. (Cantab.) in 1958, LL. B. (= LL. M.) in 1959, M. A. in 1961 and Dr. en droit (Nancy) in 1970.

During 1961-1968 he practised as solicitor in Cambridge, UK. He was appointed Secretary (1968) and later First Secretary (1972) as well as Principal Legal Secretary (1989) of International Court of Justice. In 1994 he resigned and became a Professor of International Law at the Graduate Institute of International Studies, Geneva until the year 2000.

He also served as Visiting Fellow, Lauterpacht Research Centre in International Law, University of Cambridge, and Wolfson College, Cambridge, 1999-2000; Visiting Fellow and Professor, E. M. Meijers Institute of Legal Studies, University of Leiden, 2000-2001; Visiting Professor, Graduate Institute of International Studies, Geneva, summer 2001; Visiting Professor, University of Bristol, 2001-2003; Visiting Professor, East China Normal University, Shanghai, 2002; Professor at Hague Academy of International Law, Summer 2002 (course on "Concepts, principles, rules: the structure of international legal reasoning").

His publications include *International Customary Law and Codification* (Leiden, 1971) (awarded John Westlake Prize of the Institut de droit international), *Non-Appearance before the International Court of Justice* (Cambridge, 1985) as well as numerous articles on questions of international public (and private) law, including series in particular "The Law and Procedure of the International Court of Justice, 1960-1989" in *British Year Book of International Law*; twelve parts published between 1989 and 2001, and continuing.

The Contribution of the International Court of Justice to the Development of International Law*

Hugh Thirlway

Main Contents:

Ⅰ. Introduction

Some 70 years ago, the British jurist Sir Hersch Lauterpacht gave a series of lectures at the Graduate Institute of International Studies, Geneva, entitled "The Development of International Law by the Permanent Court of International Justice", and these were then published as a book under that title. In 1958 he published an up-dated version, entitled "The Development of International law by the International Court", which is still in print today.① The idea that the Court contributes to the

---

* This paper is an edited and enlarged version of a lecture given at the University of Wuhan, China, on 22 November 2002, at the invitation of the Law Faculty of that University. My warmest thanks go to Professor Yu Minyou for the invitation and to Ms. Yao Yanxia for the very friendly and efficient organization of my visit.

① Stevens & Sons Ltd., 1958: reprinted by Grotius Publications, 1982; reprinted by Cambridge University Press 1996.

development of law is widely accepted: its decisions are to be found cited in all textbooks of international law, and are frequently relied on by counsel in argument, both before the Court itself, and before other tribunals, both national and international. In some cases, as we shall see, a decision of the Court is regarded as having been responsible for the introduction of a particular fresh aspect or rule of international law. In this lecture I intend not only to enumerate some cases of this kind, but also to consider a little more closely what is meant by "development" of law in this context, and the appropriateness of relying on the ICJ for the purpose.

For the moment, however, let us reserve the definition of "development" and simply treat the Court as having played a part in development in any areas of international law in which its decisions are considered to be a necessary part of the statement and discussion of the subject. It is appropriate first to review the position of the Court in the international system, and the special features of the law it is called upon to apply.

Ⅱ. The Functions of the International Court of Justice

The functions of the Court are defined by the Charter and the Statute; and in application of the principle of specialty,① the International Court has no powers outside those conferred or necessarily implied. The principle is usually relevant to discussion of the powers of an organization rather than an organ of an organization, but is equally applicable in the latter event. ②

Under Art. 38 of the Statute: the Court's function is "to decide in accordance with international law such disputes as are submitted to it". This function is of course law-related, but it is limited to *deciding* disputes, and to deciding only those disputes that are *submitted.* The Court's contribution to the development of law can therefore

① Most recently discussed by the Court itself in the case concerning *Legality of the Use by a State of Nuclear Weapons in Armed Conflict* (the WHO case), *ICJ Reports 1996-I*, pp. 78-9, para. 25.

② In the case of *Certain Expenses of the United Nations*, the Court contemplated acts which might be performed by the wrong organ of an organization, but which could still be directed to the purposes of the organization, and thus have some validity internationally, while contrary to the internal law of the organization (*ICJ Reports 1962*, p. 168). This approach would however not confer any validity on non-judicial action by the International Court, however much such action harmonized with or advanced the purposes of the organization.

only be sporadic and piecemeal: a legal question may be very important to the international community, and very controversial, but if no dispute to which it is relevant is brought before the Court (in contentious case or by request for advisory opinion), no judicial ruling is possible. The Court has never asserted any power to parallel (for example) the right asserted by the UN Human Rights Committee to make "General Comments". ①

Furthermore, when ascertaining the existence or content of a rule of customary law, the Court has of course to consider such material as evidence both of State practice and of the existence or otherwise of an *opinio juris*. That material is in principle limited to what is submitted to it by the parties to the case before it, even though, in application of the principle *iura novit curia*, the Court is free to examine such other information as to the law that it may be able to obtain. In this respect, it does not enjoy a benefit available to the United Nations International Law Commission. The reports and draft texts prepared by that body are available to States for comment, thus making possible a dialogue with the subjects of international law, who are evidently best placed to indicate their own practice and their own *opinio*.

The Court's role is to decide. Every decision on a dispute, except perhaps on a pure question of fact, or on a very specific provision of a bilateral treaty, involves the application of a general rule to a particular case, and thus the *statement* of a general rule, and the *statement* that it applies in this particular way. That in itself may be regarded as a development of law; but only if such a statement is compelling, or at least persuasive for other States. It is only if the statement has some impact of this kind on other States that one can speak of the Court developing the law.

The Statute draws a distinction between, on the one hand, *res judicata*, whereby the decision on the matter is final (Statute, Art. 60), but only for the parties (Art. 59); and, on the other, the persuasive significance of a judicial decision for other States. This is illustrated by Article 38 (1) (d) of the Statute, whereby judicial decisions are a subsidiary means for the determination of rules of law. The cross-reference in Article 38 to Article 59 shows that this reference includes ICJ decisions themselves. International law may be looked for in court decisions, but only as a "subsidiary means". This signifies that the formal source of a rule of law stated in

---

① Cf. also the General Comments made by the U. N. Compensation Commission, which come near to general statements of applicable law.

such a decision is not the decision itself, but must lie elsewhere, in treaty, custom or the general principles of law. The decision, while it is binding for the parties in the case in which it is given, has no compelling force in a subsequent case, even for the Court itself, and even if the facts of the two cases are legally indistinguishable.

Development of law by the Court is thus persuasive, not legislative, not even on a basis of *stare decisis*. The Court does cite its own decisions, but not on a basis of binding authority. This is clear from an important recent decision, in the *Cameroon/ Nigeria* case. In that case, proceedings had been commenced by Cameroon against Nigeria on the basis of acceptances by Nigeria and by Cameroon of the "compulsory jurisdiction" of the Court under Article 36, paragraph 2, of the Statute. However, at the date at which the proceedings were brought, Cameroon's acceptance, which had only just been deposited with the Secretary-General, had not been brought to Nigeria's notice. Any argument that this circumstance invalidated the proceedings was however met by the observation that the same thing had happened 30 years earlier, in the case of *Right of Passage over Indian Territory*, ① and the Court had then rejected the objections made by India on that basis. Nigeria argued (correctly) that the *Right of Passage* precedent was not binding on the Court, and that the Court should depart from it in the case at bar. The Court's ruling on the issue was as follows:

"[I]n accordance with Article 59 [of the Statute], the Court's judgments bind only the parties to and in respect of a particular case. There can be no question of holding Nigeria to decisions reached by the Court in previous cases. The real question is whether, in this case, there is cause not to follow the reasoning and conclusions of earlier cases." ②

Having considered the matter, the Court went on to reject the objection of Nigeria, just as it had rejected that of India in the earlier case.

The dictum quoted suggests that the Court will be more inclined than not to follow its own decisions; hence States must expect an informal use of precedent. Every decision of the Court therefore has some kind of an impact on States of non-parties. This corresponds in fact to the attitude taken by States themselves. Even in a dispute between two States neither of whom has accepted ICJ jurisdiction, the

---

① *Preliminary Objections*, *ICJ Reports 1957*, p. 125.

② *Land and Maritime Boundary between Cameroon and Nigeria*, *Judgment of 11 June 1998*, *ICJ Reports 1998*, para. 28.

background to the argument is: what would the ICJ say on this issue were it to be brought before the Court?

Of course, the Court also has power to give advisory opinions: in this respect also it is called upon to state the law, and to state it, in theory, independently of any specific dispute. In practice, there would be no request for an opinion if the point submitted to the Court were not the subject of more or less active disagreement; though, as the cases concerning nuclear weapons① showed, such disagreement may not amount to an actual inter-State dispute. An advisory opinion possesses no *res judicata*, but has nevertheless the same, or similar, persuasive authority as a judgment.

We may conclude that, in terms of functional powers, the International Court exercises an influence on international law that may be called development, but this influence can only be incidental, not purposive.

Ⅲ. The Meaning of "Development"

The limitation just referred to is in fact emphasized by Article 13 (1) (a) of the U. N. Charter: the "progressive development of international law and its codification" is there provided for as something that falls within the mandate of the General Assembly, not the Court. The General Assembly has of course set up the International Law Commission for that purpose. The Charter thus makes a distinction between "codification" and "progressive development" of international law. Since, as we have seen, the Court is called upon to decide disputes on the basis of the *existing* applicable law, its role is no more than to state the law, which corresponds to "codification". It is true that the codification/development distinction is sometimes less than realistic: the ILC itself has had difficulty keeping it sharp. However, there is, it seems clear, a distinction to be made between "development" and "progressive development". Does the Court have any function of "progressive development"? Not, apparently, in the sense that this function was conceived by the draftsmen of the Statute of the ILC, who "conceived progressive development as a conscious effort towards the creation of new rules of international law". ② Development within the

① *Legality of the Threat or Use of Nuclear Weapons, Advisory Opinion, ICJ Reports 1999.*

② *The Work of the International Law Commission, United Nations, 1996*, Fifth edition, Sales No. E.95.V.6, p.14.

functions of the Court must be something more limited.

In the work of Lauterpacht already cited, the learned author had no doubt about the desirability of development of international law by the Permanent Court and by its successor; indeed he regarded it as one of the intended functions of those bodies. He saw no need to dwell on the paradox that the Court, to inspire the confidence of States, and to comply with its Statute, must merely declare the law and not make it, i. e. , it must decide judicially and not legislatively, yet it is also expected to develop the law. He did concede that there was a limit to judicial development, considering that the Court was "powerless, without embarking on the hazardous course of judicial legislation, to effect changes in conventional or customary international law". ①

As the U. N. Charter shows, development of international law, whether "progressive" or otherwise, and by any legitimate means, is regarded as a desirable end. What are we to understand by "development"? At the least, development must imply change, and that change must, it is suggested, be either in some way for the better, or (what is not necessarily the same thing) the continuation or consummation of some existing trend.

In general (not specifically in international law), no legal system can remain static; development is often not only desirable, but inevitable. We may however distinguish three reasons for this, and thus three sorts of development:

Firstly, even in a stable society, possessing a developed legal system, unforeseen cases will arise for settlement, and will require interpretation or extension of law by way of filling in the gaps. That process may well involve simply following a current trend a logical stage further than it has previously been thought to have reached. Let us call this for convenience, development by extension.

Secondly, an existing rule of law may appear, in the circumstances of a particular case, to work injustice, in the sense that the result dictated by existing

① *The Development of International Law by the International Court*, p. 19. He went on to assert, however, that the Court could modify the law as stated in a previous decision of its own (ibid.). This is an unreal distinction. Except where the change would amount to a recognition that the earlier decision was mistaken, to modify the jurisprudence is to modify the underlying law, since the judicial decision is no more than a "subsidiary means for the determination of rules of law".

rules seems not to be in harmony with more fundamental ideas of fairness and equity. ① The law may appear to require to be limited or modified, not only for that individual case but for similar cases. Let us call this equitable development.

Thirdly, developments in technology and developments in society may mean that the law appears to be out of touch with society. Let us call the development political-oriented development.

In the first case, development by extension, the task is eminently one for judges; it is in this context that development is inevitable. If a case arises to which the law does not exactly "fit", the judge must either extend it, by analogy or otherwise, or declare that there is no law on the point, i. e., a *non liquet.* The significance of such a declaration is examined further below: however, the statement just made requires one clarification. If a claim is made resting on no established rule or right, and it does not appear justified to extend an existing rule to it by analogy, then the claim must be rejected, and this is not a *non liquet.*

An example of this is furnished by the claim of Belgium in the *Barcelona Traction* case, that diplomatic protection could be exercised on behalf of shareholders in a foreign company who had suffered loss as a result of a wrong done to the company. The Court held that it had not been established that such a right existed in customary law, and rejected the claim; it could, had it seen fit, have found that the general rules of diplomatic protection could be extended by analogy. As was expressly recognized by at least one Member of the Court, existing law could be said to be defective:② but that did not mean that the Court's finding was a *non liquet* resulting from a legal lacuna. It was not that there was no law on the point; it was that the existing law was negative on the point.

In the second case, equitable development, the problem is how far a judge may refrain from applying an established rule on the basis of abstract considerations of

① In these circumstances, the "general principles of law" of Article 38, para. 1 (c), of the ICJ Statute may perhaps be invoked; the limits of this process are however outside the ambit of this study.

② See the separate opinion of Judge Sir Gerald Fitzmaurice, *ICJ Reports 1970*, p. 78, para. 25. Note that the International Law Commission has invited comments of States on the question whether the law should be developed to give the State of the shareholders a right of action in some circumstances: http://www.un.org/law/ilc/sessions/54/54sess.htm, heading "Diplomatic Protection".

justice. In many legal systems the problem is stated as the role of equity in law.

In the third case, there is a more difficult question: who is to decide where and how the law is losing touch, and how it should be adapted? This is primarily the role of the legislator not the judge, though national systems may vary in the extent to which a judge may assume this role.

Against this background, what are the special characteristics of international law?

Firstly, it is eminently a *horizontal* system, where States are their own lawmakers; there is no superior legislator as in *vertical* systems (most national systems). Development that in a national system would be left to the legislator (political development) has to be provided some other way; but that does not mean that it is for the courts to provide it. In the international context, the International Law Commission is in fact filling this role to a considerable degree.

Secondly, the sources of law are special: primarily custom and treaty. Custom is, to a large extent, self-developing and self-adjusting; if States are not content with how customary law is operating in a particular sphere, they can change their practice, and custom will change accordingly. Against this background, a judge can "push" development by extension. Can a judge adopt the same approach to law deriving from treaty? If the parties are agreed that the treaty regime needs development, there is no problem; but if they are not, development seems prima facie to be barred. A judge can interpret and apply a treaty, but he cannot develop it, in the sense of adding to it. ①

We may recall the controversy, at the time of the preparation of the Vienna Convention on the Law of Treaties, over the proper role of interpretation. Objection was taken to the teleological approach to interpretation, and particularly to the so-called "policy-oriented" approach. The principal ground of objection was that it would transfer the power to decide what solution would best further the purpose of the treaty, from the parties (who might be thought best equipped to decide) to an international judge; such a solution is defensible on the municipal level in view of the status of judges and their integration into the society whose laws they are to

---

① The International Court seems however to have done something on these lines in its judgment in the case of the *Gabcikovo/Nagymaros Project*: see the present writer's comments in "Reflections on *lex ferenda*", 32 *Netherlands Yearbook of International Law* (2001), at pp. 22-24.

administer, but less so on the international level. The text eventually adopted as Article 31 (1) of the Convention (interpretation of the text "in the light of" the object and purpose of the treaty) amounts to a rejection of this extreme approach. By the same token, it would seem to exclude any judicial "development" of the law of the treaty regime.

A more modern notion, particularly in the human rights field, is that of a treaty that "has a life of its own". This idea has some judicial support in the context of human rights law; ① it is however a kind of equitable development. More important, the role of the judge in the human rights context, on the basis of the relevant texts and the attitude of the States making use of the Court, is arguably different from that of the International Court. ② It must remain doubtful whether an approach of this kind is open to the ICJ.

Thirdly, international law is a system in which judicial settlement is exceptional, despite greater use recently of the ICJ, and one that is based solely on consent of States. In the absence of clear indications of State consent to judicial development of the law, such development must be viewed restrictively.

As for *political development*, we can, I suggest, conclude a *priori* that is highly inappropriate for the ICJ: it is in fact synonymous with "progressive development" in the ILC sense, indicated above. Consider the developments in the law of the sea achieved by UNCLOS (though this was an extreme case): reform of the law of the sea could only be achieved by a "package deal" negotiated by States. Any attempt at judicial development of one element would have been counter-productive (as, indeed, one might consider some of the ICJ's rulings on maritime delimitation to have been). ③

---

① See for example the decisions of the European Court of Human Rights in *Tyrer* v. *United Kingdom*, Judgment of 25 April 1978, ECHR, Series A, No. 26; *Soering* v. *United Kingdom*, Judgment of 7 July 1989, ibid., No. 161, para. 102; *Selmouni* v. *France*, Judgment of 28 July 1999, ECHR Reports 199-V.

② This point is explained further in the present writer's article, "Reflections on *lex ferenda*", 32 *Netherlands Yearbook of International Law* (2001), p. 3, at pp. 24-25.

③ It has been forcibly argued by Weil that the law of maritime delimitation to be found in the Court's jurisprudence is wholly judge-made, and is out of step with the actual practice of States: see Weil, *Perspectives du droit de la délimitation maritime*, (Pedone, Paris, 1998), pp. 11-13; *Le droit international en quête de son identité*, 237 *Recueil des cours*, 1992-VI, p. 143.

Equitable development is much favoured by individual judges in their opinions,① but the Court has steered clear of it. In the *Barcelona Traction* case, for example, it was not willing to see in the application of equity a remedy for the lack of protection in international law of the Belgian shareholders. ② International law must correspond to the needs of the international community, and to the views of that community as to what is just. Any development of it must therefore work in that direction. But is the ICJ entitled to speak on behalf of the international community? Because a judge of the Court considers that an established rule of law is unjust or inequitable, does it follow that the international community would agree? Is it for the Court to determine in which direction the views of the community are developing? Some individual judges have expressed the view that this is the role of the Court, but the Court itself has —— rightly, it is suggested —— been reticent in that direction.

One may thus expect that development of the law by the ICJ has been effected within fairly narrow bounds; and the examples we can quote indicate that this is on the whole the case.

Ⅳ. Development by the ICJ in Practice

It is recognized that in a number of cases the Court has contributed to the development of the law in the sense that its decisions are cited in any discussion of the particular field of law. Some examples are the following:

· *Reparation for Injuries* (*1949*): the idea of the objective legal personality of an international organization (specifically, the United Nations); this may be regarded as recognition of an established trend in customary law.

· *Interpretation of the Genocide Convention* (*1951*): the effects of reservations to multilateral law-making treaties; the development consisted in extending to general law a trend in a particular region (the South American practice in relation to reservations to treaties).

· *Nottebohm* (*1956*): the non-opposability of a nationality lacking the "genuine link"; while seen as somewhat revolutionary, this decision could find a basis in the idea of "effective nationality" in cases of dual nationality.

---

① See for example the numerous separate or dissenting opinions of Judge (later Vice-President) Weeramantry.

② *ICJ Reports 1970*, pp. 48-50, paras. 92-101.

· *Fisheries* (*1951*): the idea of the "persistent objector"; this is a more doubtful case, but the argument was logically linked with the means of formation of customary law.

· *North Sea Continental Shelf* (*1969*): the role of equitable considerations in determining the extent of continental shelf rights; a development which, at least in its later manifestations, does not seem to have succeeded.

· *United States Diplomatic and Consular Staff in Tehran* (*1980*): responsibility of a State for conduct of persons not organs of the State, on the basis of the endorsement of that conduct by the State (which led to the inclusion of Article 11 in the ILC draft Articles on State Responsibility); a logical development of existing law.

· *Gabcikovo/Nagymaros Project* (*1997*): succession to treaties relating to territory; the relationship between treaty law and State responsibility; fundamental change of circumstances as ground for termination of treaty; application of trends already identified by the ILC and incorporated in treaty texts.

· *Arrest Warrant of 11 April 2000* (*2002*): Immunities of Ministers in relation to war crimes allegations.

These are matters of substantive law: but contributions to development of law of jurisdiction and procedure should not be overlooked, for example:

Nottebohm (*1953*): continuation of jurisdiction after expiry of title of jurisdiction; a logical corollary of the idea of consensual jurisdiction.

Monetary Gold (*1954*) (also *Nauru* and *East Timor*): the principle that a tribunal may not deal with third States' rights and duties without their consent; a similar corollary of the consent principle.

LaGrand (*2000*): the binding effect of an order of the Court indicating provisional measures; a much more doubtful case. ①

For the most part, these decisions, it is suggested, fit the paradigm indicated above as to the role of the Court in development of international law.

V. Development: to be Avoided or to be Sought out?

It is worth observing that the obligation to decide in accordance with international law clearly means the law as it is, however unsatisfactory it may seem. Thus

---

① See the present writer's comments in 72 *British Year Book of International Law* (2001), pp. 111 ff.

in the *Legality of the Threat or Use of Nuclear Weapons*, the desirability of a rule of customary law simply prohibiting such weapons was shared by almost everyone, but the Court had to rule that in customary law as it stands at present, no such rule yet exists. ① The Court may be able to develop international law, but cannot reverse its flow.

The Court must in every case state the law. Furthermore, in perhaps the majority of cases it will have to state as settled law what is in fact not entirely settled; the fact that a given dispute has been brought before it implies that more than one view is possible on the disputed point of law, or at least on how a recognized rule applies to a special set of facts. To this extent at least, development of international law is not only a possibility open to the Court; it is a duty.

This observation is however based on a tacit assumption, namely that it is not open to the Court to "refuse to give a decision on the grounds that the law is obscure or lacking". I quote those words from Article 5 of the French Civil Code, which expressly forbids French courts to take this course. Reference has already been made above to the possibility for a judge to pronounce a *non liquet*, the technical term for a declaration that there is no law on the point, so that no decision on the basis of law can be taken. There is however controversy on the point whether the ICJ, whose Statute contains nothing comparable to Article 5 of the Civil Code, ② has or has no power to do this.

It is sometimes argued that international law, as a legal system, is by definition complete, and that if a judge fills in apparent gaps, even large ones, he has the mandate to do so from international law, so that *non liquet* is neither necessary nor possible. In practice however one may well ask how a judge should have decided a dispute as to the maximum breadth of the territorial sea in the last years prior to the conclusion of the UNCLOS, when State practice had become so inconsistent that it could not be said there was any rule at all on the subject.

The choice is between a *non liquet* and a development of the law that crosses the line from the judicial to the legislative. The International Court has not yet been faced

---

① Cf. the views of Fitzmaurice in the *Barcelona Traction* case, already referred to above.

② Lauterpacht considered, and rejected, the theory that Article 59 of the Statute was intended to have this effect: see *The Development of International Law by the International Court*, p. 8, section 4.

with a clear-cut dilemma of this kind, though some aspects of the case of the *Legality of the Threat or Use of Nuclear Weapons* led it to a decision seen by some scholars as a *non liquet*. Most scholars would, I think, agree that in such a situation the Court should at least use all possible means to avoid pure judicial law-making, the difference of views being rather whether *non liquet* is or is not one of those means.

Consider however a case in which, in order to rule on a point, the Court would not have to legislate in this way, or not to this degree, but would have to come down on one side or the other of a controversial legal question. Suppose however that it would be possible to dispose of the case satisfactorily on a different ground, one involving well-settled rules of law. Which ground should the Court choose for its decision? In short, should the Court seize opportunities to develop the law, or on the contrary try not to do so unless absolutely necessary?①

This issue has been controversial between individual judges, as it applies also to judges' opinions; here it also raises the issue whether an individual judge may comment on a matter left undecided by the judgment.

It is my impression that a trend can be seen in the jurisprudence of the International Court over the last 30 or 40 years, away from a policy of what one might be called active development, and towards a sort of autolimitation, a preference for deciding cases, where a choice is legally appropriate, on the narrower and less controversial issues.

A turning point may have been marked by the *Barcelona Traction* case in 1970. On the one hand, as already noted, the Court declined to extend the principles governing diplomatic protection to enable the national State of shareholders in a company to recover from the damage suffered due to injury to the company: an example of judicial caution and reluctance to develop the law. Yet at the same time, the judgment in that case contained what is perhaps the high point of judicial activism: the famous dictum on obligations *erga omnes*:② that dictum was quite unnecessary to the Court's argument for determination of the case. It is an open secret that it was included for what one may call political reasons, as a signal concerning the

---

① I have discussed this problem elsewhere: see "Judicial Activism and the International Court of Justice", in Ando, McWhinney and Wolfrum (eds.), *Liber Amicorum Judge Shigeru Oda*, Kluwer 2002, p.75.

② *ICJ Reports 1970*, p.32, paras. 33-34; see also however ibid., p.47, para. 91.

dominant philosophy in the Court rather than the effecting of what was seen as an improvement in the law. Opinions may differ on whether it was either a good thing in itself, or a proper judicial act.

Further back in time, one may recall, as an example of judicial activism, the finding in the *Fisheries* case as to the opposability to Norway of the alleged "ten-mile rule" for bays; the dictum was unnecessary to the decision, and has set off much debate over the status of what is called the "persistent objector".

In the *Namibia* advisory opinion, one question that the Court could have left open was that of the validity of the decisions of the General Assembly and the Security Council resulting in the termination of the Mandate for South-West Africa. This is the sensitive problem of the Court's so-called "power of review". In contrast, in the *Lockerbie* cases, the Court has so far avoided ruling on the validity and effect of Security Council resolutions 748 (1992) and 883 (1993): the preliminary objection which would involve a conclusion on the point has been declared, somewhat unexpectedly, not to have "an exclusively preliminary character". ①

In three cases in the 1970s, the Court's jurisdiction was alleged to be based on the 1928 General Act for Pacific Settlement of International Disputes, a convention whose legal status was somewhat obscure, and which had (it was suggested) lapsed through desuetude. In all these cases, ② the Court was able to dispose of the case without ruling on the thorny problem of the status or continued existence of the General Act, an outcome which can hardly be coincidence.

There has subsequently been a number of cases in which Court has avoided deciding points that had been argued in the proceedings, but settlement of which was not necessary to the decision, e. g.:

· The *Gabcikovo/Nagymaros Project* case③ in 1997, in which the Court expressly refrained from expressing a view on the question whether the rule of universal succession to treaties as provided for in Article 34 of the Vienna Convention

① *Questions of Interpretation and Application of the 1971 Montreal Convention Arising from the Aerial Incident at Lockerbie*, *Preliminary Objections*, *Libya* v. *United Kingdom*, *ICJ Reports 1998*, p. 9; *Libya* v. *United States*, *ibid.*, p. 115.

② *Nuclear Tests* (*Australia* v. *France*); *Nuclear Tests* (*New Zealand* v. *France*); *Aegean Sea Continental Shelf*.

③ *Hungary/Slovakia*, *ICJ Reports 1997*, p. 7.

on Succession of States in respect of Treaties is also part of customary law, since it could, and did, dispose of the issue on the basis of the well settled rule of succession to treaties relating to territory stated in Article 12 of the same convention.

· *Kasikili/Sedudu Island*① in 1999, in which the Court was invited to rule on the status of acquisitive prescription as title to territory; it avoided doing so by finding, on the facts, that even if, in general, title to territory may be acquired by prescription, the requirements for such a title were not satisfied in the case before it. It therefore rejected Namibia's claim on this basis while carefully leaving open the general question of law. What is also striking is, first, that the parties agreed on the existence of a rule of law favouring acquisitive prescription; and secondly, that the Court measured Namibia's claim against the requirements for prescription asserted by Namibia itself, and went no further. On the basis of the established principle of *jura novit curia*, it would have been open to the Court to say whether or not it was satisfied that Namibia had correctly defined the legal requirements for acquisitive prescription. At least in theory, the Court could have said that Namibia's claim did not meet the requirements of the law as stated by Namibia, but that those requirements were too rigidly or exorbitantly stated, and that Namibia's claim could be upheld on the basis of the law as the Court found it to be.

· The case of the *Arrest Warrant*② as originally presented raised the very topical and controversial question of universal jurisdiction over accusations of war crimes; but the Court's eventual decision left this aspect entirely aside, to concentrate on the issue of immunities. It is true that the Congo decided not to press the issue of universal jurisdiction; but some of the judges expressed regret that the Court had not nevertheless ruled on it.

A very curious decision is that on the intervention of Italy in the *Libya/Malta Continental Shelf* case,③ where the Court observed that its decision could be based on two alternative interpretations of a provision of its Statute, and went on to say that it therefore did not need to say which of them was the correct one. This is however to

① *Botswana/Namibia*, *ICJ Reports 1999*, p. 1045.

② *Arrest Warrant of 11 April 2000* (*Democratic Rrepublic of the Congo* v. *Belgium*), *ICJ Reports 2002*.

③ *Continental Shelf* (*Libya/Malta*), *Application for Permission to Intervene*, *ICJ Reports 1984*, p. 3.

be explained by the need to reconcile two opposed points of view among the judges, rather than any feeling of judicial restraint.

A final point on this issue is that judicial development of the law, even if required by the case before the Court, may not always be in the interests of long-term development. The decision in the *North Sea Continental Shelf* cases,① that the equidistance method of delimitation was not required by a rule of customary law, was undoubtedly correct at the time when it was made. If the case had had to be decided a few years later, on the basis of accumulated practice, the result might have been different. As it is, it is arguable that the negative ruling checked the growth of an emerging rule of custom, which might have been the most satisfactory rule in the matter.

However, judicial decision may emphasize, or even reveal, an unsatisfactory element of existing law, so as to provoke a modification by treaty. Example: the *Lotus* case,② where the *specific* rule, that criminal jurisdiction may be asserted over acts on the high sea on the basis of the passive nationality principle, was reversed by international conventions③(see now Article 97 of UNCLOS).

Ⅵ. Conclusion

The Court has played a useful role in development of international law by extension; it has wisely kept clear of other kinds of development, namely equitable development and political development, which might endanger its credibility.

Much of the scope for development in a wider sense has been annexed by the International Law Commission, which —— as noted above —— has the advantage of State input. It is notable how often the International Court refers to treaties elaborated by the ILC (e. g. the Vienna Convention on the Law of Treaties; the Vienna Convention on Diplomatic Relations), to ILC texts that are not in force as treaties (e. g. Vienna Convention on Succession of States in Relation to Treaties), and even to texts that, at the time, were still under study (successive drafts of UNCLOS, the draft Articles on State Responsibility), in order to ascertain parallel customary law. This is a fruitful collaboration, as the ICJ can take account of subsequent

① *ICJ Reports 1969*, p. 3.

② *Judgment No. 9, PCIJ Series A, No. 10.*

③ Brussels Convention of 10 May 1952; 1958 Geneva Convention on the High Seas, art. 11.

development, and rule that a provision advanced by the ILC as development, or in respect of which it had doubts as to its customary-law status, is or has become customary law.

作者简介

曾令良

曾令良，男，1956年3月生，湖北麻城市人。1978年毕业于武汉大学外语系；美国密执安大学法学硕士（1986）；武汉大学法学硕士（1987）、法学博士（1992）；欧洲大学研究院博士研修生（1989～1990）。丹佛大学法学院福布莱特高级研究学者（1996～1997）；伯明翰大学法学院高级访问教授（1998）；香港城市大学特约教授（2003）；伊利诺斯科技大学肯特法学院高级访问教授（2004）。现任武汉大学国际法研究所教授、博士生导师、欧洲联盟法让·莫内讲座教授、武汉大学法学院院长，兼任教育部法学学科教学指导委员会副主任委员、中国法学会法学教育研究会副会长、中国法学会国际经济法学研究会副会长、中国法学会世界贸易组织法研究会副会长、中国法学会常务理事、中国国际法学会常务理事、全国司法考试协调委员会委员、世界贸易组织争端解决机构专家名单成员等职。主要著作有《欧洲共同体与现代国际法》（1992，独著）、《欧洲联盟与现代国际法》（1994，独著）、《世界贸易组织法》（1996，独著）、《21世纪初的国际法与中国》（2005，主编）。主要译著有［英］布朗利著《国际公法原理》（2003，合译、主审）。先后在国（境）内外重要学术期刊和学术会议上发表和宣读中、英文论文80余篇。先后获全国普通高等学校优秀教学成果国家级一等奖（1993）；湖北省首届社会科学优秀成果三等奖（1995）；国务院特殊政府津贴奖（1996）；全国普通高等学校第二届人文社会科学优秀研究成果二等奖（1998）；第二届全国十大“杰出中青年法学家”（1999）；教育部跨世纪人才奖（2001）；湖北省第二届社会科学优秀成果二等奖（2001）；湖北省有突出贡献中青年专家（2001）。

中国与东盟关系的国际法考量*

曾令良

目　次:

---

* 本文原是作者应邀向新加坡国立大学东亚研究所和厦门大学国际经济法研究所于 2004 年 12 月 3～4 日在新加坡举行的“中国与东盟关系：新的政治与法律问题”国际研讨会提交的论文和演讲稿，也是作者主持的教育部重大攻关项目“中国和平发展中的重大国际法律问题研究”的阶段性成果。根据中国—东盟关系的最新动态，现略有修改和增补。

一、中国与东盟关系：被忽略的国际法层面

自20世纪90年代以来，中国与东盟（Association of Southeast Asian Nations，ASEAN）之间的关系不断发展。与之相适应，有关中国与东盟关系的政治、军事、经济、文化、科技等领域的研究如火如荼地开展起来。然而，从法律角度，尤其是从国际法的角度来研究中国与东盟关系的成果，则相对冷清得多，至少在迄今的我国法学界是如此的境况。

这次，新加坡国立大学东亚研究所和中国厦门大学国际经济法研究所联合举办的“中国与东盟关系：新的政治与法律问题”国际研讨会，邀请政治、经济、法律等相关学科领域的专家同堂研讨中国与东盟关系，具有特别的意义。相邻的多学科来研究中国与东盟关系，不仅使相关的各学科相得益彰，彼此吸取研究方法和研究成果的营养，获得启迪，更重要的是，可以促使中国与东盟关系的探讨通过多角度的审视而更加全面、系统和剔透。

毋庸置疑，国际法在中国与东盟关系中扮演着不可或缺的重要角色。法律的基本功能可以依次概括为：一是在有关法律主体之间建立一定的法律关系；二是稳定有关法律主体之间已经建立的关系；三是促进有关法律主体之间关系的发展。作为法律的组成部分，国际法在中国与东盟之间在政治、军事、经济、文化、科技和社会领域的各种关系中的基本作用，同样应该概括为“建立、稳定、促进”这六个字。无论是双方的定期政治磋商，还是非传统安全领域的合作，都必须通过一定的国际法律文件形式予以确立；不论是双方建立自由贸易区，还是开展更为广泛的经济、科技和社会事务的合作，都不能脱离彼此之间已经或正在谈判缔结的国际协定。可见，国际法是中国与东盟之间建立和发展各种友好合作关系的基础和手段。因此，我们在重视中国与东盟关系的政治、军事、经济、科技和社会领域研究的同时，不可忽略其中的国际法层面。

为此，本文拟首先从国际法的角度巡视中国与东盟关系业已形成的框架和体系，并试图从中概括出若干法律特征。接着，通过研读中国与东盟关系的各种法律文件，分析其中宣示或隐含的国际法原则。最后，基于中国与东盟关系的现行法律和事实，勾列出中国与东盟关系发展中的若干法律问题，并试图提出解决这些法律问题的建议。

二、中国与东盟关系：现行法律框架巡礼

（一）1994年的《互换函件》：正式合作关系的建立

一般都认为，中国与东盟的关系始于20世纪90年代初中国相继与印度尼

西亚实现关系正常化、与新加坡和文莱建立外交关系。① 中国与所有东盟成员国建立或恢复外交关系为最终中国与东盟之间关系的建立与发展奠定了基础。更为普遍的观点认为，中国与东盟建立正式关系的标志是1991年7月前中国国务院副总理兼外交部长钱其琛应邀作为马来西亚的嘉宾出席在吉隆坡举行的东盟部长会议（ASEAN Ministerial Meeting，AMM）。这是中国领导人首次出席东盟会议。在这次会议上，钱其琛外长表示中国愿意成为东盟的对话伙伴，并有兴趣与东盟进行合作，尤其是在科技领域的合作。1993年9月，应当时外交部副部长唐家璇邀请，前东盟秘书长来北京访问并发布了关于双方探索建立协商伙伴关系会晤的联合新闻声明。② 但是，从法律角度来看，中国与东盟建立正式的合作关系应该是1994年7月23日，即当时的东盟秘书长与中国外交部长在曼谷就建立联合经济贸易合作委员会（Joint Committee on Economic and Trade Cooperation）和联合科技合作委员会（Joint Committee on Cooperation in Science and Technology）的互换函件（Exchange of Letters）。③ 此等互换函件是中国与东盟之间建立正式合作关系的法律确认。与此同时，中国与东盟开始就共同关心的政治与安全问题建立协商制度。1996年7月在第29届东盟外长会议上，东盟赋予中国完全对话伙伴地位（full dialogue partner status）。

（二）1997年《联合声明》：睦邻伙伴关系的纲领性文件

1997年12月中国与东盟举行了第一次10+1的非正式高峰会议，并发表了题为“东盟—中国合作面向21世纪”的《东盟成员国国家元首/政府首脑与中华人民共和国主席会议联合声明》（Joint Statement of the Meeting of Heads of State/Government of the Member States of ASEAN and the President of the

---

① See Lee Lai To, *China's Relations with ASEAN: Partners in the 21st Century?*, *Pacifica Review*, Volume 13, Number 1, February 2001 (electronic version); H. E. Ong Keng Yong (Secretary General of ASEAN), Keynote Address at the ASEAN-China Forum 2004, Developing ASEAN-China Relations: Realities and Prospects (electronic version), Singapore, 23 June 2004, http://www.aseansec.org/16256.htm, 2004年10月5日访问。

② See Joint Press Statement for the Meeting to Explore the Establishment of the Consultative Relationship with the People's Republic of China, Beijing, China, 13-14 September 1993, http://www.aseansec.org/5875.htm, 2004年10月8日访问。

③ 此前的1993年9月，东盟秘书长曾应邀率领东盟代表团访问北京。正是在这次访问期间，双方就建立联合经济与贸易合作委员会和联合科技合作委员会达成一致。See ASEAN-China Dialogue, Overview of ASEAN-PRC Relations, http://202.154.12.3/5874.htm, 2004年9月28日访问。

People's Republic of China）（以下简称为1997年《联合声明》）。1997年《联合声明》是双方最高领导人通过法律形式向国际社会公开发表的政治宣言和庄严承诺，在中国与东盟关系史上具有划时代的深远意义。

在1997年《联合声明》中，双方最高领导人约定，促进中国—东盟“睦邻友好关系”（good-neighbourly and friendly relations），增进高层交流，加强所有领域的对话与合作机制，以增强理解和相互信任。双方一致表示，将在平等互利原则和共同分担责任的基础上，通过加强各种双边和多边合作促进经济增长、可持续发展和社会进步，实现21世纪国家和地区的繁荣。双方承诺，将通过和平手段而非诉诸武力或以武力相威胁解决彼此间的分歧或争端；尤其在南中国海问题上，将根据公认的国际法包括1982年《联合国海洋法公约》，通过友好协商和谈判的方式解决彼此间的争端；在寻求争端解决的过程中，积极探索在有争议地区进行合作的途径；继续实行自我克制，不让现存的分歧阻碍友好关系和合作的发展。《联合声明》宣示，中国支持东盟在国际和区域事务中的积极作用，尊重和支持东盟为在东南亚建立“和平、自由和中立区”（zone of peace, freedom and neutrality）的努力，欢迎《东南亚无核武器区条约》（the Southeast Asia Nuclear Weapon-Free Zone Treaty）的生效；双方还表示将就中国加入该条约的议定书继续进行磋商。东盟各成员国再次确认继续坚持“一个中国”的政策，并相信一个稳定、和平和繁荣的中国是构成世界尤其是亚太地区的长期和平、稳定和发展的重要因素。①

（三）2002年《全面经济合作框架协定》：全面进入经贸实质合作的标志

正如现任东盟秘书长所断言的，虽然中国与东盟合作关系在20世纪90年代中期已经正常化，但是双方之间真正进行实质性的合作直到2001年才开始启动。② 在2001年11月举行的中国—东盟高峰会议上，当时的中国总理朱镕基正式提出10年之内建设中国—东盟自由贸易区的设想。东盟方面接受了这一提议。经过几轮的磋商，在2002年举行的高峰会议上，双方联合宣布了这一历史性的决定，并签署了《东南亚国家联盟与中华人民共和国全面经济合

---

① See Joint Statement of the Meeting of Heads of State/Government of the Member States of ASEAN and the President of the People's Republic of China, Huala Lumpur, Malaysia, 16 December 1997, paras. 3, 5, 8 and 9.

② H. E. Ong Keng Yong (Secretary General), Keynote Address at the ASEAN-China Forum 2004, Developing ASEAN-China Relations: Realities and Prospects (electronic version), Singapore, 23 June 2004, http://www.aseansec.org/16256.htm, 2004年10月7日访问。

作框架协定》（Framework Agreement on Comprehensive Economic Cooperation between ASEAN and the People's Republic of China on Strategic Partnership for Peace and Prosperity）（以下简称为 2002 年《框架协定》）。①

2002 年《框架协定》在中国—东盟关系史上具有划时代的意义。它是调整双方之间关系的第一个正式的条约，成为规范双方未来以建立自由贸易区为核心的全面而实质性的经济合作关系最直接的法律文件。《框架协定》涉及货物贸易、服务贸易、投资和其他相关领域。它规定了中国—东盟自由贸易区的指导方针、基本原则、范围和模式，包括早期收获和给予老挝、柬埔寨、缅甸和越南等东盟新成员国特殊和区别待遇。从 2004 年开始，中国—东盟自由贸易区正式谈判启动，计划在 2010 年以前实现中国与东盟 6 个创始成员国（文莱、印度尼西亚、马来西亚、菲律宾、新加坡和泰国）之间的自由贸易区，在 2015 年以前实现中国与东盟其他欠发达成员国柬埔寨、老挝、缅甸和越南之间的自由贸易区。与此同时，2002 年《框架协定》第二部分明确规定了双方在以下五个经济部门或领域优先开展合作：农业、信息与通讯技术、人力资源开发与投资和湄公河流域开发。此外，《框架协定》还规定应将双方的经济合作扩展到其他领域，如银行、金融、旅游、工业合作、交通、基础电讯、知识产权、中小企业、环境、生物技术、渔业、森林与森林产品、采矿、能源和次区域合作，等等。

（四）2002 年《非传统安全合作宣言》：新型安全问题合作的基本法律依据

鉴于非传统安全问题越来越成为影响亚太地区和国际和平与稳定的重要因素及其日趋加剧的严重性，考虑到非传统安全问题的复杂性和根深蒂固的背景，中国和东盟领导人认识到有必要采取政治、经济、外交、法律、科学技术和其他手段相结合的系统方式和通过区域和全球合作的机制来应对非传统安全问题带来的挑战，并相信疆域相邻的中国和东盟在应对各种非传统安全问题上具有广泛的共同利益。为此，双方于 2002 年 11 月 4 日在柬埔寨发表了《中国与东盟在非传统安全问题领域合作联合宣言》（Joint Declaration of ASEAN and China on Cooperation in the Field of Non-traditional Security Issues）（以下简称为 2002 年《非传统安全合作宣言》）。

2002 年《非传统安全合作宣言》为中国和东盟在应对日益严重的诸多非传统安全问题上开展双边合作提供了直接的法律基础，是落实 1997 年《联合

① 2003 年中国和东盟成员国代表 10 月 6 日签署了《修正东南亚国家联盟和中华人民共和国全面经济合作框架协定议定书》，对 2002 年《框架协定》的有关条款作出修改。

声明》有关“加强所有领域的对话与合作机制”政治承诺的具体行动之一。2002 年《非传统安全合作宣言》规定了此等合作的宗旨，即增强双方应对非传统安全问题的能力，促进双方稳定和发展，维护地区和平与安全。《宣言》明确地将打击非法毒品贩运、贩卖妇女儿童、海盗、恐怖主义、走私军火、洗钱、国际经济犯罪和网络犯罪等列为当前优先合作的领域或事项。《宣言》列举了以下 5 种合作形式：（1）增强信息交流；（2）增强人员交流与培训和加强能力建设；（3）增强在非传统安全问题上的实际运作；（4）增强对非传统安全问题的联合研究；（5）探索其他合作领域和模式。为此，《宣言》确定将制定中、长期合作计划和具体行动计划。

遵照 2002 年《非传统安全合作宣言》，经过一段时期的磋商，双方于 2004 年 1 月 10 日在曼谷签署了《东盟成员国政府和中华人民共和国政府在非传统安全问题领域合作谅解备忘录》（Memorandum of Understanding between the Governments of the Member Countries of the ASEAN and the Government of the People's Republic of China on Cooperation in the Field of Non-traditional Security Issues）（以下简称为 2004 年《非传统安全合作备忘录》）。该《备忘录》是进一步深化和实施 2002 年《非传统安全合作宣言》的具体法律文件。其目标是：根据各自的国内法律和规章，开发实际战略，以增强每个国家和作为整体地区应对各种非传统安全问题挑战的能力。为此，《备忘录》就《非传统安全合作宣言》中确定的 5 种合作方式逐一制定了具体的中、长期合作计划和措施，并且就实施机构、经费安排、保密事项、争端解决以及《备忘录》的中止、修订与修正、生效、期限和终止等具体事项分别作出了详细的规定。

（五）2002 年《南海各方行为宣言》：相互信任、克制和合作的庄严承诺

由于历史和现实中错综复杂的因素，中国与东盟部分成员国在南海某些岛屿问题上一直存在领土争端，而且时有摩擦发生。因此，主张对南海有关岛屿享有主权和管辖权的各方的行为，既影响有关各方之间和中国与东盟的双重关系，又影响整个亚太地区甚至全球的和平与安全。多年来，中国与东盟有关国家一直在寻求某种有利于和平和持久解决南海分歧与争端的途径。2002 年 11 月 4 日，中国与东盟成员国代表在柬埔寨举行的第八届东盟高峰会议期间签署了《南海各方行为宣言》（Declaration on the Conduct of Parties in the South China Sea）。该《宣言》的签署标志着中国和东盟本着务实的态度在有争议的南海问题上正在建立一种相互信任、相互克制和相互合作的争端处理机制。

为防止南海有争议的领土出现紧张局势，杜绝或至少减少可能出现的军事冲突，《宣言》各方确认信守《联合国宪章》的宗旨与原则、《联合国海洋法

公约》、《东南亚友好合作条约》、和平共处五项原则和其他公认的国际法原则；约定尊重和保证南海的航行自由；承诺采用和平手段而不诉诸武力来解决彼此间的领土争端；承诺对有争议的岛屿在活动上自我克制，建立和增强互信；约定防务官员之间交换意见，在自愿的基础上将军事演练活动事先通知对方，并对任何处在危险或危难的人员提供人道待遇；一致同意在海洋环境保护与科学研究、航行安全、搜寻与救助行动和打击跨国犯罪等方面进行合作。

（六）2003年中国加入《东南亚友好合作条约》：一个负责任大国的法律举措

2003年10月初，在中国—东盟高峰会议上，中国总理温家宝出席了中国加入《东南亚友好合作条约》（Treaty of Amity and Cooperation in Southeast Asia）① 的签字仪式，中国成为东南亚地区以外第一个加入该条约的大国。该条约的宗旨是，“促进缔约国人民之间的持久和平和友好与合作，增强其力量、稳定和更密切的关系”。②该条约确立了指导缔约国之间关系的如下一些基本原则：相互尊重独立、主权、平等、领土完整和民族特性；各国享有不受外来干涉、颠覆或强迫的民族生存权利；互不干涉内政；和平解决分歧或争端；放弃武力威胁或使用武力；相互开展有效合作。③

中国加入《东南亚友好合作条约》将对东南亚、亚太地区乃至整个世界的和平与安全产生积极和深远的影响。④ 中国的这一非凡举措表明中国是一个负责任的大国，有利于减轻甚至消除东盟各国对中国崛起的担忧，使“中国威胁论”不能自圆其说，因为加入该条约意味着中国继续奉行独立自主和平外交路线，说明中国愿意与世界上的国家“结伴而不结盟”。中国加入该条约有利于中国与东盟关系的可持续发展，因为这使双边关系的纵横发展增添了更加稳固的国际法基础，标志着双边和睦邻友好合作关系的条约化和制度化，表

---

① 该条约于1976年2月24日由东盟最初的5个成员国（新加坡、泰国、菲律宾、印度尼西亚和马来西亚）在印尼签署，后来加入东盟的成员国也陆续加入该条约。该条约最初只对东南亚国家开放，后经1987年和1998年两次修订，允许东南亚地区以外的国家加入。巴布亚新几内亚是第一个加入该条约的东南亚地区以外的国家。

② See Article 1, Treaty of Amity and Cooperation in Southeast Asia.

③ See Article 2, Treaty of Amity and Cooperation in Southeast Asia.

④ 参见曹云华：《远亲不如近邻——中国加入〈东南亚友好合作条约〉的意义》，载中国人民大学书报复印资料中心：《中国外交》2004年第1期；张锡镇：《中国外交的又一大手笔——中国与东盟建立战略伙伴关系并正式加入〈东南亚友好合作条约〉》，载《人民日报》2003年10月9日。

明中国与东盟永远做好邻居、好伙伴的庄严承诺，从而使中国—东盟关系更加具有稳定性和连续性。中国加入该条约有利于和平解决中国—东盟之间的各种争端，因为该条约为缔约国规定了和平解决争端的基本原则、方法和程序。中国加入该条约有利于建立全球政治经济新秩序和区域一体化，因为这显示中国有诚意并用实际行动参与国际关系的民主化与法治化进程，意味着中国作为一个正在崛起的地区大国愿意与小国、弱国平等合作，共同构建地区的和平、稳定和繁荣的美好未来。

（七）2003年《战略伙伴联合宣言》：中国与东盟关系的新蓝图

2003年10月8日在印尼巴厘岛举行的中国—东盟高峰会议的另一个重要结晶是，双方领导人共同签署了“面向和平与繁荣战略伙伴关系”的《东盟和中华人民共和国国家/政府首脑联合宣言》（Joint Declaration of the Heads of State/Government of the ASEAN and the People's Republic of China on Strategic Partnership for Peace and Prosperity）（以下简称为2003年《战略伙伴联合宣言》）。该文件的签署和发表标志着中国与东盟的关系进入了一个新的阶段，即始从协商伙伴关系，经对话伙伴关系发展到战略伙伴关系，从而使双方的睦邻友好关系上升到更高的层次。

2003年《战略伙伴联合宣言》回顾了自1997年双方领导人签署《联合声明》以来中国与东盟在政治、经济、安全、区域和国际事务等领域的关系得到了快速、全面而深入的发展。双方一致认为，东盟和中国彼此已成为重要的合作伙伴。《宣言》特别强调中国—东盟关系对于本地区和平、发展与合作的战略重要性以及对世界和平与发展的积极贡献。考虑到当今世界正在经受复杂而又深刻的变化，作为亚太地区的两个重要伙伴，加强彼此之间的合作将符合双方的目前和长远利益，并有益于本地区的和平与繁荣。为此，《宣言》庄严宣告：中国与东盟建立面向和平与繁荣的“战略伙伴关系”（strategic partnership）。

《宣言》确认，建立战略伙伴关系的宗旨是，通过在21世纪全面加深和扩大中国—东盟合作关系，促进中国与东盟之间的友好、互利合作和睦邻关系，从而为本地区的持久和平、发展和合作作出进一步的贡献。《宣言》还明确宣告，此等战略伙伴关系是非结盟的（non-aligned）、非军事的（non-military）和非排他的（non-exclusive），不妨碍各参与方与其他国家和组织发展各种友好与合作关系。《宣言》规定，中国—东盟战略伙伴关系是一种全方位的前瞻性的合作，重点是政治、经济、社会事务、安全和国际与地区事务。为此，《宣言》的最后部分就这些领域建立战略伙伴关系的主要内容和措施分别作出了原则性的规定。

三、中国与东盟关系：贯穿始终的一般国际法律准则

（一）确立国际法基本原则的支配地位

综上巡礼，中国与东盟的关系，从建立之初到发展至今，一直与一般国际法相伴而行。中国—东盟关系的每一个重要阶段、每一个重要举措，每一个重要成果，都是以一般国际法为基础，通过国际协议的形式表现出来。中国与东盟发表和签署的各种重要文件特别强调国际法基本原则在双方关系中的指导地位和作用。为此，双方发表和签署的各种宣言、声明和条约均反复重申遵守国际公认的国际关系基本准则，来深化和扩展在政治、安全、经济、社会事务和国际及区域事务等领域的合作，来处理彼此间存在的分歧和争端。

我们在分析中国—东盟关系法律文件时，不难发现它们有一个共同的特点，即在确认国际法基本原则的支配地位过程中尤其突出列出包含这些原则的重要国际条约、国际组织章程和具有普遍性或代表性的国际法基本准则的名称。1997 年《联合声明》中首次确认"《联合国宪章》、《东南亚友好合作条约》、'和平共处五项原则'和公认的国际法应作为指导其各种关系的基本规范"。① 2002 年《非传统安全合作宣言》重申这些条约或原则，只是在措辞上略有不同：双方在非传统安全领域的合作"应在遵守和平共处五项原则和《联合国宪章》及《东南亚友好合作条约》所包含的其他公认的国际法规范……的基础上进行"。② 2002 年《南海各方行为宣言》也有类似的列举："各方重申其保证遵守《联合国宪章》宗旨与原则、1982 年《联合国海洋法公约》、《东南亚友好合作条约》、和平共处五项原则和应作为调整国与国关系基本准则的其他公认的国际法原则"。③ 2003 年《战略伙伴联合宣言》一如既往地重申："东盟—中国合作将继续以《联合国宪章》、《东南亚友好合作条约》、'和平共处五项原则'和其他公认的调整国际关系的基本准则作为其指导方针"。④

---

① See Joint Statement of the Meeting of Heads of State/Government of the Member States of ASEAN and the President of the People's Republic of China, 16 December 1997, para. 2.

② See Joint Declaration of ASEAN and China on Cooperation in the Field of Non-traditional Security Issues, 4 November 2002, preamble.

③ See Declaration on the Conduct of Parties in the South China Sea, para. 1.

④ See Joint Declaration of the Heads of State/Government of the ASEAN and the People's Republic of China on Strategic Partnership for Peace and Prosperity, para. 5.

通过上述阐释，我们从中还发现一些耐人寻味的含义：

第一，上述有关中国东盟关系文件无一例外地提及《联合国宪章》，且绝大多数将其列为首位。这一方面说明《联合国宪章》是当今国际法律文件中效力和权威最高的造法条约，其载明的七项原则不仅是联合国及其会员国必须遵守的基本准则，其载明的各项宗旨不仅是联合国及其会员国必须为之努力的目标，而且是全世界所有国家、国际组织和合作机制都必须奉行的基本原则和为之努力的目标。另一方面说明中国与东盟之间在政治、安全、经济、社会事务、国际和区域事务等领域的合作关系，不论是过去的协商伙伴关系和对话伙伴关系阶段，还是现在和未来的战略伙伴关系时期，都必须与《联合国宪章》规定的宗旨相一致，以其规定的诸项原则作为最根本的行为准则。

第二，上述文件无一例外地提及“和平共处五项原则”，有的甚至将其列为首位。这充分表明：中国和缅甸、印度在 1954 年共同倡导的“和平共处五项原则”，经过半个世纪的实践检验，已经被公认为是现代国际关系基本准则的重要组成部分，甚至是最核心的内容。尤其令人瞩目的是，中国与东盟联合发表或签署的各种宣言或声明反复明确载入“和平共处五项原则”，这在中国与其他国家或国际组织之间的法律文件中是不多见的，甚至是独树一帜的。由此可见，“和平共处五项原则”在中国—东盟合作关系中的支配地位，毫无疑义地得到所有东盟成员国的认可。

第三，上述文件无一例外地提及《东南亚友好合作条约》，甚至在中国没有正式加入该条约之前所发表或签署的声明和宣言中就明确将该条约列为指导中国—东盟关系的基本文件范畴。其中的内涵是深刻的。这意味着虽然该条约不是专门规范中国—东盟合作关系的文件，甚至其缔约国向东南亚地区以外的国家开放，但是双方确认中国—东盟的各种合作关系的根本宗旨是该条约宗旨的重要组成部分，更何况该条约确立的诸项原则本身是公认的国际法基本原则的组成部分。即便如此，中国从一开始就认可《东南亚友好合作条约》在中国—东盟关系中的指导地位，尤其是在没有加入该条约之前就作出如此承诺，这在国际关系实践中同样是一种特殊的政治姿态和法律举止。从中可以看出中国旨在促进中国—东盟持久睦邻友好关系和东南亚地区持久和平、稳定和发展之诚意。

第四，上述文件无一例外地提及“其他公认的国际法原则”。这表明双方对于调整中国—东盟关系的国际法基本原则坚持的是一种开放、与时俱进的政策和立场。首先，双方不仅确认那些明确列举的国际文件所载明的国际法基本原则，而且还认可未列举的其他国际习惯法或国际文件所包含的国际法基本原则，即使中国和东盟成员国或其中一方或几方不是该文件的参与方。例如，

1955 年万隆会议《最后公报》中所载明的各国和平相处和友好合作的十项原则、1975 年欧洲安全与合作会议通过的《欧洲关于指导与会国间关系原则宣言》宣示的十项原则，无疑属于这种类型。其次，双方以一种发展的眼光来看待支配中国—东盟关系的国际法基本原则，即不仅现行的国际法基本原则是调整彼此关系的指导原则，将来形成的国际法基本原则同样是指导相互关系的基本准则。当然，这些“其他原则”，不论现行的，还是将来的，都必须是国际社会“公认的”。

第五，惟有 2002 年《南海各方行为宣言》将 1982 年《联合国海洋法公约》作为应对南海问题的一般国际法指导文件。这显然是一个理所当然的特例。1982 年《联合国海洋法公约》是现代海洋法领域最重要的造法条约，是在近代、现代海洋习惯法和条约法基础上编纂而成的。中国与部分东盟成员国有关南海的领土、资源、航行等事项的分歧和争端的解决，在遵行其他公认的国际法基本原则的同时，无疑必须遵守 1982 年《联合国海洋法公约》这一最具权威性的专门性造法公约。

那么，中国—东盟关系法律文件中反复提及的这些国际法律文件主要包含了哪些一般国际法基本原则呢？概括起来，主要有：互相尊重独立、主权、平等、领土完整和民族特性原则；互不干涉内政或内部事务原则；放弃使用武力或以武力相威胁原则；和平解决分歧或争端原则；有效合作原则，等等。①

（二）突出双方经贸合作与 WTO 原则和规则的一致性

综观中国—东盟关系，无论是从其发展的进程和规模来看，还是从其法律基础的着眼，经济与贸易合作领域一直处于领先地位。从国际法的角度出发，我们有必要对双方在这一牵头合作领域是否符合 WTO 的原则、规则和制度作些专门考量。这里有两方面的因素考虑：一方面，旨在建立中国—东盟自由贸易区为核心的 2002 年《框架协定》及其 2003 年议定书是中国与东盟之间的基本法律渊源；另一方面，WTO 是国际贸易领域具有代表性的普遍性组织，中国和东盟的多数成员国均为该组织的成员，均为该组织各种多边贸易协定的缔

① See Treaty of Amity and Cooperation in Southeast Asia, Article2; Joint Statement of the Meeting of Heads of State/Government of the Member States of ASEAN and the President of the People's Republic of China, 16 December 1997, paras. 2 and 8; Joint Declaration of ASEAN and China on Cooperation in the Field of Non-traditional Security Issues, preamble; Declaration on the Conduct of Parties in the South China Sea; Joint Declaration of the Heads of State/Government of the ASEAN and the People's Republic of China on Strategic Partnership for Peace and Prosperity, paras. 4 and 5.

约方。

1. 基本宗旨的一致性

我们可以首先从中国—东盟自由贸易区与WTO在基本宗旨方面的一致性入手进行分析。

WTO的宗旨主要包含在《建立世界贸易组织的马拉喀什协议》（以下简称为“WTO协议”)、1947年《关贸总协定》、《哈瓦那宪章》和《服务贸易总协定》等法律文件的序言之中。从中可以概括出WTO的基本宗旨如下:(1) 提高生活标准；(2) 确保充分就业和实际收入与有效需求的大量和稳定增长；(3) 扩大货物和服务的生产与贸易；(4) 允许最佳利用世界资源和确保可持续发展；(5) 确保发展中国家，特别是最不发达国家在国际贸易增长中获得与其经济发展需要相称的份额。①

中国与东盟之间以建立自由贸易区为核心的经济合作，其基本目标可以从2002年《框架协定》和上述其他相关文件中识别出来。2002年《框架协定》的序言清晰地表明，中国和东盟国家意欲建立自由贸易区和作出全面经济合作安排的目的是促进在21世纪更紧密的经济关系，即最大限度地减少壁垒；深化双方之间的经济联系；降低费用；增加区域内贸易与投资；增加经济效率；为双方的企业创造具有更多机会和更大经济规模的更大市场；增强双方对资本和智力的吸引力。该协议第1条以更加直接和简洁的措辞进一步将这些宗旨表述为:(1) 加强和增进经济、贸易和投资合作；(2) 逐步促进货物贸易和服务贸易自由化，并建立一个透明的、自由的和便利的投资制度；(3) 为更紧密的经济合作探索新的领域和开发适当的措施；(4) 为东盟新成员国提供更有效的经济融合，并在各方之间建立缩小差距的桥梁。

通过比较二者的基本宗旨，我们不难得出结论:以建立自由贸易区为基础的中国—东盟经济合作安排的宗旨，从根本上讲，完全符合WTO的各项宗旨，只不过在措辞技术上不一样。当然，WTO的宗旨是全球性的，而中国—东盟自由贸易区的宗旨是双边的或区域的。但是，两种体制之宗旨的实现又是相互支撑的。

2. 一般规则和纪律的一致性

如本文前面所阐述的，中国与东盟之间达成的各种文件特别强调国际公法的一系列基本原则在双方关系的所有领域中的支配地位。除此之外，2002年《框架协定》还专门制定了调整双方经济合作，尤其是建立中国—东盟自由贸易区的基本规则和一般纪律。所有这些规则和纪律或者与WTO相关条款的表

---

① 参见曾令良:《世界贸易组织法》，武汉大学出版社1996年版，第34~37页。

述相同或相似，或者在含义上与其保持一致。2002年《框架协定》中的有些条文甚至直接提及其与WTO规则和纪律的一致性。

最惠国待遇原则是最好的例证。中国和那些已经是WTO成员的东盟成员国在中国—东盟自由贸易区中适用最惠国待遇原则是不存在问题的，因为这个原则在WTO法律体系中是一种自动适用的原则，且具有强制性。但是，最惠国待遇原则是否在中国与那些非WTO成员的东盟成员国之间适用则是一个可谈判的事项，而且取决于中国政府一方。后者对此的态度是十分肯定的。2002年《框架协定》第9条规定："中国应从本协议签署之日起给予非WTO成员的东盟成员国以符合WTO规则和纪律的最惠国待遇"。

特殊和区别待遇原则是这方面的另一个例证。2002年《框架协定》的缔约方，"认识到东盟成员国之间经济发展的不同阶段和需要灵活性，尤其是需要提供便利以增强东盟新成员国参与中国—东盟经济合作和扩大它们的出口，包括增强其国内能力、效率和竞争力",① 承诺"向东盟新成员国提供特殊和区别待遇以及灵活性",② 以促进"更紧密的经济合作"和"缩小发展差距"。③

3. 具体措施的一致性

根据2002年《框架协定》第2条的规定，建立中国—东盟自由贸易区和开展全面经济合作的主要措施可以概括为：（1）逐步取消货物贸易的关税和非关税壁垒；（2）逐步实现服务贸易自由化；（3）建立公开和竞争性的投资制度。为此，如上所述，将给予东盟欠发达成员国一定的特殊和区别待遇以及灵活性。④ 作为保证或加强措施，缔约方还承诺建立有效的贸易与投资机制，如简化海关程序、开发相互承认安排和有效实施制度，等等。

毫无疑问，所有这些措施与WTO倡导的货物贸易、服务贸易和投资自由化的理念是一致的。这些措施甚至与相应的WTO多边贸易协议（如关贸总协定、服务贸易总协定、与贸易有关的投资措施协定，等等）的规定是相同的或具有同等效果。

此外，有些中国—东盟自由贸易区所采取的措施直接指向有关的WTO要求。在货物贸易方面，2002年《框架协定》第2（6）条明确规定，缔约各方

---

① 参见2002年《框架协定》，序言。

② 参见2002年《框架协定》，第2（4）条。

③ 参见2002年《框架协定》，第1（3）和（4）条。

④ 灵活性也将根据对等和互利原则给予所有缔约方的货物、服务和投资的敏感领域或部门。参见2002年《框架协定》，第2（5）条。

作出的有关取消关税和非关税壁垒的承诺，包括“早期收获”，“应符合 WTO 要求取消缔约方之间实质上所有贸易的关税”。该条文同时还规定，中国—东盟自由贸易区内的保障措施、补贴与反补贴纪律、反倾销措施、与贸易有关的知识产权保护等，应以关贸总协定的原则、现行的关贸总协定纪律和与贸易有关的知识产权协定为基础。在服务贸易领域，2002 年《框架协定》第 4 条要求，中国—东盟自由贸易区内消除现行歧视措施、禁止新的歧视措施和扩大服务贸易自由化应符合服务贸易总协定。

最后，在中国—东盟自由贸易区中，“早期收获计划”的任何承诺的修改、保障行动、紧急措施和其他诸如反倾销及补贴与反补贴的贸易补救措施，尽管是临时的，应依照有关的 WTO 规定来进行。①

4. 例外条款的一致性

关于例外条款问题，涉及两个层面。首先，它涉及 2002 年《框架协定》有关中国—东盟自由贸易区的例外规定，即这些例外规定与有关 WTO 规定的一致性问题；其次，它涉及中国—东盟自由贸易区本身与有关 WTO 规定的一致性，即中国—东盟自由贸易区依照 WTO 法律制度的合法性或正当性问题。

就第一个层面而言，2002 年《框架协定》第 10 条在很大程度上是关贸总协定第 20 条、第 21 条和服务贸易总协定第 14 条、第 14 条之一的一种变换措辞。2002 年《框架协定》列举了四种“一般例外”，即（1）保护国家安全；（2）保护具有艺术、历史和文化古迹价值的物品；（3）保护公共道德；（4）保护人类、动物和植物生命和健康。显然，上述第一种例外规定可与关贸总协定第 21 条和服务贸易总协定第 14 条之一所包含的“安全例外”相对应，不过措辞更加简洁。其余三项一般例外规定正好与关贸总协定第 20 条第（6）、（1）和（2）款以及服务贸易总协定第 14 条第（1）和（2）款的规定相对应。值得注意的是，2002 年《框架协定》第 10 条还规定了适用这些例外的一个重要前提，即不应“构成武断或不正当的歧视”或“对贸易的隐蔽限制”。这一前提规定与关贸总协定第 20 条和服务贸易总协定第 14 条的序言是类似的。②

让我们将讨论转移到中国—东盟自由贸易区依照 WTO 的合法性或正当性问题。从实质上讲，建立自由贸易区与多边贸易体制最基本的原则——最惠国待遇是相悖的。但是，多边贸易体制从一开始就允许自由贸易区作为最惠国待

① 参见 2002 年《框架协定》，第 6.3（4）条。

② 关于 WTO 例外规定的全面、系统和详细分析，参见陈卫东：《WTO 例外条款解读》，对外经济贸易大学出版社 2002 年版。

遇原则的一种例外而存在。与此同时，它也为这种例外规定了一些实质和程序上的条件。这种例外的法律依据和相关的条件主要体现在关贸总协定第24条、1979年“授权条款”和服务贸易总协定第5条。可见，建立中国—东盟自由贸易区依照WTO法律制度是一种合法的例外，如果它符合WTO上述条款规定的条件。

中国—东盟自由贸易区或WTO成员之间的任何其他自由贸易区或关税同盟或二者的过渡安排，其合法性或正当性的要求可以从上述条款和WTO争端解决机构所建立的法理中概括出如下几点：(1) 贸易的实质性涵盖；(2) 消除缔约方之间实质上所有货物贸易的关税和非关税壁垒和实质上服务贸易的所有现行歧视；(3) 禁止缔约方之间任何新的关税和非关税壁垒和任何新的或更加严厉的歧视措施；(4) 禁止提高对非缔约国货物贸易和服务贸易的总体壁垒水平；(5) 及时通知WTO。

从上述最先列举的两个要求来看，2002年《框架协定》已作出了适当的规定，如该协议第3 (1) 条和第4条。前者明确规定：“对于缔约方之间实质上所有货物贸易的关税和其他商业限制性规定……应予以取消。”后者类似地确认，有关的谈判应指向“逐步取消缔约方之间在服务贸易方面实质上所有的歧视和禁止缔约方之间新的更加严厉的歧视措施”。至于上述第四个要求，虽然2002年《框架协定》中没有直接提及，但是似乎没有理由去怀疑中国—东盟自由贸易区在这方面的一致性。同样地，一旦中国—东盟自由贸易区得以建立，缔约方将会及时通知WTO。

四、中国与东盟关系：法律上的欠缺和改进建议

一般认为，中国—东盟战略伙伴关系的快速发展主要是政治利益和经济利益的驱动。同样正确的是，这种战略伙伴关系的建立与发展不仅对双方来说是一件双赢的事，而且对于亚太地区甚至整个世界的稳定、安全和繁荣都具有重大意义。但是，我们必须牢记的是，这种具有深远意义的合作关系，如果在法律层面上不作出不断的努力，是不可能开展和深化的。因此，有必要经常地检讨中国—东盟关系的法律构架并使之不断完善。

(一) 尚存的法律欠缺

我们可以自豪地断言：目前中国—东盟的双边关系是历史上的最好时期。但是，依笔者看来，这种双赢关系的法制建设落后于其政治和经济层面。考察现行的中国—东盟关系的法律规制，其不足主要表现在如下几个方面：

首先，中国—东盟战略伙伴关系的各个领域之间在法律调整方面显然是不

平衡的。一般说来，有关自由贸易区和其他经济合作部门的法律规制与政治、安全和社会合作领域相比，要先进一些，不论是从法制建设的速度来衡量，还是从法律的慎密程度来考究。

其次，从现行调整中国—东盟关系的法律渊源来看，硬法相对较少，大部分法律文件在表现形式和具体内容或措辞上属于软法性质。诚然，中国—东盟关系中的那些联合宣言、联合声明和备忘录等不只是具有政治意义，而且是一种能产生法律效果的政治承诺。① 尽管如此，这些文件在法律形式、内容和约束力等方面是不可与条约或协议相比拟的。除了《东南亚友好合作条约》之外，真正调整双方战略伙伴关系的条约目前只有 2002 年《框架协定》及其 2003 年议定书。

再次，从整体上看，目前中国—东盟关系的法律水平还处于初级阶段，缺乏系统的、可操作性的实施性法律规范和机制。检讨中国与东盟之间现行法律文件的内容，我们不难感受到，几乎每一个文件主要都只是确立宗旨、原则、指导方针、一般纪律或总体计划，等等，期望以后能制定相应的实施措施。

最后，中国—东盟关系的法律层面中缺乏系统的争端解决机制。迄今为止，双方在这一方面只是达成了一些一般原则，即承诺通过友好协商和谈判解决彼此间的分歧和争端。有些文件甚至排除其他和平解决争端的方式。例如，2004 年《非传统安全合作备忘录》第 8 条规定，“有关本《谅解备忘录》的解释/实施/适用的任何争端或分歧，应通过缔约方之间的友好协商/谈判解决，不诉诸任何第三方”。虽然 2002 年《框架协定》第 11 条规定“缔约方应在本协议生效的一年内为本协定的目的建立适当的正式争端解决程序和机制”，但是这种正式的程序和机制即使建立了，也只限于有关该框架协议适用的范围，不涉及战略伙伴关系的其他领域。

总之，迄今为止，中国—东盟关系的法律调整在整体上还没有达到形成一个法律体系的阶段。其完善需要双方今后不断地作出努力。

（二）若干完善的建议

为了使中国—东盟战略伙伴关系在现有的法律框架基础上，建立一个稳定的、系统的和可操作性的法律机制，笔者拟提出如下若干改进建议：

第一，双方有关部门及官员应制定适当计划为现有法律文件制定相应的实

---

① 所谓软法，就是指那些法律文件虽然本身在法律上不具有约束力，但是可以产生法律效果，即这些法律文件的签署方通常在实践中信守他们先前在这些文件中所作出的政治承诺。

施措施，尤其是那些已经作出如此明确要求的文件，更应加紧通过相关的实施性措施。这些实施措施应该尽可能详细和具有可操作性。诚然，制定实施措施的任务是相当艰巨的，其难度有时甚至超过了先前框架文件的制定，因为具体承诺的谈判往往要比原则性承诺的谈判要困难得多。而且，随着中国—东盟关系的不断扩展，制定实施措施的任务就会越来越繁重。仅以中国—东盟自由贸易区为例，在货物贸易、服务贸易和投资领域，还需要双方在很多具体事项上谈判和缔结大量的子协定，如关税减让表、非关税取消、原产地规则、海关估价、保障措施、紧急措施、反倾销、补贴与反补贴措施、标准与相符评估、技术壁垒、投资便利，等等。

第二，既然法律基础在经济合作领域尤其是在建立自由贸易区领域相对更加稳固，可以考虑率先在这些领域制定系统的可操作性措施，然后逐渐扩展到其他合作领域，如非传统安全、社会事务和南中国海行为，等等。这种“从易到难”的法律制定技术路线在深化中国—东盟关系的法律调整过程中，不失为一个务实的选择。

第三，在中国—东盟自由贸易区的法律制度中引进国民待遇原则似乎是一种可取的选择。既然国民待遇与最惠国待遇一起，已经成为多边贸易体制和各种区域一体化安排的基本规范，似乎没有更具有说服力的理由将国民待遇这一国际经济交往中普遍认可的原则排除适用于中国—东盟自由贸易区。当然，目前将国民待遇原则同时适用于自由贸易区的货物贸易、服务贸易和投资便利也许不太现实，但是至少可以从一个领域的适用逐步扩展到另一个领域。总之，有开端总比不作为好。

第四，随着中国—东盟关系的不断深化和加强，一些合作领域的软法最好升级为硬法，以增强相关合作领域的法律基础。以《南海各方行为宣言》为例。正如本文先前所提及的，该宣言无疑是各方的庄严承诺以保证和平处理领土争端和制定基于自我克制、不使用武力或以武力相威胁和航行自由等原则的非正式行为法典。但是，由于这一庄严承诺是通过宣言的形式表现的，一些评论者将它视为一种非正式的和不具有约束力的行为法典。① 因此，在不远的将来，各方以条约或协定的形式取代现行的宣言，从法律角度来看，无疑是最佳的选择。

---

① See Ralf Emmers, *ASEAN*, *China and the South China Sea*: *an Opportunity Missed*, *Perspectives*, Institute of Defence and Strategic Studies, Nanyang Technological University, Singapore, www. ntu. edu. sg/ idss/ Prospectives /Research-050228. htm, 2004 年 10 月 5 日访问。

第五，从长远来看，在中国—东盟战略伙伴关系的法律规制中建立一个动态的、有多种政治或外交方式和法律程序构成的争端解决机制，实属必要。长期以来，中国政府一直主张通过友好协商和谈判解决国与国之间的争端。几十年来，中国与外国签订的各种双边条约和协定在有关争端解决条款中总是将这一主张明确地予以规定。毫无疑问，友好协商和谈判方式在诸如营造争端解决气氛、争端解决的灵活性和争端方掌握争端解决的主动权等方面具有一定的优越性。但是，这种单一的争端解决模式似乎显得略为单调和僵硬，与当今国际争端解决方法、程序和机制的多样化趋势不相适应，势必也难于适应中国—东盟关系纵横发展的趋势。更重要的是，这种单一模式无法应对现实中的如下情势：有关争端通过友好协商和谈判仍然得不到解决。

诚然，友好协商和谈判在未来争端解决机制中应该是首选和必选的方式。但是，无论如何，将它规定为排他的方式是不可取的，应该有其他的政治或外交方法紧随其后，供当事方选择，如斡旋、调停、调解、调查委员会，等等。此外，仲裁和某种形式的准司法方法或程序也可供当事方利用。

五、结束语

如果说中国—东盟战略伙伴关系的法治一路顺风，显然是不切实际的。但是这条法治之路一直朝着稳步、积极的方向完善，则是有目共睹的事实。2004年11月29~30日在万象举行的第十届东盟高峰会议上，中国与东盟领导人签署和通过了一系列新的法律文件。① 所有这些新的法律文件都是这些年来双方签署或发表的协定、议定书、宣言、联合声明或备忘录的实施措施。它们向世界发送了一个最新的、强有力的信号：中国—东盟战略伙伴关系正在不断深化，将越来越朝着全面法治的方向发展。

从法律层面来观察，如下的一些最新迹象尤为引人瞩目：

在政治与安全合作领域，双方在原有基础上，进一步承诺增强《东南亚友好合作条约》的作用，将该条约确定为东南亚国家间关系的行为法典，并共同激励其他东盟对话伙伴国家加入该条约，以促进地区和平、安全、繁荣和

① 这些文件主要有：(1)《实施东盟—中国战略伙伴关系联合宣言行动计划》；(2)《第八届东盟—中国峰会主席声明》；(3)《东盟成员国政府与中华人民共和国政府交通合作谅解备忘录》；(4)《东盟与中国全面经济合作框架协议货物贸易协定》；(5)《东盟与中国全面经济合作框架协议争端解决机制协定》，等等。See http://www.aseansec.org/4979.htm，2005年2月10日访问。

彼此间的信任。① 我们欣喜地看到，继中国和印度之后，韩国和俄罗斯不久前也加入了《东南亚友好合作条约》。② 中国承诺支持东南亚实现无核化努力，并重申将尽早签署《东南亚无核武器区条约议定书》，同时在鼓励所有核武器拥有国签署该议定书方面进行合作。③ 在实施《南海各方行为宣言》方面，一个重要的举措是，将建立一个工作组，起草实施该宣言的指导原则，并向东盟—中国高级官员会议提供政策与实施问题方面的建议。而且，还承诺在协商一致的基础上，致力于最终通过南中国海行为法典。④ 在非传统安全合作方面，将共同制定2005年的工作计划和今后的年度工作计划，以实施双方在这一领域先前达成的合作备忘录，其中特别强调依照各自的国内法，以适当的方式促进刑事执法机关和检察机关以及相关法律机制的联系与合作。⑤

在经济合作领域，东盟—中国自由贸易区建设在法律上取得了如下实质性的突破：一是签署了《货物贸易协定》，制定了关税减让和取消的双轨模式，即“通常轨道模式”（modality in the normal track）和“敏感轨道模式”（modality in the sensitive track），⑥ 并且制定了东盟—中国自由贸易区原产地规则。⑦ 二是签署了《争端解决机制协定》，为解决2002年《框架协定》实施

① Plan of Action to Implement the Joint Declaration on ASEAN-China Strategic Partnership for Peace and Prosperity, para. 1.3. http://www.aseansec.org/16806.htm, 2005年2月10日访问。

② Chairman's Statement of the 8th ASEAN + China Summit, Vientiane, 29 November 2004, para. 4. http://www.aseansec.org/16749.htm, 2005年2月10日访问。

③ Plan of Action to Implement the Joint Declaration on ASEAN-China Strategic Partnership for Peace and Prosperity, para. 1.4. http://www.aseansec.org/16806.htm, 2005年2月10日访问。

④ Plan of Action to Implement the Joint Declaration on ASEAN-China Strategic Partnership for Peace and Prosperity, para. 1.5. http://www.aseansec.org/16806.htm, 2005年2月10日访问。

⑤ Plan of Action to Implement the Joint Declaration on ASEAN-China Strategic Partnership for Peace and Prosperity, para. 1.6. http://www.aseansec.org/16806.htm, 2005年2月10日访问。

⑥ Agreement on Trade in Goods of the Framework Agreement on Comprehensive Economic Cooperation between the ASEAN and China, Annex I and Annex II. http://www.aseansec.org/4979.htm, 2005年2月10日访问。

⑦ Agreement on Trade in Goods of the Framework Agreement on Comprehensive Economic Cooperation between the ASEAN and China, Annex III. http://www.aseansec.org/4979.htm, 2005年2月10日访问。

中的各种争端提供了系统的规则、程序和方法。该协定是中国同外国或国际组织之间在争端解决机制方面签署的第一个全面、系统的专约。协定在争端解决方法和程序规定方面尤其值得赞许：既坚持协商程序，又不排斥由第三方介入的调解或调停。协定关于仲裁的条款最多，篇幅最长，从仲裁庭的组成、建立、职责、程序、第三方参与、仲裁程序中止与结束、仲裁裁决实施、减让或利益的补偿与终止，均作出了较详尽的规定。可以预见，该协定的意义将远远超过中国—东盟战略伙伴关系本身。这意味着中国在对待国际争端解决方法的政策上正在发生重大变化，即在继续重视友好协商这一政治和外交方法的同时，注重争端解决方法和程序的多样性以及法律的强制方法在解决国家间争端的重要地位与作用。

最后，对中国具有特殊政治、经济和法律意义的是，东盟领导人同意承认中国的完全市场经济地位，并承诺在东盟每一个成员国与中国的贸易关系中，不适用《中国加入 WTO 议定书》第 15 条和 16 条以及《中国加入 WTO 工作组报告》第 242 段有关中国非市场经济地位的特殊规定。① 这一庄严承诺无疑将极大地促进中国在国际上获取完全市场经济地位的普遍承认，从而尽早改变中国在遭受其他 WTO 成员在实施反倾销、反补贴和保障措施中所施加的歧视性待遇。

---

① Chairman's Statement of the 8th ASEAN + China Summit, "Deepening ASEAN-China Strategic Partnership", Vientiane, 29 November 2004, para. 15. http://www.aseansec.org/16749.htm，2005 年 2 月 10 日访问。

作者简介

肖永平

肖永平，1966年2月生，湖北麻城人，1984～1988年在西南政法学院法律系学习。1988年考取武汉大学法学院国际私法研究生，1990年提前攻读博士学位，师从韩德培先生。1993年毕业后留武汉大学法学院国际法系任教，历任讲师（1993年）、副教授（1995年）、教授（1997年）和博士生导师（1998年）。1998～1999年在美国哈佛大学作高级访问学者，2000年4～5月在德国马克思—布朗克国际私法与外国私法研究所从事合作研究，先后多次参加在国内外举行的国际学术会议。现任武汉大学珞珈特聘教授、教育部人文社会科学重点研究基地武汉大学国际法研究所执行所长、武汉大学法学院副院长，兼任中国国际私法学会常务副会长，西南政法大学、澳门科技大学、西北政法学院等高校兼职教授，中国国际经济贸易仲裁委员会、武汉仲裁委员会等仲裁机构仲裁员，《中国国际私法与比较法年刊》主编，中国国际法学会理事、湖北省法学会常务理事等职。肖永平教授出版了《国际私法原理》、《肖永平论冲突法》、《冲突法专论》、《中国冲突法立法问题研究》、《中国仲裁法教程》等6部个人专著，主编了15部教材、著作、论文集，并在《中国社会科学》、《中国法学》、《法学研究》、《中国国际法年刊》、《中国国际私法与比较法年刊》、（荷兰）《国际私法年刊》（英文）、《美国比较法杂志》（英文）、《二十一世纪》（中国香港）、《华岗法粹》（中国台湾）等权威、核心刊物上发表中英文论文120余篇。主持完成了7项省部级科研课题，作为主要成员参加了10余项省部级以上课题。他的多项成果曾获得武汉市社会科学优秀成果一等奖，司法部优秀科研成果一等奖，武汉大学优秀科研成果一等奖，湖北省首届社会科学优秀成果三等奖，霍英东教育基金会第五届高等院校青年教师基金奖等。肖永平教授在2000年获教育部首届“优秀青年教师奖”，并于2001年享受国务院特殊津贴。

国际私法条约规则在我国的适用

肖永平

目　次：

(二) WTO 协议在我国的适用方式

(三) WTO 协议在我国的优先适用问题

(四) WTO 协议在我国的直接效力问题

六、关于“国际私法条约的适用”的立法建议

(一) 我国的习惯性规定

(二) 评论

(三) 结论：具体建议案文

国际条约在国内的适用实质上涉及国际法与国内法的关系问题，如果要作出立法上的明确规定，应该在一个国家的宪法层面上解决这个问题。① 但作为国际私法渊源的国际条约也是可以在一国的国际私法立法中规定的，因为这类条约主要是指国家间缔结的协调彼此间国际私法规范，以实现缔约国间在某一或某些国际私法领域法律统一的协议，我们可以称之为国际私法条约。在研究国际条约在我国的适用②问题时，我国大多数学者没有根据不同种类的国际条约的特点分别讨论它们在国内的适用，这常常使其观点不够全面，不利于问题的解决，也使我国的立法机关无所适从。本文将在区分国际公法条约、国际私法条约和 WTO 协议的基础上探讨适用国际私法条约的一般规则和实体法条约、冲突法条约、程序法条约以及 WTO 协议在我国适用的规则，并对我国如何规定国际私法条约的适用规则进行了设计。

一、适用国际私法条约的一般规则

(一) 国际条约在国内适用的一般方式

现代国际法确立的“约定必须信守”原则要求国际条约的“当事国不得援引其国内法规定为理由而不履行条约”，但一个国家如何履行条约义务则由该国国内法自行裁量。从各国的实践来看，国际条约在国内的适用方式可概括为三种：(1) 转化（transformation）方式，即条约规定经过国内立法机关的立

---

① See Francis G. Jacors & Shelley Roberts, *the Effect of Treaties in Domestic Law*, xxiv (1st ed. 1987).

② 就国际条约在国内的实施而言，条约缔约国的立法机关、司法机关和行政机关都有适用国际条约的义务和机会。本文探讨的国际条约的适用，仅指司法机关对国际条约的适用，讨论司法机关能否和怎样根据国际条约中的规定裁判私人当事人之间的权利义务关系。

法行为转变为国内法，才能在国内由行政机关和司法机关予以适用。如按照英国普通法，英国法院不适用未经国会以法律转变为国内法的条约。（2）并入或采纳（adoption）方式，即由国内宪法或部门法作出原则性规定或通过立法机关的行为（如通过批准条约、公布条约、司法判例等），从总体上承认国际条约是国内法的组成部分并可在国内直接适用。（3）混合方式，即一个国家同时采用转化和纳入两种方式来适用条约，根据条约的性质和内容的不同，有的条约只以采纳方式在国内直接适用，另一些条约必须经过立法机关立法转化后才能在国内直接适用，美国是运用混合方式的典型代表。①

对于国际条约在中国的适用问题，我国宪法没有统一规定，但许多法律、法规和司法解释对该问题作了明文规定。概括起来，主要有三种方式：

1. 一些部门法明确规定直接适用国际条约，即将国际条约纳入国内法予以直接适用。如《民法通则》第142条第2款、《民事诉讼法》第238条等。这些法律还明确规定，当有关国内法与国际条约相冲突时，国际条约具有优先适用的效力。此外，最高人民法院的一些权威性司法解释要求各级法院直接适用国际条约的规定，如最高人民法院1989年《关于印发〈全国沿海地区涉外涉港澳经济审判工作座谈会纪要〉的通知》明确指出："鉴于我国已经加入1980年《联合国国际货物销售合同公约》，承担了执行该公约的义务，自1988年1月1日起，我国公司同该公约的其他批准国的公司订立的合同，如未另行选择所适用的法律，将自动直接适用该公约的有关规定。法院应当按该公约规定处理它们之间的合同纠纷。"最高人民法院1987年《关于执行我国加入的〈承认与执行外国仲裁裁决公约〉的通知》，要求各级法院"切实依照执行"这一公约。

2. 既允许直接适用有关国际条约，又将该国际条约的内容制定成国内法予以实施。这种方式以《维也纳外交关系公约》和《维也纳领事关系公约》为典型，中国于1975年和1979年分别加入这两个公约以后很长一段时间，没有将这两个公约的规定制定成相应的国内法，而是直接适用。到1986年，全国人大常委会制定了《外交特权与豁免条例》；1990年，全国人大常委会又制定了《领事特权与豁免条例》，这两个条例将上述两个公约中的规定转化成国内法予以实施。与此同时，这两个公约仍可在我国直接适用。因此，这两个公约在我国的适用，出现了转化方式和纳入方式并存的情况。

3. 只允许以转化方式适用国际条约。这种情况比较少见，但《中华人民

① 参见王铁崖：《条约在中国法律制度中的地位》，载《中国国际法年刊》1994年卷。

共和国香港特别行政区基本法》规定了这种特殊制度，该法第 39 条第 1 款规定："《公民权利和政治权利国际公约》、《经济、社会与文化权利的国际公约》和国际劳工公约适用于香港的有关规定继续有效，通过香港特别行政区的法律予以实施。"可见，两个人权公约和国际劳工公约不能直接在香港特别行政区适用，必须通过转化方式在香港实施。①

由此可见，我国在适用国际条约方面，对国际私法条约主要采取并入方式，对国际公法条约则主要采取转化方式，并兼采并入方式。

（二）国际公法条约、国际私法条约与 WTO 协议的区分

要在我国立法中正确规定国际条约在我国的适用规则，有必要区分国际公法条约、国际私法条约和 WTO 协议，只有这样，才能根据它们的不同特点确定不同的适用规则。这是我们在国内立法中规定国际条约的适用规则的理论前提。对于国际公法条约和国际私法条约的区分标准，应该考虑下列因素：(1) 国际条约所调整的社会关系。如果国际条约调整的只是国家间的关系，或者国家与国际组织的关系，它就是国际公法条约；如果国际条约调整的主要是私人间的关系，即自然人之间、法人之间或者它们相互之间的关系，它就是国际私法条约。(2) 国际条约所规定的内容。这就是要看条约统一的法律规则属于国际公法范畴还是国际私法范畴。很显然，大部分国际条约根据这个标准是可以区分为国际公法条约和国际私法条约的。(3) 国际条约是否直接赋予私人当事人具体的权利和义务。一般说来，国际公法条约不直接赋予私人当事人具体的权利和义务，国际私法条约则正好相反。因此，可以说，国际公法条约的规定约束的是国家，需要通过国家行为（包括立法、司法、行政行为等）来实施；而国际私法条约的规定约束的对象可以直接是自然人和法人，一个内国法院可通过司法行为直接实施该公约。(4) 国际条约的规定的抽象性程度。一般说来，国际公法条约的规定比较抽象，也不便在内国法院直接得到适用；国际私法条约的规则相对比较具体，规定了当事人的具体权利和义务，可以成为定案的根据。(5) 私人的自治性权利问题。国际公法条约一般不会赋予私人以自治权，但国际私法条约有时会给私人较大的自治权。因此，综合考虑上

① 参见王丽玉：《国际条约在中国国内法中的适用》，载《中国国际法年刊》1993 年卷，第 293～295 页。

述多种因素，是可以对国际公法条约和国际私法条约作适当区分的。①

但是，按上述标准区分 WTO 协议的性质还有相当的难度。我个人认为，WTO 协议的性质更接近于国际公法条约，但与典型的国际公法条约有较大的区别，其范围的广泛性、规范的复杂性、部分规范对私人当事人权利的赋予等又使它带有国际私法条约的性质，这也是我国学者在讨论 WTO 协议在我国的适用时观点为什么不一致的原因。因此，为了讨论国际条约规则在我国的适用，有必要把 WTO 协议作为第三类国际条约专门讨论。

（三）“自执行条约”与“非自执行条约”的区分

根据国际条约能否在国内法体系中直接适用，可将它分为“自执行条约”（self-executing treaty）和“非自执行条约”（non-self-executing treaty）。所谓“自执行条约”是指“可以在国内法体系中无须求助于国内立法即可实施”的国际条约；而“非自执行条约”是指“在一国之内发生效力之前，要求制定使其能够实施的法令”的国际条约。② 对于区分“自执行条约”与“非自执行条约”的理由，根据李浩培先生的总结，主要包括：“第一，有些条约明文规定缔约国须以立法予以执行，在这种情况下，缔约国以补充立法执行该条约，是它从条约本身承担的义务。第二，有些条约，如同盟互助条约，是政治性的，这些条约所规定的权利义务，原则上只涉及缔约国政府本身，而与自然人和法人无关，所以，把这类条约的效力扩及自然人和法人，就需要补充立法予以规定。第三，有些条约的规定只是大纲性的，不够详细和缜密，也须以立法作补充规定。第四，有些条约所用的语文不是本国语文，还须译成本国语文，并以法律予以公布。”③

美国是把国际条约区分为“自执行条约”和“非自执行条约”的典型代表。《美国宪法》第 6 条第 1 款把条约规定为与美国宪法、法律具有同等效力的美国最高法律。但在 1929 年，美国最高法院法官马歇尔就在福斯特诉尼尔森案的判决中宣告：“条约按其本质是两个国家之间的契约，而不是立法行

---

① 当然，在一部国际条约中，既有国际公法性质的规则，也有国际私法性质的规则是常见的。所以，本文作此区分不是就整部国际条约而言的，更准确地说，是以国际条约中的规则为区分对象的。简言之，本文是以规则为中心的（rules-oriented）。

② 许多学者称之为“自动执行条约”（automatic-incorporating treaty）和“非自动执行条约”（non-automatic-incorporating treaty）。由于大多数英文表达是 self-executing treaty，在 2001 年武汉大学召开的一次国际学术会议上，有学者主张将 self-executing treaty 译为“自执行条约”，我觉得有一定道理，故采用。

③ 李浩培：《条约法概论》，法律出版社 2003 年版，第 319 页。

为……美国确立了一个不同的原则。我们的宪法把条约宣布为国家的法律。因此，当条约无须任何立法规定的助力而自动施行时，在法院中应把它认为是与立法行为的等同物。但是，当条约规定的文字意含一个契约，当缔约任何一方承诺履行一个特定行为时，该条约是针对政治部门而不是司法部门的；在该条约能成为对法院来说是一个法律规定以前，必须先由立法机关执行该契约。"①此后，美国法院在一系列判决中依循这个先例。例如，在藤井诉加利福尼亚案②中，一个日本人藤井没有资格取得美国国籍，1948 年，他在加利福尼亚州取得了一块土地的所有权。但按照《加利福尼亚州外国人土地法》规定，土地所有权转让给无资格取得美国国籍的外国人时，该土地应无偿归属国家。这样，他取得的土地应无偿转归加利福尼亚州所有。因此，藤井向加利福尼亚州法院起诉，请求宣告该法无效。该州地方上诉法院判决认为，该法与美国参加的《联合国宪章》第 55 条和第 56 条的规定相抵触；按照《美国宪法》第 6 条第 2 款，美国所参加的条约是美国的最高法律，与之抵触的州法无效。因此，该土地并不无偿转归加利福尼亚州所有。很显然，该判决认为《联合国宪章》的上述两条规定具有自动执行性，美国法院可以直接予以适用。在上诉中，该州最高法院虽然维持了原判，但其理由认为加州的土地法的规定违反了《美国宪法》第 14 修正案的平等保护条款，专横地歧视日本人，因而无效。与此同时，该判决否定了原判决对于《联合国宪章》上述两条规定的性质的断定。对于《联合国宪章》上述两条规定是否具有自动执行性，不仅上述两个法院的判决持不同见解，美国学者的认识也有分歧。由此可见，自执行条约和非自执行条约的区分不是很精确。

但一般说来，一个条约，除非含有需要立法执行的明文规定，或者由于其涉及必须经美国国会立法才能实施的政府行动，因而按其性质是不能径直适用的那类条约，就是非自执行条约。在实践中，需要美国支付金钱的条约、规定关税的条约、需要改变美国现行国内法的条约、处分美国财产的条约、任命政府委员会的条约，都是非自执行条约；而引渡条约、规定领事权利的条约、规定最惠国待遇的条约、惩治走私的条约等，都是自执行条约。为了解决一个具体条约是否具有自执行性，美国学者主张探求下列因素：（1）条约起草者和参加者的意图；（2）一国的宪法对缔结自执行条约的权力是否有限制；（3）

① 李浩培：《条约法概论》，法律出版社 2003 年版，第 319 页。

② SEI FUJII v. STATE, Supreme Court of California, 1952. 38 Cal. 2d 718, 242 P. 2d 617. See Henry J. Steiner, Detlev F. Vagts and Harold Hongju Koh, *Transnational Legal Problems: Materials and Text*, 553-555 (4th ed. 1994).

原告是否依据条约的规定主张权利；(4) 条约的目的是否调整私人的行为；① (5) 对于私人的权利和豁免，条约是否约束法院和立法部门；(6) 一般说来，条约是否为自执行条约与国际法庭没有关系，因为缔约国有义务执行条约的安排。②

我国虽然没有将国际条约区分为"自执行条约"与"非自执行条约"的法律制度，也没有因将国际条约认定为"非自执行条约"而拒绝在国内法中直接适用的实例，但从前面介绍的我国现有的立法和司法解释来看，我国也是根据条约的不同性质采取不同的适用方式的。参考上述标准可知，中国目前允许在国内法中直接适用的国际条约大体属于民事类和行政管理类。这类条约往往涉及国内有关机关和人员的权利和义务，内容较为具体，政治性不强，基本上符合上述"自执行条约"的特征。可以说，国际私法条约基本上都是"自执行条约"。

(四) 统一实体法条约、统一冲突法条约和统一程序法条约的区分

根据国际私法条约所统一的对象，可将它分为统一实体法条约、统一冲突法条约和统一程序法条约。如果国际条约统一的对象是实体私法，这种条约便属于统一实体法条约，如《统一国际航空运输某些规则的公约》、《联合国国际货物销售合同公约》。③ 统一冲突法条约是指对冲突法规范进行统一的国际公约，海牙国际私法会议制定的许多国际私法条约便属于这种类型。规定国际民事诉讼程序和国际商事仲裁程序的国际条约便是统一程序法条约，如海牙国际私法会议制定的一些调整法院管辖权、诉讼文书送达和域外取证等问题的公约属于这类条约。④ 由于这些国际条约所规定的法律规范的性质不同，它们在国内的适用规则也有一些差别，不能一概而论。本文后面就是以此为基础分门别类地讨论这些条约在我国的适用问题。

(五) 国际私法条约的直接适用规则

条约在国内法中的直接适用是指一国的司法机关及其他适用法律的专门机

---

① 当然，这个因素并没有决定性意义，有些并不调整私人行为的条约可能是自执行条约。

② See Henry J. Steiner, Detlev F. Vagts and Harold Hongju Koh, *Transnational Legal Problems: Materials and Text*, 556-560 (4th ed. 1994).

③ 值得注意的是，这种分类是从总体上来说的，并不意味着这些条约中的所有规则都是统一实体法规则。

④ 参见李双元主编：《国际私法学》，北京大学出版社 2000 年版，第 99 ~ 101 页。

关，以条约的规定作为其适用法律的根据，并以适用国内法的同样方式适用条约的规定。根据中国宪法的规定，缔约权和立法权在很大程度上是一致的，它们主要由全国人民代表大会及其常务委员会行使。《中华人民共和国宪法》第67条第14款规定，全国人民代表大会常务委员会“决定同外国缔约的条约和重要协定的批准和废除”。《中华人民共和国缔结条约程序法》第7条进一步明确规定：“条约和重要协定的批准由全国人民代表大会常务委员会决定。前款规定的条约和重要协定是指：（1）友好合作条约、和平条约等政治性条约；（2）有关领土和划定边界的条约、协定；（3）有关司法协助、引渡的条约、协定；（4）同中华人民共和国法律有不同规定的条约、协定；（5）缔约各方议定须经批准的条约、协定；（6）其他须经批准的条约、协定。”《中华人民共和国立法法》第7条规定：“全国人民代表大会和全国人民代表大会常务委员会行使国家立法权。”因此，全国人民代表大会常务委员会是中国的主要缔约机关，它同时在立法方面行使主要的权力，这给国际私法条约在国内法的直接适用带来了宪法体制上的便利。

当然，在中国国内法中直接适用国际条约通常需要完成一定的法律程序，除了完成批准程序外，通常应以某种行政行为为前提，如在政府公报上予以公布等。《中华人民共和国缔结条约程序法》规定了条约的公布程序，即经全国人民代表大会常务委员会决定批准或者加入的条约和重要协定，由全国人民代表大会常务委员会公报公布；其他条约、协定根据国务院规定的方法公布。中国缔结的条约和协定由外交部编入《中华人民共和国条约集》。但该法没有规定国际条约的“公布”是否属于其在中国直接适用必须完成的法律程序。

前面讲过，中国宪法对国际条约的直接适用没有明文规定，但不少部门法律作了规定。1966年《国境河流外国籍船舶管理办法》第16条规定：“外国籍船舶所属国家政府已经同我国政府签订有商船通航协定的，可以仍按协定执行；协定中未规定的，按照本办法执行。”这可以说是中华人民共和国法规中第一次作出直接适用条约的规定。但这项《办法》不是全国人大或其常务委员会通过的法律，而最早在法律中明确规定直接适用国际条约的是1982年《民事诉讼法（试行）》第189条：中华人民共和国缔结或者参加的国际条约同本法有不同规定的，适用该国际条约的规定。但是，我国声明保留的条款除外。以后，《商标法》、《继承法》、《涉外经济合同法》、《民法通则》、《民事诉讼法》、《合同法》等法律、法规和相关司法解释等都确立了国际私法条约的直接适用规则。

（六）国际私法条约的优先适用规则

当国际条约与国内立法存在冲突时，国际法规定“当事国不得援引国内法规定为由而不履行条约”，这为一国国内法院优先适用国际条约奠定了基础，但“履行条约”并不等于一国法院应该优先适用国际条约，因为“履行条约”的方式可以是多样的。对于国际条约与国内法在国内法体系中的冲突，取决于各国的具体规定。① 解决这种冲突的做法也有所不同，有的修改国内法或国际条约，消除两者之间的冲突；有的适用“解释一致”规则消除国际条约与国内法之间不一致的情况；有的规定国际条约调整的事项不再适用国内法，从而避免国际条约与国内法之间的冲突；有的规定优先适用国际条约。②我国主要采取后两种方式。

（1）规定国际条约调整的事项不再适用国内法，从而避免国际条约与国内法的冲突。如 1985 年《继承法》第 36 条第 3 款规定：“中华人民共和国与外国订有条约、协定的，按照条约、协定办理。”这表明有关事项如果属于国际条约的调整范围，就应适用国际条约，不适用有关的中国法律。《继承法》的这一制度为《中华人民共和国公民出境入境管理法》第 18 条，《渔业法》第 8 条，《国境卫生检疫法》第 25 条等法律和行政法规采纳。此外，《中华人民共和国专利法》第 18 条规定：“在中国没有经常居所或者营业所的外国人、外国企业或者外国其他组织在中国申请专利的，依照其所属国同中国签订的协议或者共同参加的国际条约，或者依照互惠原则，根据本法办理。”这条规定表明，对外国人在中国申请专利的，如果申请专利的外国人所属国与中国订有国际条约，就适用该国际条约的规定；只有当两国之间没有关于专利事项的国际条约时，才可以依照互惠原则适用中国法律。

（2）规定优先适用国际条约。最早明确规定国际条约与中国法律有不同规定时应优先适用国际条约的法律是 1982 年《民事诉讼法（试行）》第 189 条：中华人民共和国缔结或者参加的国际条约同本法有不同规定的，适用该国际条约的规定。但是，我国声明保留的条款除外。该条规定对我国后来的立法和司法实践产生了广泛影响，此后，优先适用国际条约的规定出现在中国许多

---

① 有的规定国内法的地位优越于条约；有的规定国内法与条约的地位相等；有的规定条约的地位优越于国内法；还有的规定条约的地位优越于宪法。参见李浩培：《条约法概论》，法律出版社 2003 年版，第 324～330 页。

② See Francis G. Jacors & Shelley Roberts, *the Effect of Treaties in Domestic Law*, 275-279 (1st ed. 1987).

法律、行政法规和其他规范性法律文件之中。如《民法通则》第142条、《外交特权与豁免条例》第27条、《国境卫生检疫法》第24条、《邮政法》第42条、《水法》第51条、《外商投资企业和外国企业所得税法》第28条、《海商法》第268条、《水污染防治法实施细则》第37条，均规定了优先适用国际条约的规则。

值得注意的是，中国上述法律、法规中关于优先适用国际条约的条款，都含有“中国声明保留的条款除外”或类似的文句。这是符合《维也纳条约法公约》第19～23条的规定的。因为保留是指一国在签署、批准、接受、核准或者加入条约时所作的单方声明。不论具体的措辞或名称如何，只要其目的是将条约的某些规定在对该国的适用上排除或改变其法律效果，就构成条约法上的保留。① 因此，保留对保留国的法律效果有两种：一是使保留所涉条款不适用于保留国，二是保留所涉条款虽然适用于保留国，但适用的法律效果发生了变化。也就是说，一国提出保留的目的是为了免除该国的某项义务或变更该国的某项义务。因此，保留所涉条款不能在保留国与其他缔约国之间得到适用，更不能得到优先适用。

（七）当事人选择适用国际私法条约

国际私法条约的直接适用和优先适用的前提条件是：某一具体案件中的争诉问题属于该国际条约的适用范围，如双方当事人所属国均是该条约的缔约国。如果中国不是某一国际私法条约的缔约国，或者具体案件中的外方当事人所属国或营业地所属国不是条约的缔约国，该条约就不能在中国得到直接适用，更不能优先适用。但是，如果双方当事人在签订合同时，或在发生争议以后，共同选择适用某一国际私法条约，只要这种选择符合下列条件，该国际私法条约也可以得到适用。

（1）当事人的选择是共同的明示选择，其具体形式既可以是书面的，也可以是口头的。这强调的是当事人的合意，并且是明确表达出来的共同意思表示。

（2）具体案件的争讼问题属于该国际私法条约调整的范围。这个条件说明国际私法条约的有关规定可以用来解决具体案件中的有关问题，客观上属于该条约的适用范围。

（3）当事人的选择不违反我国法律中的强制性规则和公共秩序。这是各国冲突法限制适用当事人意思自治原则的普遍做法，有些国际条约本身也规定

① 参见李浩培：《条约法概论》，法律出版社2003年版，第125页。

了这个条款。所谓“强制性规则”（mandatory rules），就是不依赖于当事人的意志而必须支配当事人行为的规则，尽管各国立法和学理对此并无一致的认识，但每个国家出于自己特殊国情的考虑而赋予某些法律以强制适用的效力，这些具有强制适用效力的法律规范便是强制性规则。一般说来，国家关于经济管制的法律规范和对某些利益进行特殊保护的法律规范均属于强制性规则，通常包括关于外贸管制的法律规范、关于金融税收的法律规范、关于公司成立及活动和工商管理的法律规范以及关于某些特殊合同或特殊交易活动的法律规范，如有关消费者交易合同、雇佣合同和合资企业合作生产合同等的法律规范。① 公共秩序对当事人意思自治原则的限制一般是在当事人选择了内国法以外的法律，如果适用当事人选择的法律，其结果将会违背国内的公共秩序的情况下适用的。也就是说，当事人选择法律的实际效力是以其不违背内国公共秩序为必要条件的。对于当事人意思自治原则的这种条件性限制，人们一般并无异议。②

（4）被当事人选择的国际私法条约应该是国际统一实体法条约，一般不包括统一程序法条约和统一冲突法条约。因为程序法问题通常涉及国家的公共利益，一般不会赋予私方当事人以自治权；而冲突法规则本身没有相应的确定性，当事人一般不会选择适用。

另一个值得注意的问题是：如果双方当事人所属国都是某个国际私法条约的缔约国，而当事人明确合意选择其中一个国家的国内法作为准据法，法院能否适用该国际条约呢？例如，第十届 Willem C. Vis 国际商事仲裁模拟比赛的案例可以很好地说明这个问题。基本案情是：A 公司（卖方）所在国是 1980 年《联合国国际货物销售合同公约》（CISG）的缔约国，B 公司（买方）所在国没有参加 CISG。2000 年 12 月 15 日，A 与 B 签订一份分 4 期交货的 200 吨货物销售合同，该合同的法律选择条款规定：“适用 A 公司所属国的国内商法（domestic law）。” 2001 年 4 月 3 日，A 与 B 通过电话讨论再购买 1350 吨，分 9 期交货的合同。双方约定：除调整数量、装船日期及报价以外，其他类似条款

---

① 从理论上讲，强制性规则有三类：内国强制性规则、外国强制性规则和统一强制性规则。由于它们的强制性来源不同，内国司法机关对于它们的适用态度也是不同的。这里不涉及外国强制性规则的适用问题，但似乎可以包括统一强制性规则，即载于国际条约中的强制性规则。参见邵景春：《国际合同法律适用论》，北京大学出版社 1997 年版，第 65～72 页。

② 但是，如果当事人的法律选择只是违反了某外国的公共秩序，内国法院是否可以根据公共秩序保留否定该法律选择的效力呢？大多数国家的实践对这个问题的态度是不清楚的。

(other similar terms) 与2000年12月15日的合同一样。后来，双方因价格条款中的折扣发生争议，对2001年4月3日的口头合同是否成立发生了争执。A向仲裁机构提起仲裁。A公司所属国的国内法规定，CISG是其国内法的一部分，并用来调整国际商事合同关系。①

要回答这个问题，取决于下列多个因素的考量：(1) 双方当事人的真实意图——他们是否想通过选择一个国家的国内法来排除该国际条约的适用；(2) 国际条约本身关于其约束力的具体规定——国际条约是否允许当事人排除该条约的适用；(3) 有关国家关于国际条约在其国内法律体系中的地位——只有该国认为它所参加或缔结的国际条约构成其法律体系的一部分，该国法院才可能适用该国际条约；(4) 如果当事人的意图不明确，应根据当事人法律选择条款的措辞、合同缔结的客观情况和当事人提供的各种情况判断当事人的意图，如果能查明他们意图排除该国际条约的规定，就不适用该国际条约；(5) 如果一国法律中没有解决案件中具体法律问题的规定，尽管当事人明确或默示地排除国际条约的适用，我认为该国际条约中的有关规定可以作为国际惯例得到适用。所以，该问题不便于在立法层面上形成统一的明确规则，只能根据每一个条约和案件的实际情况分别作出决定。

二、国际统一实体私法条约在我国的适用

(一) 国际统一实体私法条约的概念和特点

国际统一实体私法条约是国家之间缔结的统一某领域实体私法规范的协议，它具有如下特点：(1) 这种条约的调整对象为国际实体私法关系，也就是国际民商事关系当事人之间的实体权利义务关系，直接赋予私人实体法上的权利和义务。(2) 这种条约大多规定商事事项，② 较少涉及一般民事事项。因此，商人自治得到了极大的尊重。(3) 这种条约通常由有关统一国际私法的专门组织准备和制定，然后由缔约国签署和批准，充分体现了各国民商法共有的一般规则。(4) 这种条约政治性不强，而具有较强的法律尤其是私法的

① 参见肖永平：《国际私法原理》，法律出版社2003年版，第309页。

② 各国法律对“商事”的含义规定不同，但一般尽可能作广义的解释。1985年《联合国国际商事仲裁示范法》对该词的说明就是：“‘商事’一词应给予广义的解释，以便包括产生于所有具有商业性质的关系的事项，不论这种关系是否为契约关系……”

专业性。①

进入20世纪80年代以来，我国缔结或加入的有关国际统一实体私法的条约逐年增多。在外国人民事法律地位方面，缔结或参加的公约有：1925年《本国工人与外国工人关于事故赔偿的同等待遇公约》、1951年《关于难民地位的公约》及1967年《关于难民地位的议定书》、1979年《关于消除对妇女一切形式歧视的公约》等。在实体法方面，我国参加的国际条约较多，主要集中在国际货物买卖、国际货物运输、知识产权的国际保护等方面，如1980年《联合国国际货物销售合同公约》、1966年《国际船舶载重线条约》、1972年《国际海上避碰规则公约》、1974年《联合国班轮公会行动守则公约》、1969年《国际油污损害民事责任公约》、1929年《关于统一国际航空运输某些规则的公约》及1955年《关于修订统一国际航空运输某些规则的公约的议定书》、1883年《保护工业产权巴黎公约》、1886年《保护文学艺术作品伯尔尼公约》、1891年《商标国际注册马德里协定》、1952年《世界版权公约》、1967年《成立世界知识产权组织公约》等，此外，我国还同许多国家签订了双边投资保护协定、贸易协定等。其中也包含了大量的调整涉外民事关系的实体法规范。②

（二）国际统一实体私法条约在我国的适用

对于国际统一实体私法条约在我国的适用，应根据每个条约的具体规定和具体案件当事人所属国是否为缔约国以及是否涉及中国当事人等情况分别确定其适用规则。

1. 根据条约的不同规定采用不同的方式

（1）有些条约规定缔约国有义务把条约纳入国内法，如1930年《统一汇票及本票法公约》、1931年《统一支票法公约》③ 和1964年《国际货物买卖统一法公约》等。如1964年《关于国际货物买卖统一法公约》第1条规定，各缔约国保证在不迟于公约在各该国生效之日，按照本国的立法程序，把国际货物买卖统一法纳入本国的法律。这样做的结果是，当缔约国把条约规定的统

---

① 黄进：《论国际统一实体私法》，载《中国国际私法与比较法年刊》（1998年创刊号），法律出版社1998年版，第9页。

② 参见韩德培主编：《国际私法》，高等教育出版社2000年版，第30～31页。

③ 这两个公约第1条均规定："各缔约国应将本公约第一附件所制定之统一法，以原文或该国文字通令所属境内采用。"但这一规定是否要求缔约国以国内立法的形式将统一法纳入国内法律体系，人们可能有不同的看法。

一实体规范纳入国内法后，该国国内法中只有一种国际货物买卖法，它不仅适用于缔约国国民，同样适用于非缔约国国民。

（2）有些国际条约没有规定缔约国有义务把条约的内容纳入国内法，如1924年《统一提单的若干法律规则的国际公约》（《海牙规则》）、① 1956年《国际公路货物运输合同公约》等。这类公约可以被缔约国纳入国内法，也可以不被缔约国纳入国内法。如果缔约国不把这类公约纳入国内法，该缔约国在有关法律领域就存在两套法律：一套是国际条约规定的统一私法，缔约国有义务将之适用于所有缔约国国民，但没有义务适用于非缔约国国民；另一套是缔约国自己制定的有关国内法，它可以适用于非缔约国国民，但不适用于缔约国国民，除非该国际条约允许私方当事人排除公约的适用而选择适用缔约国自己制定的国内法。②

2. 如果具体案件中的争诉问题属于某一国际条约的适用范围，③ 不论有没有中国当事人，相对于我国法律中的冲突规范，条约中的实体规范应得到优先直接适用。这是现代国际私法关于直接调整方法和间接调整方法相互关系的理论的必然要求。因为作为调整国际民商事关系的国际私法，其主要目的是为了解决不同国家民商事法律之间的冲突，直接适用国际条约和利用冲突法正是代表了两种不同的调整方法。冲突法方法是从分析国际民商事关系的性质入手，来确定该民商事关系应适用何国法律。因此，它不直接规定当事人的权利与义务。而直接适用国际条约的方法，其思维方式恰好相反，它不需要冲突规范的援引，而是直接适用国际条约中的规定确定当事人的权利和义务。因此，它避免了在不同国家的法律之间作出选择，从而更全面、更直接、更彻底地解决了不同国家间的民商事法律冲突。所以，国际条约中的实体法规定相对于国内法中的冲突规范来说，要优先得到适用。否则，直接调整方法就起不到应有的作用。④

再进一步分析，国际条约中的实体法规则为什么可以优先于国内法中的实体法规则呢？因为国际社会由国家组成，国家由个人组成，国家是个人与国际社会之间联系的纽带。透过这一社会结构可以发现，国家处于中心地位，它负

---

① 该公约在签字议定书中规定：各缔约国得以给予本公约以法律效力，或将本公约采用的规则以适合于本国立法的形式纳入该国法律的方式，使之生效。

② 参见沈达明、冯大同编著：《国际贸易法新论》，法律出版社1989年版，第5~6页。

③ 例如，案件当事人所属国都是某一国际条约的缔约国等。

④ 肖永平：《肖永平论冲突法》，武汉大学出版社2002年版，第185页。

责维系着国际社会的整体利益、作为一个独立社会和实体的国家利益和具体案件当事人的利益之间的平衡：国家通过与其他国家的合作维护和促进国际社会的整体利益；国家通过合理合法的手段认可和保护私人的利益；国家通过维护国际社会的整体利益和保护私人的个人利益，建立适合自身存在和发展的外部环境和内部环境，以此增进国家自身的利益。所以，国家间通过国际条约对一些共同关心的民商事法律问题进行规范，以便减少当事人的交易成本，促进相互间的合作与交往。这既是建立和维护国际社会民商事秩序的需要，也是增加国家和个人福利的需要，反映了上述三个层次利益的一致性。所以，无论是从国际社会的整体利益考虑，还是为国家自身利益考量，或者是为当事人个体利益着想，国家都需要遵守和执行其缔结和参加的国际条约。从表面上看，这是国际条约对缔约国的约束力使然，实质上是任何一个国家追求国际社会利益、国家利益和个人利益最大化的要求。

3. 如果我国不是某一国际条约的缔约国，该条约不能优先直接适用。当中国法院审理这一类案件时，必须首先适用中国法中相应的冲突规范，① 如果中国的冲突规范指引适用某国法律，而该国是某一国际条约的缔约国，中国法院可以适用该国际条约的规定，当然也可以不适用，这取决于该外国国内法关于国际条约在其国内法体系的地位的规定和国际条约本身的规定。也就是说，如果某国际条约本身作了规定，像《联合国国际货物销售合同公约》第 1 条第 1 款（b）项②那样，而该外国把其参加的国际条约视为国内法律体系的一部分，中国法院就可以适用该国际条约的规定。

4. 如果具体案件的当事人所属国都不是某一国际私法条约的缔约国，该条约当然不能直接适用，但当事人可以选择适用此种统一实体法条约。因为这时的国际条约可以看成是某一法律领域国际惯例的证明。我国法律也确立了这种选择的有效性。③ 通常，谈起法律选择，人们首先想到的是选择某国的法律。这是自然的，因为正是由于不同国家法律制度的差异，才产生了法律选择的需要。但如果仅仅把法律选择局限于国内法，这种认识未免落后于时代。因为在统一实体法与各国国内法并存以及同一法律领域中不同的统一实体法并存的今天，统一实体法也是合同当事人进行法律选择的对象。因为：（1）在合

① 对于国际私法案件来说，一个基本的理论前提，如果没有统一实体法可供适用，法院应适用本国的冲突规范寻找适当的准据法。

② 它规定：如果国际私法规则导致适用某一缔约国的法律，本公约适用于营业地在不同国家的当事人之间所订立的货物销售合同。

③ 肖永平：《冲突法专论》，武汉大学出版社 1999 年版，第 222～226 页。

同当事人选择国内法的意见分歧、相持不下的情况下，选择统一实体法可以使他们找到一条解决问题的新出路。作为协调不同国家利益冲突的产物，统一实体法往往使合同当事人易于接受。(2) 统一实体法，特别是作为国际惯例的统一实体法，也容易被法院所接受，并可以在较大程度上保证在不同国家的法院起诉时，对同一国际合同法律适用的一致和判决的一致。(3) 与选择外国的国内法相比，证明统一实体法的内容往往也比较容易。①

（三）特别观察：《联合国国际货物销售合同公约》在我国的适用

从《联合国国际货物销售合同公约》的制定、通过、核准到生效，我国始终采取积极的态度。1980 年 4 月，我国政府派代表参加在维也纳举行的外交会议，并签署了该公约。其后，我国政府又于 1986 年 12 月 11 日向联合国交存批准文书，成为该公约的缔约国。与我国同一天交存核准书的有美国、意大利（在此之间有 8 个国家核准加入），公约因此从 1988 年 1 月 1 日起生效。截至 2006 年 2 月，公约已对中、美、意、法等 68 个缔约方生效。② 而在 1983 年，就包括了 22 个欧洲及其他西方发达国家、11 个南美国家、7 个非洲国家、11 个亚洲国家以及 11 个社会主义国家。我国在交存核准书时依公约规定作了两项保留：(1) 不受公约第 1 条第 1 款（b）项的约束；(2) 对公约第 11 条、第 29 条及有关规定提出保留。为了执行该公约，我国对外经济贸易部在 1987 年 12 月 4 日发布了《关于执行〈联合国国际货物销售合同公约〉应注意的几个问题》。根据公约的内容、特点以及我国所作的保留和对外贸易部发布的意见，我国在适用公约时除了要考虑本文第一部分的一般规则以外，还应注意下列问题：

1. 公约的非强制性适用问题

公约第 6 条规定，当事人可以全部排除公约的适用，也可以删减或改变公约的任何规定的效力。这就是说，公约的适用并不具有强制性，即使合同双方

① 参见邵景春：《国际合同法律适用论》，北京大学出版社 1997 年版，第 55～56 页。

② 这 68 个缔约方是阿根廷、澳大利亚、奥地利、巴拉圭、白俄罗斯、比利时、波斯尼亚和黑塞哥维那、保加利亚、布隆迪、加拿大、智利、中国、哥伦比亚、克罗地亚、古巴、塞浦路斯、捷克共和国、丹麦、厄瓜多尔、埃及、爱沙尼亚、芬兰、法国、格鲁吉亚、德国、加纳、希腊、几内亚、洪都拉斯、匈牙利、冰岛、伊拉克、以色列、意大利、韩国、吉尔吉斯共和国、拉脱维亚、莱索托、立陶宛、卢森堡、毛里塔尼亚、墨西哥、摩尔多瓦、蒙古、利比里亚、荷兰、新西兰、挪威、秘鲁、波兰、罗马尼亚、俄罗斯、圣文森特和格林纳丁斯、南斯拉夫联盟共和国、新加坡、斯洛伐克、斯洛文尼亚、西班牙、瑞典、瑞士、叙利亚、乌干达、乌克兰、美国、乌拉圭、乌兹别克斯坦、委内瑞拉、赞比亚。

当事人的营业地分处不同的缔约国，本应适用该公约，但如果他们在合同中规定不适用该公约，而选择公约以外的其他法律作为合同的准据法，就可以完全排除公约的适用。如果营业地分别处在不同缔约国的双方当事人，在他们订立的合同中没有排除公约的适用，公约就自动适用于他们所订立的合同。

当事人也可以在买卖合同中作出规定，部分地排除公约的适用，或改变公约中的任何一条规定而代之以合同中作出的规定。但是，当事人的这一权利有一定限制，即如果当事人营业地所在国在批准公约时作出了保留，当事人必须遵守该项保留。例如，营业地在我国的当事人就不能以口头方式订立合同或以口头修改、废止合同，因为我国对此作了保留。①

如果当事人仅在合同中选择适用某一国际惯例所规定的贸易术语，不能认为排除了公约的适用。因为这些贸易术语主要是用来确定买卖双方在交货方面的责任、费用与风险划分等问题，它们不能解决对货物品质的责任、违约及对违约的救济方法等问题，而公约对这些问题作了具体规定。因此，公约与贸易术语是相互补充的，并不相互排除。②

2. 书面保留问题

依照公约第 11 条规定，国际货物销售合同不一定要以书面形式订立或以书面来证明，在形式方面也不受任何其他条件的限制。因此，国际货物销售合同无论采取口头形式还是书面形式都是有效的。这一规定与我国在加入公约时有效的《涉外经济合同法》关于涉外经济合同必须采取书面形式订立的要求不一致。因此，我国在核准公约时，对此提出了保留，即中国坚持认为，国际货物销售合同必须采用书面方式，包括电报和电传。但是，随着《中华人民共和国合同法》③ 的生效和《涉外经济合同法》的废止，我国的国内法与该条约的规定相同，我国的这一保留也就失去了存在的法律和理论基础，我国应尽快撤销这一保留。当然，在我国正式撤销这一保留之前，我国法院仍应坚持国际商事合同必须采取书面形式。

3. 第 1 条第 1 款（b）项的保留问题

公约强调它只适用于国际性的货物销售合同，即营业地处于不同国家当事人之间所订立的货物销售合同。因此，公约在认定合同是否具有国际性时，惟一的标准是当事人的营业地，至于双方当事人的国籍是否不同，或者合同的性

---

① John Shijian Mo, *International Commercial Law*, 85-86（3rd ed. 2003）

② 参见韩德培主编：《国际私法》，高等教育出版社 2000 年版，第 341～343 页。

③ 因为《合同法》第 10 条规定：“当事人订立合同，有书面形式、口头形式和其他形式。”而该法同时适用于国际商事合同。

质是民事性质还是商事性质，对公约的适用来说，则不予考虑。因此，当事人的营业地在不同国家的事实，如果从合同中，或者从订立合同之前的任何时候或订立合同时当事人之间的任何交易或当事人透露的情况均看不出来的话，就不能适用该公约。在口头合同的情形下，证明营业地在不同国家有时会发生困难。

如果当事人有一个以上的营业地或没有营业地，应该如何确定当事人的营业地在不同国家呢？公约第10条规定："（1）如果当事人有一个以上的营业地，则以与合同及合同的履行关系最密切的营业地为其营业地，但要考虑到双方当事人在订立合同前任何时候或订立合同时所知道或所设想的情况；（2）如果当事人没有营业地，则以其惯常居所地为准。"但是，如何确定"与合同的履行有最密切关系的营业地"，并没有统一的标准，这只能由法官自由裁量，有些具体案件可能还比较困难。①

除了合同当事人的营业地处于不同国家以外，还必须符合下列条件之一，公约才适用于他们所订立的货物销售合同：（1）这些国家都是该公约的缔约国；或（2）如果当事人的营业地所在国不是缔约国，则须依据国际私法规则导致适用某一缔约国的法律。

上述第1条第1款（b）项规定的目的是为了扩大公约的适用范围，使公约不仅适用于缔约国的当事人之间订立的买卖合同，也可能适用于非缔约国的当事人所订立的买卖合同。这里所谓的"国际私法规则"是指对法院有约束力的冲突规则，可以是法院国内法中的冲突规则，也可以是对法院有约束力的国际统一冲突法规则。例如，营业地在甲国的当事人同营业地在乙国的当事人之间的货物销售合同，假设甲国为公约的缔约国，乙国不是公约的缔约国，按照第一项的规定，由于乙国不是缔约国，该公约不适用于他们所订立的合同。但是，如果根据第二项的规定，只要国际私法规则导致适用甲国的法律（可能因为甲国是合同的订立地或履行地等），由于甲国是公约的缔约国，该公约就适用于他们之间所订立的买卖合同。对于这一点，我国提出了保留，即我国仅同意对双方的营业地所在国均为缔约国的当事人之间所订立的货物销售合同才适用该公约。

对于第1条第1款（b）项的设立，理论界一直存在争论。由于该项的设立使公约既代替了内国法的适用，也代替了外国国内法的适用，这对一个国内立法不适应国际贸易发展的国家来说是有积极意义的，也有利于扩大公约的适用范围，但它不可避免地导致公约适用的不确定性，这与公约作为统一法的宗

① John Shijian Mo, *International Commercial Law*, 80-82 (3rd ed. 2003).

旨背道而驰。也正因为如此，公约第 95 条规定缔约国可以对该项提出保留。事实上，按照第 1 条第 1 款（b）项适用公约的情形主要有：（1）当事人的营业地或惯常居所在不同国家，法院地国家是当事人之一的营业地或惯常居所地所在国，同时也是没有根据该公约第 95 条作出保留声明的缔约国，依据对该法院有约束力的冲突规则，有关的货物销售合同适用法院地法，从而最终导致该公约的适用。（2）其他条件与第（1）种情形一样，但依据对法院有约束力的冲突规则，有关的货物销售合同适用作为公约缔约国的第三国法律，也可导致该公约的适用。（3）当事人的营业地或惯常居所在不同国家，但并不在法院地国，当事人之一的营业地或惯常居所所在地是缔约国，法院地国是没有根据公约第 95 条作出保留声明的缔约国，依据对法院地国有约束力的冲突规则，有关的货物销售合同适用法院地的法律，从而导致该公约的适用。（4）其他情形与第（3）种情形一样，但依据对法院有约束力的冲突规则，有关的货物销售合同适用作为公约缔约国的第三国法律，也导致该公约的适用。（5）当事人的营业地或惯常居所在不同国家，但这些国家既不是公约的缔约国，也不是受理案件的法院地国，法院地国是没有根据公约第 95 条作出保留声明的缔约国，依据对法院地有约束力的冲突规则，有关的货物销售合同适用法院地法，从而导致该公约的适用。（6）其他情形与第（5）种情形一样，但依据对法院有约束力的冲突规则，有关的货物销售合同适用作为缔约国的第三国法律，也最终导致该公约的适用。因此，第 1 条第 1 款（b）项可以扩大该公约的适用范围，并在公约缔约国之间比较彻底地取代了各国相应的国内法。①

但是，中国是否有必要对此提出保留值得进一步研究。就中国法院受理的当事人不是都在该公约缔约国设有营业所的国际货物销售合同案件来说，如果中国的冲突规范导致适用中国法，不作此保留就要适用该国际条约，随着我国合同法制度的完善，其与国际条约中的制度差别不大。因此，其结果对我国国家利益和当事人的利益也没有害处；如果中国的冲突规范导致适用另一个公约的缔约国的法律，不作此保留就要适用该国际条约，这对减轻中国法院的负担和维护中国有关当事人的利益是有好处的，因为它避免了适用外国的国内法。另外，随着该公约的缔约国越来越多，该项的作用也越来越小，对缔约国国内法的影响也越来越小。所以，我国可以考虑取消这个保留。

4. 缔约国的保留声明对适用公约的影响

由于公约是一项旨在协调各大法系货物销售合同法律制度差异的统一实体

① 参见邵景春：《国际合同法律适用论》，北京大学出版社 1997 年版，第 216～218 页。

法，为了使尽量多的国家参加该公约，公约第92条规定了保留制度，规定缔约国可以声明它不受公约第二部分或者第三部分的约束。公约第二部分和第三部分是关于合同的订立和货物的买卖（包括买卖双方的义务、违约的救济、风险的转移等问题），这是公约的实质性核心内容。这样，作出此种保留声明的缔约国，在该声明适用部分所规定的事项上，不得视为该公约第1条第1款范围内的缔约国。这会导致同一个当事人订立的国际货物销售合同，就一部分而言，其营业地所属国是缔约国；但就另外一部分来说，它又不是缔约国。这对该公约的适用会产生直接的影响。例如，卖方的营业地在甲国，买方的营业地在乙国，甲乙两国都是公约的缔约国，若甲国根据公约第92条对该公约第二部分作了保留声明，买卖双方的货物销售合同就只能受公约第三部分的支配，而不受第二部分的支配。因为就第二部分而言，甲国已经不再是缔约国了，卖方的营业地也不再位于缔约国内了。在上述条件下，如果乙国也根据公约第92条作了保留声明，但不是就公约第二部分作出的，而是就第三部分作出的，买卖双方的货物销售合同就完全不受该公约的支配了。因为在此情况下，甲国不再是公约第二部分事项的缔约国，乙国也不再是公约第三部分事项的缔约国。这样一来，甲乙两国虽然可以被称为《联合国国际货物销售合同公约》的缔约国，但就买卖双方的销售合同而言，它们的营业地不能被认为位于公约的缔约国境内。① 因此，我国法院或仲裁机构必须谨慎地查明该公约缔约国在参加、接受、核准公约时所作的保留、声明或者变更等，以便准确适用公约。②

---

① 参见邵景春：《国际合同法律适用论》，北京大学出版社1997年版，第214～215页。

② 该公约规定，缔约国在批准或加入公约时，根据公约第12条和第96条规定声明，公约第11条、第29条或第二部分任何条款，凡准予通过协议形式签订销售合同或进行修改或终止，或以书面形式以外的任何形式提出要约、承诺或表示意向者，概不适用于任何当事方在其各自国家内设有营业地点的销售合同。一些国家作出的保留是：（1）中华人民共和国政府在认可公约时声明，不受第1（1）（b）条和第11条的约束，也不受公约内与第11条内容有关的规定的约束。（2）丹麦、芬兰、挪威和瑞典政府在批准公约时根据第92（1）条的规定声明，它们不受公约第二部分（合同的订立）的约束。丹麦、芬兰、挪威和瑞典政府在批准公约时根据第94（1）和94（2）条声明，公约不适用于营业地点设在丹麦、芬兰、瑞典、冰岛或挪威的当事方的销售合同。在2003年3月12日生效的一份通知中，冰岛根据第94（1）条的规定声明，公约不适用于营业地点设在丹麦、芬兰、冰岛、挪威或瑞典的当事方的销售合同及合同的订立。（3）德国政府在批准公约时声明，对于已经声明不适用第1（1）（b）条的任何国家，德国也不适用第1（1）（b）条。

5. 缔约国参加的其他国际协议对适用公约的影响

国际条约之间的冲突是一个非常复杂的问题。如果先后两个条约的缔约国完全相同，一般可以根据后法优于前法的原则，适用新条约，因为当事国有权以新条约废除、补充或变更旧条约。但是，如果先后两个条约的缔约国部分相同，部分不同时，如何选择适用这些不同的条约，学者们提出了许多不同意见，①《维也纳条约法公约》第 30 条规定：在这两个条约都是当事国与仅是其中一个条约的当事国之间，权利和义务依两国都是当事国的那个条约决定。这说明公约采用的是条约当事国必须善意履行条约的原则和条约相对效力原则，即条约对第三国既无利也无害的原则。② 不过，新条约不能改变旧条约中的强制性规定，而条约本身关于其优先地位的规定对该问题有重要影响。因此，在具体适用公约解决当事人的营业地位于我国和其他缔约国的货物销售合同纠纷时，还要考虑公约和其他国际协议的关系。好在公约尊重其他国际协议的效力，其第 90 条明确规定："本公约不优于业已缔结或可能缔结并载有与属于本公约范围内事项有关条款的任何国际协议，但以双方当事人的营业地均在这种协议的缔约国内为限。"因此，如果两个当事人的营业地所在国同时参加公约和其他调整国际货物销售合同关系的国际协议，后者应优先适用。我国最高

---

① 例如，（一）《哈佛条约法公约草案》第 22 条第 2 项规定：一个多边条约的两个或者多个当事国相互间拟缔结一个后条约以代替前条约时，必须符合下列两个条件：（1）前条约的规定并不禁止后条约的缔结；（2）后条约并不与前条约的总目的不相容到这样的程度，以致大概会破坏该条约的目的。（二）劳特派特则主张：一个双边或多边条约或其任何规定，如果其履行必然使一个或几个缔约方违反其以前负担的条约义务，即属无效；但该原则不适用于下面后订的多边条约：（1）该后订的多边条约具有一定程度的一般性，从而具有正当影响国际社会全体成员的立法的性质，或该后订条约是为了国际利益而缔结的；（2）后订条约是修订前多边条约的，且其修订是依照前多边条约的规定进行的，或在没有这种规定的场合，是由前多边条约绝大多数当事国进行的。（三）菲茨摩里斯则把多边条约规定的义务分为三类：（1）互惠性（reciprocating）的，即每一当事国对另一当事国负担某种义务，而从后者得到相应的权利；（2）互赖性（interdependent）的，即每一当事国的履行义务以所有其他当事国履行条约义务为条件；（3）全体性（integral）的，即每一当事国的义务是当然存在的、绝对的、固有的，其履行不以其他当事国的相应履行为条件。对于后两类条约，如果后条约在一个重要的个别部分与前条约直接抵触时，在抵触的范围内，应为无效。（四）沃尔多克主张：在后条约的当事国不完全包括前条约当事国的情况下，与前条约抵触的后条约并非无效，而只是前条约对后条约处于优先地位，后条约的当事国因而可能违反前条约规定的义务而负担国际责任。但违反前条约强行法规定的后条约当然无效。详见李浩培：《条约法概论》，法律出版社 2003 年版，第 256 ~ 260 页。

② 参见李浩培：《条约法概论》，法律出版社 2003 年版，第 260 ~ 261 页。

人民法院在转发对外经济贸易部《关于执行〈联合国国际货物销售合同公约〉应注意的几个问题的通知》中明确指出：我国和匈牙利虽然是《联合国国际货物销售合同公约》的缔约国，但是由于彼此之间存在“交货共同条件”，所以仍然优先适用该交货条件，因为该交货共同条件可以看成是该公约的特别安排。

6. 公约在非缔约国当事人之间适用的可能性

如果非缔约国的当事人通过意思自治选择适用公约，公约能够得到适用吗？公约对此没有作出明确规定。其实，1964 年《国际货物买卖统一法公约》第 4 条明确规定：双方当事人选择公约作为合同准据法的，不管他们的营业地或惯常居所地是否位于不同国家，也不管这些国家是否在 1964 年 7 月 1 日以前成为《国际货物买卖统一法公约》的缔约国，公约都可以适用，只要不违反在当事人没有选择公约时本应适用的法律的强制性规定。但在制定本公约的过程中，国际贸易法委员会删除了这一条，原因是该条中的“强制性规定”在许多缔约国法律中的含义和范围是不同的。委员会试图全面允许当事人选择适用公约，但又担心在没有“强制性规定”的情况下有可能导致适用于某些消费合同，从而减损本应适用的国内法对消费者提供的特殊保护。正是由于这个两难选择，公约放弃了对该问题的规定。但这并不表明公约禁止当事人选择适用公约，当然也不希望当事人的意思自治减损本应适用的国内法的强制性规定。①

所以，对于非缔约国的当事人选择适用公约的有效性问题，除了根据我国冲突法中关于当事人意思自治原则的限制性条件进行判断以外，还要考虑当事人是否在公约调整范围以外的合同中选择适用该公约、② 当事人的营业地是否位于同一个国家等因素。公约对这个问题既没有明确的否定，也没有明确的肯定，而是保持沉默，看来是一个缺陷。例如，下列合同可以仅仅因为当事人的选择而适用公约：

（1）当事人的营业地或者惯常居所在同一国家内的货物销售合同，但当事人的国籍不同，或者他们的合同履行地可能涉及不同的国家等，如果当事人选择适用该公约，该公约应该予以适用。这样既尊重了当事人的意思，又扩大

---

① 参见邵景春：《国际合同法律适用论》，北京大学出版社 1997 年版，第 220 ~ 227 页。

② 因为公约第 2 条明确排除下列合同的适用：（1）供私人和家庭使用的买卖合同；（2）以拍卖方式进行的买卖；（3）根据法律执行令状或其他令状进行的买卖；（4）股票、投资证券、流通票据或货币的买卖；（5）船舶或飞机的买卖；（6）电力的买卖。

了公约的适用范围，有利于形成一个统一的法律秩序。

(2)对于营业地或惯常居所在不同的非公约缔约国的当事人之间的货物销售合同,如果当事人选择了该公约,只要这种选择符合法院地国的冲突规则,应该肯定这种选择的效力。因为根据该公约第1条第1款b项,如果当事人选择了该公约某缔约国的法律,只要对法院有约束力的冲突规则肯定了当事人的此种法律选择,就可以适用该公约,当事人直接选择适用公约就更应该得到支持。

(3)对于拍卖交易中的货物销售合同,如果当事人选择了该公约,应该肯定当事人的选择,并适用该公约;在拍卖地国家是公约的缔约国时更应该如此。这样做除了是尊重当事人的意思以外,更是便于买卖双方当事人,因为在拍卖交易的场合,买卖双方可能并不了解拍卖行所在地国家的法律,只有拍卖行和拍卖人熟悉当地的法律,给予当事人选择适用该公约的权利,自然方便双方当事人。

但是，对公约第2条排除的其他种类的合同，即使当事人选择适用公约，一般也不应该适用该公约。因为这些事项都具有比较特殊的商业性质或法律性质，公约中的规定往往不适合于对它们的调整。①

总而言之，《联合国国际货物销售合同公约》的适用情况可以概括为下列四类：(1) 对于相关营业地在公约不同缔约国的当事人，如果他们签订的合同属于公约的适用范围，公约自动成为该合同的准据法，除非当事人选择其他的法律。(2) 如果仅有一方当事人的营业地在公约的缔约国，而公约缔约国的国内法是合同的准据法，也可以适用公约的规定。(3) 如果合同双方当事人的营业地都不在公约的缔约国境内，因当事人的选择，公约的原则也可以得到适用。(4) 在仲裁实践中，即使合同当事人的营业地都不在公约缔约国境内，当事人也没有在合同中选择该公约，公约的原则有时也得到了适用。这时，公约是作为国际惯例起到了补缺作用的。②

---

① 参见邵景春:《国际合同法律适用论》，北京大学出版社1997年版，第222~224页。

② General information on the application of the CISG: (1) For parties with their relevant places of business in different Contracting States, where their contract falls within the scope of the CISG, the contract is automatically governed by the CISG, unless the parties indicate otherwise. (2) The above conclusion and recommendation can also apply when only one of the parties has his relevant place of business in a Contracting State. (3) There are also cases in which principles of the CISG can apply to transactions between parties neither of whom has his relevant place of business in a Contracting State. (4) In addition, there are situations in which principles of the CISG can be deemed applicable even when neither party has his relevant place of business in a Contracting State and the parties have made no reference to the CISG in their contract. See http://www.cisg.law.pace.edu., 2004年10月27日访问。

（四）个案分析

1. 公约规则的自动直接适用

德国A公司与我国B公司已经做过多笔买卖。在履行前一个合同后，德国A公司又寄来一张订单，规定一切有关的交易条件按上次合同办理。以往，我国B公司接到订单后立即表示承诺，然后发行货物。这次，B公司未予回答，事隔不久，德国A公司依据惯常做法通过银行将信用证开到B公司。我国B公司仍置之不理。到此，德国A公司要求B公司履行合同，否则需要赔偿损失，其理由是B公司的沉默是对要约的默认，因此合同已成立。A、B公司双方的合同中没有选择法律，仲裁庭注意到A公司所在地德国和B公司所在地中国均是1980年《联合国国际货物销售合同公约》的成员国。

该案的主要争诉点是合同是否成立。如果案件由我国法院或仲裁庭负责处理，我国法院或仲裁庭应该首先适用1980年《联合国国际货物销售合同公约》的有关规定，不管该公约的规定与我国《合同法》的规定是否一致。这是国际条约优先直接适用的必然要求。只有当国际条约没有规定，或有关规定不能适用或不能解决问题时，我国法院或仲裁庭才应根据我国《合同法》或《民法通则》中规定的有关合同法律适用的冲突规则在中国法、德国法或其他国内法中选择一个解决本案纠纷。对于本案来说，1980年《联合国国际货物销售合同公约》第18条可以用来判断合同是否成立。该条第1款首先规定，沉默和不作为本身不构成承诺；而该条第3款规定的例外是：如果根据要约或当事人之间确定的习惯做法或惯例，受要约人可以作出某种行为来表示同意，无须向要约人发出通知。本案中当事人之间的习惯做法是受要约人接到订单后“立即表示承诺”，但我国B公司既没有“立即表示承诺”，也没有作出一定的行为，没有有效的承诺，合同因此没有成立。

2. 冲突规则导致公约规则的适用

我国某出口公司于某年8月3日应中东一中间商的询盘，发了一个供应某商品10万磅的实盘，规定自当年11月至第二年3月平均每月各装2万磅，单价为C&F每磅1.38美元，目的港为西非某港口，发盘的有效期至8月8日止。8月7日收到对方来电称：“你3日电已说服客户接受你方价格，请考虑数量12万磅，10月至次年3月平均装，电告合同号码（YC3RD CONVINCED CLIENTS ACCEPTING YOUR PRICE PLEASE CONSIDER QUANTITY 120000 LBS SHIPMENT OCTOBER TO MARCH EQUALLY CABLE CONTRACT NUMBER）。”

此时，公司发现原盘单价因核算错误，每磅少报了0.14美元，倘若按此达成交易，10万磅共少收汇1.4万美元。随即对来电内容进行分析，从中研究是否还有挽回损失的余地。在分析来电内容过程中，有两种意见：一种认为，该商仅表示接受我方发盘中的价格；接受一词用的进行时“ACCEPTING”，意指“正在接受中”而非“已经接受”，有不肯定的意思；对数量和装运期虽用了“请考虑”字样，但实质上作了变更；“请电告合同号码”则是请我方接受的表示，也是对方转告其客户凭办进口许可手续所需，所以应视做还盘。另一种意见认为，该商已接受我方发盘，10万磅的交易已经达成，另外要求增加2万磅，只是把两笔交易混在一起（一笔是我方10万磅发盘的“接受”；另一笔是对方要求增供2万磅的“发盘”）。至于对方仅表示接受我方价格，而“接受”一词又用了进行时“ACCEPTING”，这是中东商人经常使用的一种用语，不能作为否定其接受有效性的依据。所以，倘若以对方变更条件为理由作还盘处理，从而宣告我方8月3日发盘已经终止效力，势必引起纠纷，而且最终可能带来对我方不利的结果。

后来，我国出口公司在复电中没有提发盘的价格，而是增加了两个条件。假设该中东中间商所属国没有加入1980年《联合国国际货物销售合同公约》，双方对合同是否成立发生了争执，起诉到我国有管辖权的法院。

我国法院在查明中东中间商所属国不是《联合国国际货物销售合同公约》的缔约国以后，就不能适用该条约，必须首先适用中国法中的冲突规范。看当事人有没有合法选择合同适用的法律；没有选择的，就根据最密切联系确定应适用的法律。如果中国法院认为应该适用中国法，尽管中国是《联合国国际货物销售合同公约》的缔约国，由于中国对该公约第1条第1款B项作了保留，中国法院只适用国内合同法解决合同是否成立问题。①

3. 当事人选择适用公约规则

中国内地A公司向中国香港B公司发出要约，要约规定，供应100匹马力的拖拉机50台，每台CFR香港3500美元，订立合同后两个月装船，不可撤销信用证付款。B公司收到要约后，立即电复承诺，表示接受A公司的要约，并要求订立合同后立即装船。但A公司未作任何答复，也没有提交货物。事后，B公司以A公司违反合同为由要求损害赔偿。双方在仲裁申请书、答辩状中均引用1980年《联合国国际货物销售合同公约》的条款为自己申辩，仲裁庭在进一步确认后，认为当事人双方协议选择适用该国际公约，决定适用《联合国国际货物销售合同公约》。

---

① 参见韩德培、肖永平：《国际私法学》，人民法院出版社、中国社会科学出版社2004年版，第226～227页。

由于B公司的承诺改变了要约中的装船日期，那么，装船日期的改变对承诺的有效性是否有影响呢？根据1980年《联合国国际货物销售合同公约》第19条的规定，如果承诺对要约内容作了实质性改变，则这种接受就不构成承诺。依据公约的解释，所谓实质性改变，是指承诺对要约中有关货物价格、付款、货物质量和数量、交货地点和时间、赔偿责任范围和解决争端的改变。由此看来，装船日期作为交货时间是合同的实质性条件。所以B公司的承诺因实质性改变要约的内容而不能产生法律效力，因而也不能导致合同的成立。所以仲裁庭裁定A公司不承担任何赔偿责任。

4. 公约规则的补充适用

如果一份国际货物买卖合同的当事人的营业地都不是1980年《联合国国际货物销售合同公约》的缔约国，当事人也没有通过明示或默示的方式选择适用该公约，当法院或仲裁庭适用有关的冲突规则选择适用某一国内法，但该国内法没有相关规定或不能适用时，《联合国国际货物销售合同公约》的规定也可以国际惯例得到补充适用。

5. 保留对公约规则适用的影响

假设甲、乙、丙、丁4个国家。甲为内国，同时是1985年《国际货物销售合同法律适用公约》和1980年《联合国国际货物销售合同公约》的缔约国；乙、丙、丁为外国，其中，乙仅是1985年《国际货物销售合同法律适用公约》的缔约国，丙仅是1980年《联合国国际货物销售合同公约》的缔约国，丁与甲一样，同时是1985年《国际货物销售合同法律适用公约》和1980年《联合国国际货物销售合同公约》的缔约国。在这样的条件下，从甲国角度出发，对于不同场合的国际合同应按不同方法解决其法律适用问题：如果争议中的国际合同是与甲、乙两方有关的，应根据《国际货物销售合同法律适用公约》的规定确定合同应适用的法律，不直接适用《联合国国际货物销售合同公约》；如果争议中的国际合同与甲、丙有关，则直接适用《联合国国际货物销售合同公约》，而不适用《国际货物销售合同法律适用公约》；如果争议中的国际合同是与甲、丁有关的，尽管该合同同时属于这两个国际条约的适用范围，由于统一实体法比统一冲突法应该优先适用，因为其目的就是为了避免冲突的发生，因此应该直接适用《联合国国际货物销售合同公约》。①

三、国际统一程序法条约在我国的适用

国际民事诉讼程序规则的统一对于一国法院顺利审理国际民商事案件具有

① 参见邵景春：《国际合同法律适用论》，北京大学出版社1997年版，第174页。

重要意义。我国目前参加的程序法方面的条约主要有：1987 年参加的 1958 年《承认和执行外国仲裁裁决公约》（简称《纽约公约》）、1991 年加入的 1965 年《关于向国外送达民事或商事司法文书和司法外文书公约》（简称《海牙送达公约》）、1992 年加入的 1965 年《关于解决国家与他国国民之间的投资争端的公约》（《华盛顿公约》）、1997 年加入的 1970 年《关于从国外调取民事或商事证据的公约》（《海牙取证公约》）。此外，自 1987 年，我国开始和外国缔结司法协助方面的双边条约。截至 2003 年 6 月，我国已与 45 个国家谈判缔结了 60 个有关司法协助方面的双边条约，其中 44 个条约已经生效实施。① 这些

① 在这些条约中，仅仅关于民事的双边司法协助条约有 11 个：(1)《中华人民共和国和法兰西共和国关于民事、商事司法协助的协定》；(2)《中华人民共和国和比利时王国关于民事司法协助的协定》；(3)《中华人民共和国和泰王国关于民商事司法协助和仲裁合作的协定》；(4)《中华人民共和国和意大利共和国关于民事司法协助的条约》；(5)《中华人民共和国和西班牙王国关于民事、商事司法协助的条约》；(6)《中华人民共和国和保加利亚共和国关于民事司法协助的协定》；(7)《中华人民共和国和摩洛哥王国关于民事和商事司法协助的协定》；(8)《中华人民共和国和匈牙利共和国关于民事和商事司法协助的协定》；(9)《中华人民共和国和新加坡共和国关于民事和商事司法协助的条约》；(10)《中华人民共和国和突尼斯共和国关于民事和商事司法协助的条约》；(11)《中华人民共和国和阿根廷共和国关于民事和商事司法协助的条约》。关于民事和刑事的双边司法协助条约有 18 个：(1)《中华人民共和国和波兰人民共和国关于民事和刑事司法协助的协定》；(2)《中华人民共和国和蒙古人民共和国关于民事和刑事司法协助的条约》；(3)《中华人民共和国和罗马尼亚关于民事和刑事司法协助的条约》；(4)《中华人民共和国和古巴共和国关于民事和刑事司法协助的协定》；(5)《中华人民共和国和俄罗斯联邦关于民事和刑事司法协助的条约》；(6)《中华人民共和国和乌克兰关于民事和刑事司法协助的条约》；(7)《中华人民共和国和白俄罗斯共和国关于民事和刑事司法协助的条约》；(8)《中华人民共和国和哈萨克斯坦共和国关于民事和刑事司法协助的条约》；(9)《中华人民共和国和希腊共和国关于民事和刑事司法协助的协定》；(10)《中华人民共和国和吉尔吉斯共和国关于民事和刑事司法协助的条约》；(11)《中华人民共和国和塔吉克斯坦共和国关于民事和刑事司法协助的条约》；(12)《中华人民共和国和乌兹别克斯坦共和国关于民事和刑事司法协助的条约》；(13)《中华人民共和国和立陶宛共和国关于民事和刑事司法协助的条约》；(14)《中华人民共和国和越南社会主义共和国关于民事和刑事司法协助的条约》；(15)《中华人民共和国和老挝人民民主共和国关于民事和刑事司法协助的条约》；(16)《中华人民共和国和土耳其共和国关于民事、商事和刑事司法协助的协定》；(17)《中华人民共和国和阿拉伯埃及共和国关于民事、商事和刑事司法协助的协定》；(18)《中华人民共和国和塞浦路斯共和国关于民事、商事和刑事司法协助的条约》。其他都是关于刑事、引渡和被判刑人移管方面的条约。详见最高人民法院外事局编：《中国国际司法协助条约与实施手册》，外文出版社 2004 年版。

条约极大地便利了中国同其他缔约国在民商事领域开展司法协助。

（一）国际统一程序法条约的直接适用规则

由于各国把程序法都看成是公法问题，从国际社会的普遍实践来看，程序问题适用法院地法一直是各国法院审理国际民商事案件的基本原则。而国际统一程序法条约一般都没有要求缔约国把条约的规定转化为国内法规定，这样一来，国际统一程序法条约一般应该通过直接适用的方式得到实施。从统一程序法条约的内容来看，其规则大部分是就某一方面的内容规定缔约国法院或其他诉讼参与人之间的“手续”要求或合作义务，一般是比较具体的规则，能够成为法院和诉讼参与人进行诉讼的具体准则。这为国际统一程序法条约在国内的直接适用提供了可能。特别从我国同其他国家订立的双边司法协助条约来看，它们更是直接为中国与有关国家间开展司法协助提供了具体的规则。例如，《中华人民共和国和法兰西共和国关于民事、商事司法协助的协定》就直接对两国间转递和送达司法文书及司法外文书的方式、送达请求书的格式和文字、送达回证的要求、费用的免除以及拒绝送达的理由等问题作了具体规定；对代为调查取证的范围、方式、调查取证请求书的格式、取证费用的安排和结果的通知以及拒绝协助取证的理由等作了明确规定；对相互间请求承认和执行法院判决和仲裁裁决的提出、材料要求、程序、效力以及拒绝承认和执行的理由都作了安排。这些规定甚至比我国《民事诉讼法》的有关规定还具体、还明确，并有针对性。所以，该双边条约第 4 条规定：“缔约双方在本国领域内实施司法协助的措施，各自适用其本国法，但本协定另有规定的除外。”① 这表明，只要是该双边条约规定的事项，就应该直接适用条约的规定，不适用缔约国的国内法。由此可见，国际统一程序法条约在一国国内法院是应该并可以得到直接适用的。

（二）国际统一程序法条约的优先适用规则

由于不同国家关于条约与国内法的关系的理论和主张不同，也直接影响了国际统一程序法条约在这些国家能否得到优先适用。但可以肯定的是，绝大多数国家坚持国际统一程序法条约的优先适用规则。例如，美国最高法院在 1987 年对法国航空工业公司诉美国依阿华南区联邦地方法院案中认定，美国虽已批准《海牙取证公约》，但公约的适用不是强制性的和排他性的，美国法

① 最高人民法院外事局编：《中国国际司法协助条约与实施手册》，外文出版社 2004 年版，第 615～620 页。

院只在基于“礼让”的范围内适用公约所规定的域外取证制度，并可以自由裁量不适用公约，而根据美国的联邦诉讼程序规则进行域外取证，包括可由美国律师直接到外国进行取证活动。该项判决一经作出，立刻在国际上掀起了轩然大波，许多国家指责美国的这种做法明显违背了公约的宗旨，损害了他国的司法主权。①

统一程序法条约为什么能够得到优先适用呢？除了“条约必须信守”的一般国际法原则以外，由于国际统一程序法条约一般是就国际民事诉讼程序中的特殊问题作出特别的安排，相对于一个国家的民事诉讼法律制度来说，它是特别法。所以，即使一个国家认为国际条约与国内法具有平等的地位，根据“特别法优于普通法”的原则，国际统一程序法条约也应该得到优先适用。这个规则除了得到了许多国家的立法和司法实践的支持以外，一些国际条约也作了明确规定。例如，1965 年《海牙送达公约》第 1 条规定：在所有民事或商事案件中，如有需送达司法文书或司法外文书以便向国外送达的情形，均应适用该公约。各国一致理解该条款意味着公约在缔约国之间的适用是排他性的，亦即缔约国向另一缔约国境内送达公约所指的文书时，不得采取公约以外的方法。就是美国最高法院也在 1988 年对大众汽车股份公司诉舒隆克案中确认，《海牙送达公约》在缔约国之间的适用应是排他性的。②

从统一程序法条约的实践来看，条约与国内法不一致的情况大致有两种：一种是条约和国内法在同类事项上的规定不同；另一种则是条约和国内法中，一个对某问题作了规定，另一个没有对该问题作出规定。造成这种不一致的原因主要是：（1）由于制定条约和国内法的主体不同，一国在制定国内法时，完全根据本国的政治、经济制度，风俗习惯和法律传统等客观情况；但在缔结和参加国际条约时，由于各方平等的法律地位和不尽相同的实际需要，各国都要作出一些让步。可以说，完全将一国的法律制度纳入国际条约是办不到的。（2）由于条约和国内法的调整对象不同，对某些问题规定的侧重点也不一样，它们的规定也就会有差异。（3）由于各国程序法方面的差异和对法律概念的不同解释，即使国际条约使用了与国内法同样的术语，内涵有时也有很大差别。例如，上述公约对“民商事”概念的界定与许多国家的国内法的含义就有差别。不过，一国参加的国际条约与其国内法之间的差异，一般并非本质上的冲突。因为一国在批准或加入条约时，都要考虑条约与本国宪法和法律的基本原则是否吻合，尽量避免产生冲突；在原则冲突不可避免时，它可以自由选

---

① 参见徐宏：《国际民事司法协助》，武汉大学出版社 1996 年版，第 46～47 页。

② Gary B. Born, *International Civil Litigation in United States Courts*, 804 (3rd ed. 1996).

择不参加条约或在条约允许的范围内作出保留；在参加条约以后进行国内立法时，缔约国也应该注意与条约的规定相协调，不能通过修改国内法的方式改变其依条约承担的国际义务。从我国的实际情况看，国内法的有关规定是我国对外订立国际条约的依据，而国际条约的规定，又是对国内法的进一步完善和补充，是实现国内法规定的有效保障，两者之间是一种相互衔接、相辅相成的关系，共同构成我国国际民商事法律制度的整体。因此，当我国参加的国际条约与国内立法存在差异的时候，并不会对我国的司法实践带来很大的困难。这也是我国在《民事诉讼法》第238条中明确规定优先适用国际条约的实际原因。

（三）国际统一程序法条约与当事人意思自治

由于国际统一程序法条约规范的主要是缔约国之间在司法管辖权、司法协助、法院判决和仲裁裁决的相互承认与执行等问题上的合作和协调关系，尽管它们也会涉及私方当事人的诉讼权利和诉讼义务，但国家间关系的“公法”性质没有改变。所以，在这类国际条约的适用问题上，当事人的意思自治不能发挥作用，也就是说，当事人不能通过合意排除这类国际条约的适用，也不能选择适用这类公约。

（四）特别观察：1965年《海牙送达公约》在我国的适用

海牙国际私法会议于1965年11月15日通过的《关于向国外送达民事或商事司法文书和司法外文书公约》（简称《海牙送达公约》）是国际上迄今关于域外送达方面最完备、影响最大的公约。截至2003年11月，公约的成员除中国、中国香港特别行政区、中国澳门特别行政区以外，还有其他48个国家和地区。① 中国于1991年3月2日批准加入该公约，除指定中华人民共和国司法部为中央机关以外，还作了四点保留声明：（1）只有在文书须送达给文书发出国国民时，才能采用公约第8条第1款规定的直接通过其外交或领事代表机构向身在中华人民共和国境内的人完成文书的送达。（2）反对采用公约第10条规定的方式在中华人民共和国境内进行送达，而第10条规定的方式

---

① 这些成员是：阿根廷、白俄罗斯、比利时、保加利亚、加拿大、塞浦路斯、捷克共和国、丹麦、埃及、爱沙尼亚、芬兰、法国、德国、希腊、爱尔兰、以色列、意大利、日本、韩国、拉脱维亚、立陶宛、卢森堡、墨西哥、荷兰、挪威、波兰、葡萄牙、俄罗斯、斯洛伐克、斯洛文尼亚、西班牙、斯里兰卡、瑞典、瑞士、土耳其、英国、美国、委内瑞拉、安提瓜和巴布达、巴哈马、巴巴多斯、博茨瓦纳、科威特、马拉维、巴基斯坦、圣马力诺、塞舌尔、乌克兰。

有：通过邮寄途径直接送达、通过文书发出国和送达目的地国的司法助理人员、官员或其他主管人员之间的合作送达、利害关系人直接通过送达目的地国的司法助理人员、官员或其他主管人员完成送达。（3）根据公约第15条第2款声明，在符合该款规定的各项条件的情况下，即使未收到任何送达或交付的证明书，法官仍可不顾该条第1款的规定，作出判决。①（4）根据第16条第3款的声明，被告要求免除丧失上诉权效果的申请只能在自判决之日起的一年内提出，否则不予受理。我国在适用该公约时，有两点值得注意：

1.《海牙送达公约》的排他性适用问题

《海牙送达公约》第1条规定："在所有民事或商事案件中，如有须递送司法文书或司法外文书以便向国外送达的情形，均应适用本公约。"这一条款意味着公约在缔约国之间的适用是排他性的，即缔约一国向缔约另一国境内送达公约所指的文书时，不得采用公约以外的方法。这从该条使用的明显带有强制性的措辞"shall apply in all cases, in civil or commercial matters, where there is occasion to transmit a judicial or extrajudicial document for service abroad"可以清楚地看出来：缔约国的共同意思就是让公约得到排他性适用。大多数缔约国在实践中也是这样做的。如美国Arizona上诉法院在Kadota v. Hosogai（1980）案（下文案例将详细介绍）中就认为：《海牙送达公约》对美国国内法规定的送达方式来说具有排他性，只能适用《海牙送达公约》的规定。美国最高法院在Volkswagenwerk v. Schlunk（1988）案（下面案例将详细介绍）中再次重申了《海牙送达公约》规定了排他性的域外送达方式。不过，由于它通过分析美国福克公司与德国大众公司之间的密切关系，确认可将传票送达福克公司，从而不需要域外送达，达到了排除《海牙送达公约》的适用的目的。这在国际上引起了广泛的关注，受到了许多国家和学者的抨击。可见，《海牙送达公约》的排他性适用得到了国际社会的普遍同意。

《海牙送达公约》之所以得到了各国的广泛接受，是因为它较好地平衡了

---

① 公约第15条规定："如须根据本公约向国外递送传票或类似文书，以便送达，而被告没有出庭，则在确定下列情况之前，不得作出判决：（1）该文书已依文书发往国的国内法所规定的国内诉讼中对在其境内的人送达文书的方法予以送达；或（2）该文书已依本公约规定的其他方法被实际交付被告或其居所。并且，在上述任何一种情况下，送达或交付均应在能保证被告进行答辩的足够时间内完成。每一缔约国均可声明，只要满足下述条件，即使未收到送达或交付的证明书，法官仍可不顾本条第1款的规定，作出判决：（1）已依本公约所规定的一种方法递送该文书；（2）法官根据具体案情认为自递送文书之日起不少于6个月的适当期间已满；（3）尽管为获取证明书已通过文书发往国的主管机关尽了一切合理的努力，但仍未收到任何种类的证明书。"

各国的关注。一方面，将送达视为行使司法权行为的国家，可以通过公约规定的排他性适用，使其司法主权得到切实保护；另一方面，将送达视为私人行为的国家，可以通过公约规定的简易程序，使本国民事诉讼中的文书能在外国顺利送达，而不致引起外国的抗议。其实，我国法院要适用《海牙送达公约》的送达方式并不总是程序烦琐、费时费力，因为公约除了规定了代为送达制度以外，只要受送达国认可，邮寄送达、通过使领馆送达、直接委托司法助理人员送达等都是可以采取的方式。

但是，我国实际工作部门可能对这个公约的排他性适用认识不足，甚至以为要优先适用国内法规定的送达方式。如广东省高级人民法院编的《中国涉外商事审判实务》认为："通过《海牙送达公约》送达是司法文书送达的一种方式，受送达人所在国为公约缔约国或参加国时，法院并不必然适用公约进行送达，是否有适用公约的需要，应根据具体情况而定。一般情况下，能通过公告送达以外的其他方式送达的，就不必再适用公约规定的方式送达；法院能合理推断出通过公约规定的方式仍不能完成送达的，也没有必要启动《海牙送达公约》进行送达。"该书总结可以启动海牙送达公约进行送达的条件是："1. 通过相对简便的方式（公告送达除外）无法完成送达，确实存在公约规定的'有须递送司法文书或司法外文书以便向国外送达的情形'；2. 受送达人所在国是公约的缔约国或参加国，且与中国没有缔结司法协助协定或者缔结的司法协助协定中没有关于司法文书送达方面的安排。"① 这种理解是不符合公约的规定的。因为按照公约第1条的规定，在所有的民事或者商事案件中，只要符合下列条件：（1）有向其他公约缔约国送达文书的情形；（2）受送达人地址明确，我国就必须启动《海牙送达公约》。

2.《海牙送达公约》与其他双边司法协助条约的关系

当一个多边国际条约的缔约国之间缔结了双边条约时，只要多边国际条约没有特别的规定，双边条约一般应该得到优先适用。因为双边条约是多边条约缔约国之间的特别安排，根据特别法优于普通法的一般原则，当然应该适用双边条约。我国最高人民法院、外交部、司法部《关于执行〈关于向国外送达民事或商事司法文书和司法外文书公约〉有关程序的通知》第7点就明确规定："我国与公约成员国签订有司法协助协定的，按协定的规定办理。"

① 参见广东省高级人民法院编：《中国涉外商事审判实务》，法律出版社2004年版，第23页。

（五）特别观察：1970 年《海牙取证公约》在我国的适用

为了协调各国不同的取证制度，尽可能减少纷争，海牙国际私法会议在 1970 年 3 月 18 日通过了《关于从国外调取民事或商事证据的公约》（简称《海牙取证公约》）。截至 2003 年 11 月，该公约的成员有 41 个。① 我国于 1997 年 7 月 3 日批准加入了该公约，该公约已经在中国与荷兰、卢森堡、捷克共和国、以色列、波兰、芬兰、德国、意大利、美国、斯洛伐克共和国、法国、丹麦、西班牙、澳大利亚、挪威、阿根廷、爱沙尼亚、瑞士、瑞典之间生效。② 我国在加入该公约时作了两点保留：（1）根据公约第 23 条声明，对于普通法国家旨在进行审判前文件调查的请求书，仅执行已在请求书中列明并与案件有直接密切联系的文件的调查请求。（2）根据公约第 33 条声明，除第 15 条以外，不适用公约第 2 章的规定。而第 2 章是关于外交官员、领事代表和特派员取证，第 15 条规定的是外交官员或领事代表在不采取强制措施的情况下向本国国民调取证据。这表明，我国只接受向本国国民取证的外交官员途径和领事代表途径，而不接受特派员取证制度和其他形式的外交官员取证和领事代表取证。除了注意这些保留和公约在我国与相关国家之间的生效以外，我国在适用该公约时应注意下面两点：

1.《海牙取证公约》的优先适用

与《海牙送达公约》不同，由于《海牙取证公约》并没有明文规定该公约“必须”适用于需域外取证的“所有”民商事案件，③ 对于公约是否具有排他性适用的效力，在国际上引起了广泛的争论。在 1987 年以前，美国各法

---

① 成员名单是阿根廷、澳大利亚、白俄罗斯、保加利亚、中国、中国香港特别行政区、中国澳门特别行政区、塞浦路斯、捷克、丹麦、爱沙尼亚、芬兰、法国、德国、以色列、意大利、拉脱维亚、立陶宛、巴巴多斯、新加坡、卢森堡、墨西哥、摩纳哥、荷兰、挪威、波兰、葡萄牙、俄罗斯、斯洛伐克、斯洛文尼亚、南非、西班牙、斯里兰卡、瑞典、瑞士、土耳其、英国、美国、委内瑞拉、科威特、乌克兰。

② 参见最高人民法院外事局编：《中国国际司法协助条约与实施手册》（第 1 卷），外文出版社 2004 年版，第 614 页。

③ 该公约第 1 条规定：“在民事或商事案件中，每一缔约国的司法机关可以根据该国的法律规定，通过请求书的方式，请求另一缔约国主管机关调取证据或履行某些其他司法行为。”（in civil or commercial matters a judicial authority of a Contracting State may, in accordance with the provisions of the law of that State, request the competent authority of another Contracting State, by means of a Letter of Request, to obtain evidence, or to perform some other judicial act.）

院关于《海牙取证公约》与国内法的关系的立场很不相同，大部分州法院认为：《海牙取证公约》并非排他性适用，但如果美国法院诉讼程序中的当事人要求域外当事人提供文件，回答讯问或作证，应优先适用公约规定的程序，只有在按公约规定无法取证时，才可适用法院地的诉讼程序规则；大部分联邦法院则认为，公约的规定完全是任择性的，它没有优先适用的效力；也有少数法院认为，《海牙取证公约》规定的域外取证方式是排他性的，即使依公约规定的程序无法取证，法院也不能下令直接到域外取证。① 为了统一各法院的不同做法，美国最高法院在1987年法国航空工业公司诉美国依阿华南区联邦地方法院案中详细阐述了美国最高法院对这个问题的立场（下面的案例将详细介绍）。其中心观点是：公约对其适用范围所采用的措辞是灵活的，公约因此不是排他性或强制性的，它并不排除在向域外当事人获取证据时适用联邦民事诉讼程序规则。

针对美国的上述立场，在海牙国际私法会议1989年特委会会议上，各国展开了激烈的争论。瑞士、法国、德国等许多国家认为：缔约国在进行域外取证时，应保证适用海牙取证公约；公约中采取灵活措辞，并不意味着公约是任意性适用的，而只是允许缔约国在采用公约规定的请求书方式、领事方式或特派员方式这三者之间进行选择，如采用其他方式必须得到取证国的事先许可；美国最高法院的这一判决直接与条约必须信守原则相抵触，与公约的宗旨也不符，违背了各缔约国协调各自取证制度的初衷；未经取证地国同意，外国机构或个人直接获取在其境内的证据，是对该国司法主权的侵犯，应该受到严格禁止。② 经过交锋，会议没有取得一致意见，但作为妥协，会议通过了下列5点结论，供各缔约国执行公约时参考：（1）特委会强调，公约制定者的主要目的是在大陆法系国家和普通法系国家的取证制度之间建立一种联系；（2）特委会注意到在公约是否排他性适用问题上的观点仍有分歧；（3）然而，考虑到公约的目的，特委会认为不论各缔约国对公约的排他性适用问题持何观点，其在需从域外取证时应优先适用公约所提供的程序；（4）为便于优先适用公约，特委会鼓励根据第23条已作保留的国家限制该保留的范围；（5）如果一缔约国司法机关为获取处于另一缔约国境内的证据仍依其本国诉讼程序规则采取强制措施，特委会敦促该司法机关尊重其他国家依第23条作出限制性保留

① See Gary B. Born, *International Civil Litigation in United States Courts*, 903 (3rd ed. 1996).

② 参见徐宏：《国际民事司法协助》，武汉大学出版社1996年版，第206~207页。

的精神。① 由此可见，该公约的优先适用（first use of the convention）② 得到了绝大多数国家的普遍支持。

2.《海牙取证公约》与其他双边司法协助条约的关系

与《海牙送达公约》和其他双边司法协助条约的关系一样，《海牙取证公约》的缔约国如果缔结了双边司法协助条约，只要双边司法协助条约能够适用，就应该先适用双边条约。其道理和理由是一样的。

（六）特别观察：1958 年《纽约公约》在我国的适用

1958 年 6 月 10 日，联合国在纽约通过了《承认和执行外国仲裁裁决公约》（简称《纽约公约》），其目的是在国际上建立统一的规则，促进外国仲裁裁决的承认及执行，以避免执行过程中不可预见的障碍。该公约是迄今为止最为成功的一个国际条约，已有 121 个国家和地区参加了该公约。③ 我国于 1986 年 12 月 2 日决定加入《纽约公约》，该公约在 1987 年 4 月 22 日对我国生效。我国在参加 1958 年《纽约公约》时作了互惠保留声明和商事保留声明。所谓“互惠保留”，是指我国只承认和执行在缔约国领土内作成的仲裁裁决。所谓“商事保留”，是指我国只承认和执行属于契约性和非契约性商事法律关系争议作成的仲裁裁决。我国最高人民法院于 1987 年 4 月 10 日发布的《关于执行我国加入的〈承认和执行外国仲裁裁决公约〉的通知》中，进一步明确了我国所作的互惠保留和商事保留声明。特别指出“契约性和非契约性商事法律关系”是指由于合同、侵权或者根据有关法律规定而产生的经济上的权利义务关系，例如货物买卖、财产租赁、工程承包、加工承揽、技术转让、合资经

---

① 参见徐宏：《国际民事司法协助》，武汉大学出版社 1996 年版，第 208 ~ 209 页。

② 这意味着公约规定的方法可以优先适用，但不是排他性适用（the Hague Convention might be interpreted to require first, but not exclusive, use of its procedures）。

③ 关于《纽约公约》缔约国家和地区的数量，我国公开出版物上的记载很不一致：高祥法官统计为到 2001 年 7 月 10 日是 125 个国家和地区（见万鄂湘主编：《中国涉外商事海事审判指导与研究》2001 年第 1 卷，人民法院出版社 2001 年版，第 350 页）；王生长先生统计为 140 个国家和地区（见王生长：《外国仲裁裁决在中国的承认和执行》，载《国际经济法论丛》第 2 卷，法律出版社 1999 年版，第 471 页）；韩健教授 2000 年统计为 145 个国家和地区（见韩健：《现代国际商事仲裁法的理论与实践》，法律出版社 2000 年修订版，第 537 ~ 544 页）；李双元教授等统计：到 1999 年 5 月 31 日，其成员国和地区是 148 个（见李双元等编：《国际私法教学参考资料选编（中册程序法）》，北京大学出版社 2003 年版，第 1245 页。广东省高级人民法院编的《中国涉外商事审判实务》统计到 2001 年 7 月 10 日其成员国和地区是 127 个（见该书第 40 页）。这个数字是作者于 2004 年 11 月 5 日访问联合国网站获得的：http：//untreaty. un. org/english/。

营、合作经营、勘探开发自然资源、保险、信贷、劳务、代理、咨询服务和海上、民用航空、铁路、公路的客货运输以及产品责任、环境污染、海上事故和所有权争议等，但不包括外国投资者和东道国政府之间的争端。除了上述保留问题以外，我国在适用《纽约公约》时还要注意下列问题：

1.《纽约公约》的直接优先适用

同其他国际私法条约一样，由于《纽约公约》规定了缔约国承认和执行外国仲裁裁决的义务，并提供了一些具体的明确规则。毫无疑问，该公约在缔约国之间是可以得到直接优先适用的，这为所有缔约国所支持，并在实践中得到了很好的执行。我国最高人民法院在《关于执行我国加入的〈承认和执行外国仲裁裁决公约〉的通知》第1条就明确规定："根据我国加入该公约时所作的互惠保留声明，我国对在另一缔约国领土内作出的仲裁裁决的承认和执行适用该公约。该公约与我国民事诉讼法有不同规定的，按该公约的规定办理。"这就明文确立了直接优先适用规则。

2.《纽约公约》与国内法的合并适用

由于《纽约公约》的不少条款明确规定要依赖于相应的国内法制度解决有关问题，例如，第3条规定："在以下各条规定的条件下，缔约国应承认仲裁裁决具有约束力，并依照裁决需其承认或执行的地方的程序规则予以执行。"第5条第1款第1项规定："第2条所称协议的当事人，依对其适用的法律有无行为能力情形的，或者根据双方当事人选择的法律，或没有这种法律选择时，根据裁决作出地的法律，上述协议是无效的。"第5条第1款第4项规定："仲裁庭的组成或仲裁程序和当事人的协议不符，或者当事人没有这种协议时，与仲裁地的法律不符的。"第5条第2款第1项规定："依该国法律，争议事项是不能通过仲裁方式解决的"，等等。这些条款明确要求缔约国根据相应的国内法规则作出判断，也就是将《纽约公约》规则与国内法规则合并适用。这是适用《纽约公约》的一个特别之处。

3.《纽约公约》与其他公约的关系

适用《纽约公约》的另一个特别之处是该公约与其他国际条约关系的处理。《纽约公约》第7条规定："本公约的规定不影响缔约国订立的有关承认和执行仲裁裁决的多边或双边协定的效力……1923年《关于仲裁条款的日内瓦议定书》和1927年《关于执行外国仲裁裁决的日内瓦公约》，对本公约缔约国受本公约约束后，在其受本公约约束的范围内失效。"由此可见，除了1923年《关于仲裁条款的日内瓦议定书》和1927年《关于执行外国仲裁裁决的日内瓦公约》以外，《纽约公约》对其他同类双边和多边条约没有优先适用的效力。这种处理和安排在国际私法条约中也是很少见的。

4. 我国适用《纽约公约》的几个程序性问题

根据我国最高人民法院于1987年4月10日发布的《关于执行我国加入的〈承认和执行外国仲裁裁决公约〉的通知》，我国适用《纽约公约》的程序性问题是：

（1）根据1958年《纽约公约》第4条规定，申请我国法院承认和执行在另一缔约国领土内作出的仲裁裁决，是由仲裁裁决的一方当事人提出的，对于当事人的申请，应由我国下列地点的中级人民法院受理：第一，被执行人为自然人的，为其户籍所在地或者居所地；第二，被执行人为法人的，为其主要办事机构所在地；第三，被执行人在我国无住所、居所或者主要办事机构，但有财产在中国境内的，为其财产所在地。

（2）我国有管辖权的人民法院接到一方当事人的申请后，应对申请承认和执行的仲裁裁决进行审查，如果认为不具有1958年《纽约公约》第5条第1、2两项所列的情形，应当裁定承认其效力，并且依照我国《民事诉讼法》规定的程序执行；如果认定具有第5条第2项所列情形之一的，或者根据被执行人提供的证据证明具有第5条第1项所列情形之一的，应当裁定驳回申请，拒绝承认和执行。

（3）申请我国法院承认和执行的仲裁裁决，仅限于1958年《纽约公约》对我国生效后在另一缔约国领土内作出的仲裁裁决。申请人须提出书面申请，并附有裁决书正本。如申请人为外国当事人，其申请书须用中文提出。申请执行的期限，双方或一方当事人是自然人的为1年，双方是法人或其他组织的为6个月。

（4）关于不予执行涉外仲裁裁决的报告制度。最高人民法院于1995年8月28日公布的《关于人民法院处理与涉外仲裁及外国仲裁事项有关问题的通知》确立了关于不予执行涉外仲裁裁决或拒绝承认和执行外国仲裁裁决的报告制度：凡一方当事人向人民法院申请执行我国涉外仲裁机构裁决，或者向人民法院申请承认和执行外国仲裁机构的裁决，如果人民法院认为我国涉外仲裁机构裁决具有民事诉讼法第260条情形之一的，或者申请承认和执行的外国仲裁裁决不符合我国参加的国际公约的规定或者不符合互惠原则的，在裁定不予执行或者拒绝承认和执行之前，必须报请本辖区所属高级人民法院审查；如果高级人民法院同意不予执行或者拒绝承认和执行，应将其审查意见报最高人民法院。待最高人民法院答复后，方可裁定不予执行或者拒绝承认和执行。

（七）个案分析

1.《海牙送达公约》的排他适用

Kadota v. Hosogai [608 P. 2d 68 Ariz. App. (1980)]

上诉人角田宏（Kadota）是一个日本人，在发生于亚利桑那州的一起车祸中，他将被上诉人细谷（Hosogai）的丈夫撞死，并使被上诉人脑部受伤。细谷于1976年3月25日在美国法院对角田宏提起诉讼，并先后3次向角田宏送达传票和诉状。第一次是由一个美国私人送达员进行送达，并由该送达员向法院提交宣誓证明书；第二次由一位日本律师进行送达，并由该律师向法院提交宣誓证明书；第三次是将文书交给被告的诉讼监护人。初审法院认为送达已经完成，并判决角田宏承担225000美元的赔偿。角田宏提出上诉。上诉法院认为，由于日本和美国都是《海牙送达公约》的缔约国，向身在日本的被告送达文书只能按照《海牙送达公约》规定的方式进行，而不能采用美国法律规定的其他方式。因此，本案进行的3次送达都是无效的。据此，上诉法院撤销了原审法院的判决。①

2.《海牙送达公约》的适用条件

Volkswagenwerk Aktiengesellschaft v. Schlunk [486 U. S. 694 (1988)]

舒隆克（Schlunk）是居住在伊利诺斯州的美国公民，由于他的父亲在一起车祸中丧生。他在伊利诺斯库克县的巡回法院对美国福克公司和德国大众公司提起产品责任诉讼。为了完成对德国大众公司的送达，舒隆克没有直接向德国境内的大众公司进行送达，而是将传票交给美国福克公司。大众公司主张，这种送达违反了《海牙送达公约》的规定，是无效的。要求撤销对它的起诉。当初审法院和上诉法院驳回其主张后，大众公司又上诉到美国最高法院。最后，美国最高法院确认了初审法院和上诉法院的裁判。理由是：福克公司的财产百分之百属于大众公司所有，两公司的董事会存在实质上的重叠，福克公司的业务有赖于大众公司，它的活动受大众公司支配。正因为两公司之间存在如此密切的控制与被控制关系，足以认定福克公司可作为替大众公司接受送达的“非自愿代理人”，舒隆克的送达是有效的。美国最高法院认为：《海牙送达公约》尽管强制适用于域外送达的所有情形，但公约并没有对决定是否有必要向域外转递文件方面规定统一的标准。因此，对此问题应适用法院地法。这实际上将是否存在需向域外送达文书的情形的解释指向适用国内法，从另一个角度绕开了公约的排他性适用。

---

① 参见徐宏：《国际民事司法协助》，武汉大学出版社1996年版，第141~142页。

因此，该案在国际上引起了广泛关注。在1989年海牙国际私法会议特别委员会会议上，各国对此进行了深入的讨论。许多国家的专家指出，只在分支机构被其总部指定有权代总部接受送达时，方可向其送达文书。舒隆克案中所体现的基于分支机构与总部之间的密切联系而向分支机构进行的送达，只在非常特定的案件中才能成立。① 我国最高人民法院于2002年在《关于向外国公司送达司法文书能否向其驻华代表机构送达并适用留置送达问题的批复》中指出："人民法院可以根据民事诉讼法第147条第5项的规定向受送达人在中华人民共和国领域内设立的代表机构送达诉讼文书，而不必根据海牙送达公约向国外送达。根据民事诉讼法第247条的规定，人民法院向外国公司的驻华代表机构送达诉讼文书时，可以适用留置送达的方式。"

3. 《海牙取证公约》的优先适用

Societe Nationale Industrielle Aerospatiale v. U. S. District Court [482 U. S. 522 (1987)]

该案起因于一起产品责任诉讼。法国国家航空公司是法国的国有公司。一架该公司设计、制造并经销的飞机于1980年8月19日在美国依阿华州失事，致使一名飞行员和一名乘客丧生。据此，三名美国公民在依阿华南区联邦地方法院提起诉讼，指控被告制造并销售了有瑕疵的飞机，应承担过失责任。被告出庭应诉，未对法院管辖权提出异议，但在取证阶段，被告拒绝提供原告所要求的文件，并请求法院发布保护性命令。其理由是：(1) 法国的"障碍法规"(blocking statute) 禁止其执行美国的取证请求。(2)《海牙取证公约》的规定对于在法国境内的取证应排他性适用。但法院驳回了被告的主张。在上诉中，美国联邦第八巡回上诉法院确认了联邦地方法院的决定，并指出："如果联邦法院对于外国当事人具有管辖权，海牙公约就不适用于要求该当事人提供其拥有的证据的情形，尽管有关文件和情形可能实际处于签署该公约的外国境内。"被告于是上诉到美国最高法院。

美国最高法院在作出判决时认为：(1) 公约对其适用范围所采用的措辞是灵活的，因此，公约不是排他性的或强制性的，它并不排除在向域外当事人获取证据时适用联邦民事诉讼程序规则。(2) 公约并未区分对当事人和证人的取证，因此，上诉法院关于《海牙取证公约》不适用于向美国诉讼中的当事人取证的观点是不正确的。在美国法院对外国当事人具有管辖权的情况下，仍可适用公约所规定的取证程序。(3) 公约所规定的请求书方式在许多情况下会造成不适当的时间浪费和费用支出，并且难以确保所需的证据得到提供。

---

① 参见徐宏：《国际民事司法协助》，武汉大学出版社1996年版，第149~150页。

因此，公约所规定的取证方式并不比国内法所规定的方式更为优先，法院应根据个案的具体情况，逐一决定采用何种方式更为适宜。在作出此种决定时，应进行国际礼让分析，即对有关案件所涉及的具体事实、主权利益、取证方式的有效性等事项作具体分析。

不过，美国最高法院的这一判决是以5:4的微弱多数通过的。4位持反对意见的法官虽然对判决的前两点意见也表示同意。但他们认为，法院的第3点意见是不正确的，因为公约规定的取证程序，很大程度上减少了美国法律与外国法律在取证方面的冲突。如果由低级法院逐案自行决定是否适用公约程序，等于无视公约在协调各国不同利益方面的重要成果，无视美国政府部门参加公约的谈判和批准公约时的政策，将会损害美国的国家利益和国际利益，而且，美国法院在平衡外国利益和美国利益方面的能力是有限的。因此，公约规定的程序应得到优先适用。

前面已经介绍了，该项判决一经作出，立刻在国际上掀起了轩然大波，许多国家指责美国的这种做法明显违背了公约的宗旨，损害了他国的司法主权。①

4.《纽约公约》与国内法的合并适用

设一外国公司A向中国法院申请承认和执行在一《纽约公约》缔约国作成的仲裁裁决，作为被申请人，中国公司B向法院提出抗辩：仲裁的事项不能通过仲裁方式解决。中国法院必须适用《纽约公约》第5条第2款第1项和中国仲裁法的有关规定，判断仲裁的事项是否属于“不可仲裁”。如果是不可仲裁的事项，裁定拒绝承认与执行；如果不是不可仲裁事项，应裁定承认与执行。这是国际条约规则与国内法规则的合并适用。

总结上面的分析，关于我国法院适用统一程序法公约的规则，可以得出下列几点结论：(1) 如果案件双方当事人所属国是某一条约的缔约国，只要属于该条约的适用范围，该条约所确立的规则应优先得到直接适用。(2) 如果案件的外方当事人所属国是某一条约的非缔约国，而中国是缔约国，中国法院依照该条约关于适用范围的规定可以适用条约中的程序法规则，也可以不适用条约中的规则而适用我国民事诉讼法中的规则。(3) 如果中国是某一条约的非缔约国，不管案件的外方当事人所属国是不是缔约国，中国法院均不适用条约中的程序法规则，而应适用中国民事诉讼法中的有关规定。(4) 当中国法院适用某一统一程序法条约时，不允许当事人排除该公约的部分或全部适用，也不允许当事人选择适用条约中的规定。

---

① 参见徐宏：《国际民事司法协助》，武汉大学出版社1996年版，第46~47页。

四、国际统一冲突法条约在我国的适用

海牙国际私法会议是目前国际上最主要的统一冲突法的常设的政府间国际组织。自1893年第1届海牙国际私法会议召开到1951年第7届海牙国际私法会议通过《海牙国际私法会议章程》为止，海牙国际私法会议从性质上说还不能称为国际组织，实际上是一种临时性的国际会议。《海牙国际私法会议章程》的通过，标志着它已演变成一个常设的政府间国际组织。我国已于1987年7月3日正式加入海牙国际私法会议，从而成为该组织的成员国，并派代表参加了在1988年10月3日至20日召开的第16届海牙国际私法会议。海牙国际私法会议的成员国已从1951年的17国发展到现在的62国，并且已由少数欧洲大陆法系国家参加的会议发展到现在由来自五大洲不同法系的国家组成的国际组织。百余年来，海牙国际私法会议已举行了18届例会和两次特别会议，通过了三十多部关于国际经济贸易、婚姻、家庭、继承、扶养、国际民事诉讼程序等方面的国际公约。由于海牙国际私法会议的公约起草组的成员多由各国政府代表和国际私法专家组成，在公约通过前还征求各国政府的意见。因此，公约比较集中地反映了各国国际私法的立法和司法实践，代表着当代国际私法的发展趋势。不过，我国到目前为止还没有参加一部冲突法方面的国际条约。

（一）冲突法条约的特殊性

讨论统一冲突法条约在国内的适用问题同样需要明确这类条约的特殊性：（1）这类条约的目的是为了协调不同国家关于冲突法的不同政策，逐步统一冲突法规则，但其实质不是调整国家间的关系，也不是调整国家与个人之间的关系，而是与私人间的权利与义务关系有实质性的密切联系。① （2）不少冲突法条约的缔约国很少，它们只起到示范法（Model Laws）的作用，对一些国家的国内立法有一定的影响。（3）冲突法条约所规定的冲突规则主要用来指令法院或其他纠纷解决机构选择适当的准据法，所以，它主要对法院的司法行为产生影响，应该具有直接适用的效力。（4）几乎所有的冲突法条约既没有规定其适用具有排他性，也没有规定当事人是否有权排除或选择其适用，但20世纪60年代以后的冲突法条约都规定了公共秩序保留条款，即国内法院可能以公共秩序为由排除条约中冲突规范的适用。这是其他种类的国际条约所少见的。

---

① See Francis G. Jacors & Shelley Roberts, *the Effect of Treaties in Domestic Law*, 223-225 (1st ed. 1987).

（二）冲突法条约在我国的适用规则

考虑到国际条约在国内适用的一般规则和冲突法条约的上述特殊性，冲突法条约在我国的适用规则应该是：（1）直接适用，因为这类条约规定的规则实质上关系到私人的权利与义务，又是对法院的指令，特别当我国国内法没有相关规定时，当然应该也可以适用条约中的规则。（2）优先适用，如果我国今后参加的国际条约同国内立法有差异时，除了因为“条约必须信守”原则以外，即使我国把国际条约看做是与国内立法有同等效力的法律，根据“新法优于旧法”的原则，后参加的国际条约也应该得到优先适用。（3）当事人不能意思自治选择适用冲突法条约，因为冲突规范本身具有不确定性，它同时涉及私人和国家的利益，当事人的意思自治应该不能发挥作用。（4）公共秩序保留原则，即我国法院在具体案件中可以公共秩序保留为由排除公约中冲突规范的适用，这在国际社会得到了普遍的认同。①

总结上述论述，我们可以把冲突法条约在我国的适用规则归纳如下：（1）对于双方当事人所属国均是某一冲突法条约缔约国的案件，该国际条约应该优先直接适用。假如我国有这样一条冲突规范：人的身份依其本国法。而我国1982年加入的《关于难民地位的公约》第12条第1款规定：“难民的个人身份，应受其住所地国家的法律支配，如无住所，则受其居所地国家的法律支配。”这两条规定是不同的，我国法院在处理涉及难民身份的案件时，如果案件的具体情况属于公约的适用范围，就应适用《关于难民地位的公约》中的统一冲突规范，而不是我国国内法中的冲突规范。不过，到目前为止，我国尚未缔结或参加任何有关统一冲突法的国际条约，我国已经缔结或参加的国际条约也很少有统一冲突规范的条文。但国际上有关统一冲突规范的条约正在增多，随着我国加入WTO和对外开放的不断深化，我国必将逐渐参加一些有关统一冲突规范的国际条约。因此，优先适用统一冲突规范的情况也将日益增多。（2）如果案件的外国当事人所属国是某一冲突法条约的缔约国，中国不是该条约的缔约国，中国法院应适用中国的冲突规范选择应适用的法律；如果中国没有相应的冲突规范，中国法院可以参照适用该条约中的冲突规范。（3）如果案件的当事人所属国和中国都不是某一冲突法条约的缔约国，中国法院既不会适用该条约中的冲突规范，也不允许当事人选择适用该条约中的冲突规范，而只适用中国法中的有关冲突规范。

① See J. G. Castel, *Introduction to Conflict of Laws*, 58-59 (3rd ed. 1998).

五、WTO 协议在我国的适用

我国已成为 WTO 的正式成员国，因此，如何保证 WTO 协议在我国的正确适用，使我国的各项法律、规章及行政程序与 WTO 协议相一致，是我国面临的一个重要的现实问题。

（一）WTO 协议的含义和法律性质

与一般的国际条约不同，WTO 协议是一个广义和能动的概念。从广义的概念出发，WTO 协议不仅指《乌拉圭回合最后文件》中关于建立 WTO 的协议，还包括该协议所附的各项协议及部长决定和宣言，同时包括关于中国加入 WTO 议定书及其附件。从能动的概念来看，WTO 协议不仅指现行的各种 WTO 协议和规范性文件，还包括在 WTO 体制中将达成的各项协议和规范性文件。

WTO 协议在本质上是一种契约。在这种契约中，各成员政府交换贸易权利与义务，具体说来，每个 WTO 成员在贸易政策方面作出并接受许多具体承诺，而每一项承诺均构成其贸易伙伴的一项权利。如果某个 WTO 成员不遵守 WTO 规则，其他 WTO 成员就可以撤销其对该成员的义务。为此，WTO 协议还建立了一种统一适用于所有规则的强制实施和争端解决机制。因此，与一般的国际条约相比，WTO 协议有以下特殊性：

1. 尽管 WTO 协议在某些方面是独一无二的，但它的各项规则，如其他国际条约一样，只有在国内法中生效后，才能对其成员境内的公民和法人强制实施。公民和法人不能直接根据 WTO 协议采取行动，如法人不能向 WTO 投诉某个外国政府的规章或政策，但可说服本国政府代表它采取行动。在这方面，不同国家有不同的方法，但绝大多数成员政府制定了与 WTO 协议规定一致的国内法而没有把 WTO 协议本身纳入国内法。

2. WTO 成员资格是开放的，除了政府以外，任何控制自己贸易与关税政策的实体均可成为 WTO 成员，即便它没有国家那样的主权。但个人和法人不能成为 WTO 成员，不过，它们可利用 WTO 协议对它施加影响，在许多国家，条约需经国会批准，这使行政部门（政府）在条约签署前向公民和法人提供机会以发表其对谈判目标的看法。

3. WTO 协议是一种规定 WTO 各成员政府在制定与实施国际贸易立法和规章方面的具体权利和义务的国际条约，它可谓是由多项国际贸易协定组成的一个多边条约体系。这个条约体系不仅使 WTO 成员的重要贸易权利获得了保障，也使其政府的贸易政策在其同意的范围内受到了约束。作为一个条约体系，WTO 协议不仅得到了 140 多个成员的广泛接受，并且涉及国际贸易关系的广泛领域，还建立在一套核心原则的基础之上并拥有一个统一的强制实施和解决争端的机制。这种统一性和WTO成员的广泛性是其他国际条约所罕见的。①

（二）WTO协议在我国的适用方式

WTO协议在其成员国的实施不外乎三种方式：一是直接并入方式，其好处是实际操作简便，只需公布WTO协议或在有关国内法中写入WTO协议的内容或用专门条款规定"当国内法与WTO法相抵触时，WTO法优先"即可；另一个好处是这种方式最受WTO及其成员的欢迎，可最大程度地避免中国不遵守WTO协议的嫌疑。但其弊端是，中国的市场经济法律体系还不很完善，如果一次性地直接并入WTO协议，有的可能不符合中国实际。二是转化方式，其好处是可以结合国内有关部门或领域的实际适用WTO协议，从而将WTO协议的履行与我国社会主义市场经济法律体系的完善这一系统工程有机结合起来，相辅相成。其不利之处是，WTO协议的内容十分庞杂，如果都通过转化方式，中国国内的立法任务繁重、费时，而且有些转化式立法难免与WTO协议不一致。三是维护现状，等发生争议后再根据WTO争端解决机构的裁决修改、补充相关的国内立法。这是一种被动方式，也最不受WTO及其成员的欢迎，但在我国现行的市场经济立法不很完善的情况下，适度采用这种方式也未尝不可。

因此，考虑到我国的实际情况和其他WTO成员的普遍实践以及WTO协议的不同领域和规定，我国应采取并入与转化相结合，并辅之以个案修改和补充的方式。具体说来，并入方式可以适用于下列情形：（1）WTO协议中的基本原则；（2）我国适用WTO协议所规定的规则不存在难度或难度不大的领域或部门；（3）我国新近颁布和即将颁布以及修改不大的有关法律、法规，也可以采用并入法。转化方式适宜于下列情况：（1）有关的WTO协议本身不完备，而是框架安排、过渡性安排、原则性安排，如原产地协议、服务贸易总协定等；（2）WTO有关协议本身要求各成员制定相应的国内法律、法规或行政措施保护其实施，如倾销与反倾销协议，装运前检验协议、TRIPS协议等；（3）需要结合中国实际制定系统的实体规范和程序规范的部门或领域，如反倾销、反补贴等。而个案修改和补充方式主要适用于：（1）现行国内法和措施中今后被其他WTO成员指控与WTO法相悖、并经WTO裁决必须修改或补

---

① 参见余敏友：《论世贸组织（WTO）的几个法律问题》，载《中国国际私法与比较法年刊》（2001年卷），法律出版社2001年版，第299～302页。

充的规定；（2）今后被其他 WTO 成员指控没有适当履行 WTO 义务并经 WTO 裁决必须予以补救的国内法真空领域。①

（三）WTO 协议在我国的优先适用问题

由于我国调整市场经济的法律不很完善，与 WTO 规则相抵触的现行国内法律的废止、修改与调整还需要一定的时间，而制定与 WTO 法相符的新法律更需要一个相当长的过程。在此情况下，我国国内法与 WTO 法相冲突的情况很容易发生，我国法院应采取下列原则解决这种冲突：（1）同等法律效力原则，即要坚持 WTO 法与我国普通法具有同等的法律效力；（2）WTO 法优先原则，即有关国内法或 WTO 协议如果明文规定优先适用 WTO 规则，WTO 法就应优先得到适用；（3）后法优于前法原则，即当有关国内法或 WTO 协议没有规定何者优先时，则适用生效时间在后的法律规则；（4）特别法优于一般法原则，即当有关国内法或 WTO 协议没有规定何者优先时，法院将 WTO 协议视为特别法，依“特别法优于一般法”适用 WTO 协议。

（四）WTO 协议在我国的直接效力问题

1. 条约的直接效力的含义

所谓条约的直接效力，是指条约的某一缔约国国内的个人是否可以援用条约的规定在该国法院提起诉讼，主张自己在条约项下的权利。它与条约的直接进入、条约的直接适用、条约的优先效力等概念的内涵不同。直接进入是指个人能够像国家一样在国际司法机构中援用条约起诉，乃是“个人是国际法的主体”这一观点的重要理论内核。直接适用是指在条约的缔约国，该条约可以无须转化立法而直接以并入方式被接受为国内法的一部分。优先效力则是指在国内法与条约的规定发生冲突时，条约的规定优于国内法。②

2. WTO 协议的直接效力问题

所谓 WTO 协议的直接效力，是指在一定条件下，WTO 的某一成员国或地区内的个人可以援用 WTO 协议的规定在该国或地区法院提起诉讼，主张自己在 WTO 协议项下的权利。学术界对此问题有三种不同主张：

（1）肯定说主张 WTO 协议具有直接效力。如杜姆里赫（Tumlir）提出了

---

① 参见曾令良：《WTO 协议在中国的适用及我国法制建设的革命》，载《中国法学》2000 年第 6 期。

② 参见陈卫东：《论 WTO 协议的直接效力》，载黄进、肖永平主编：《展望二十一世纪国际法的发展》，湖北人民出版社 2001 年版，第 750 ~ 751 页。

将国际贸易规则“国内宪法化”的主张，他将个人的自由贸易权提升为基本人权，并将贸易条约看做对抗国内法律体系中固有的贸易保护主义倾向的武器。为防止国家权力对个人权利的侵蚀，他主张应当给个人在他们的国内法院中援用贸易条约条款的权利。

（2）否定说认为WTO协议没有直接效力。如杰克逊（Jackson）认为，政府尽管有义务遵守它们作出的国际承诺，但可援用性对于确保这一义务的遵守并不是必须的。如果给予个人在国内法院援用条约的权利以及条约效力优于国内法，这对民主理念来说是危险的。因此，贸易条约的可援用性必须由各国政府自行决定。

（3）折中说否定WTO协议的直接效力，但肯定WTO争端解决机构的裁定具有直接效力。如皮尔·埃克霍特（Piet Eeckhout）认为，有关否定WTO协议的直接效力的各项理由，无论是其协议条文措辞的灵活性，或是立法与司法的权力分配，还是对适当的争端解决场所的尊重，对一般规则的效力尚可适用。但WTO争端解决机构裁定的效力与WTO协议的效力不同，如果WTO争端解决机构裁定某一成员的国内法或国内措施不符合WTO协议的规定，该成员国法院就应确保遵守WTO争端解决机构的该具体裁决。

从司法实践来看，各国对这个问题的解决也没有一致的主张。欧盟一再宣称GATT的规则没有直接援用的效力。尤其是在著名的香蕉案中，欧洲法院重申了其以前的判例法立场，即排除任何个人对GATT法的援用。美国近期三个重要的自由贸易协议均包含明确排除该协议自执行力的条款。这同样体现在美国的WTO执行立法中，该法令明确禁止依WTO的规则在国内法院由个人或州提起诉讼。

我们认为，WTO协议是否具有直接效力主要取决于WTO协议的具体内容和各个成员国国内法的安排。由于WTO协议大部分规则是原则性和框架性的，且其权利义务仅及于各成员政策。即便是那些小部分具体规则，也没有明确各成员具体履行义务的标准，就WTO各协议中的司法审查条款来说，它只是一种个人对特定事项可以要求司法复审的程序性权利，而不是给予个人依据WTO协议的规定在国内法院起诉的权利。因此，从总体上说，WTO协议在我国没有直接效力。当然，也不排除个别WTO协议中的具体规定在我国具有直接效力的可能性。

六、关于“国际私法条约的适用”的立法建议

《中华人民共和国民法（草案）》第9编第3条在综合、借鉴和采纳《民法通则》第142条和《民事诉讼法》第238条的基础上规定：“中华人民共和

国缔结或者参加的国际条约同中华人民共和国民事法律有不同规定的，应当适用国际条约的规定，但中华人民共和国声明保留的条款除外。中华人民共和国法律和中华人民共和国缔结或者参加的国际条约没有规定的可以适用国际惯例。"

（一）我国的习惯性规定

从立法学和该条的措辞方面来分析，国际私法条约在我国优先适用的条件是：（1）中国是该条约的缔约国，并对案件所涉及的问题没有作出保留，但没有限定案件当事人所属国是否必须是该公约的缔约国。（2）该条约的规定与中国的法律规定不同，但没有明确国际条约的规定与中国法相同时，是否也应当适用国际条约。（3）这里的"国际条约"应该是指"国际统一实体法条约"，因为它是在与"民事法律"的对比中使用的，使人有理由相信它仅指实体法方面的国际条约。所以，该条是否适用于程序法条约和冲突法条约是不明确的。（4）该条第 2 款规定的是国际惯例的适用条件，这实际上与第 4 条第 2 款有部分重复。

（二）评论

尽管这条规定复制了我国现行法律中的有关规定，但我国制定民法典的目的应该是完善和发展相关的法律制度，不能简单地照搬现行的法律规定。我认为《民法（草案）》第 9 编第 3 条存在下列不足：

1. 把国际条约的适用和国际惯例的适用放在一个条文中规定，显得比较零乱，不符合一条一个问题的立法技术要求，建议第 3 条专门规定国际条约的适用规则，而第 4 条专门规定国际惯例的适用规则。

2. 上面的研究已经明确，中国缔结或者参加的国际条约只有在处理该条约缔约国之间的关系时才具有优先的直接适用效力，我国的立法应该明确这个条件。但现在的案文表明只要中国是某一国际条约的缔约国，当其规定与我国立法不同时，就优先适用国际条约的规定，这似乎认定中国参加的国际条约的法律效力高于我国的基本法，在我国宪法没有明确采纳这个原则的情况下，最好不要这样简单规定。

3. 对于国际条约与我国立法相同时的法律适用问题，该条也应该作出规定。我认为，在这种情况下，国内立法可以看成是为了实施国际条约转化而来的，因此应该适用国内立法，在必要的情况下，也可以合并适用国际条约和国内立法。

4. 应该明确《民法（草案）》第 9 编第 3 条中的"国际条约"所包括的范围。我主张至少包括国际统一实体法条约和冲突法条约，但不能包括 WTO

协议。至于程序法条约，由于《民事诉讼法》第238条已有规定，而这次制定《民法（草案）》第9编又不涉及程序法问题，所以第3条也可以不包括程序法条约。不过，我倾向于在第3条中对所有的国际私法条约在我国的适用规则作出规定。

（三）结论：具体建议案文

第三条　国际私法条约的适用

中华人民共和国缔结或者参加的国际私法条约被转化为国内立法后，除非该国际条约与我国的立法不同，应当适用我国的法律。

中华人民共和国缔结或者参加的国际统一实体法条约在转化为国内立法以前，对其调整范围内的缔约国当事人之间的关系具有直接优先的适用效力。

如果当事人选择适用中华人民共和国没有参加的国际统一实体法条约，只要符合本编规定的关于当事人意思自治原则的条件，也可以适用该国际条约的规定。

中华人民共和国缔结或者参加的国际统一程序法条约对该公约范围内的缔约国之间的事项具有排他性的优先适用效力。

中华人民共和国缔结或者参加的国际统一冲突法条约对公约范围内的缔约国之间的事项具有直接优先的适用效力。

本条不适用于世界贸易组织协议在我国的适用。

作者简介

徐崇利

徐崇利，1966年2月生，浙江平阳人，法学博士。1987年本科毕业于厦门大学法学院国际经济法专业；1990年硕士研究生毕业于上海社会科学院法学研究所国际私法专业；1991～1996年在厦门大学法学院在职攻读国际经济法专业博士学位。1994年和1997年被破格提拔为厦门大学法学院副教授、教授；1998年起担任厦门大学法学院国际法专业博士生导师。1997～1998年度美国坦普尔大学法学院福布莱特项目访问学者。主要从事国际经济法及国际私法的研究，为厦门大学国际法学国家重点学科青年学术带头人之一。现任中国国际经济法学会常务理事兼秘书长及中国国际私法学会常务理事、中国国际法学会理事、中国法学会世贸组织法研究会理事，兼任中国国际经济贸易仲裁委员会仲裁员。曾在《中国社会科学》、《中国法学》、《法学研究》、《中外法学》、《比较法研究》、《中国国际法年刊》等海内外权威和核心刊物上发表学术论文40余篇。先后承担国家级和部委级科研课题9项。主撰的《MIGA与中国：多边投资担保机构述评》于1998年获福建省第三届社会科学优秀成果奖一等奖，并获教育部普通高校第二届人文社会科学研究成果奖三等奖；因教学和科研成绩突出，分别于1998年和2002年两次获教育部霍英东教育基金会全国高校青年教师奖；2005年入选教育部首批“新世纪优秀人才支持计划”。

国际关系理论与国际经济法律秩序的构建

徐崇利

目　次：

晚近，随着经济全球化趋势的日益深入，国际经济立法活动开始更趋活跃。首先，从经济全球化的深度来看，经济全球化意味着各国间在经济上的相互依赖关系愈加密切。随着各国间交往频率的加快和密度的增大，创制更多的国际经济法律制度将有利于减少各国经济交往的成本。其次，从经济全球化的维度来看，经济全球化已波及贸易（包括货物贸易、服务贸易、技术贸易等）、投资、金融等各个经济领域，原属各国国内法管辖的经济问题不断跨国化，并进入国际经济法的视野，需要制定相应的国际经济法律规则予以调整。乌拉圭回合达成的WTO“一揽子协议”，就是在进入全球化时代之后各国首次在国际经济领域进行大规模立法活动的产物。国内外许多学者认为，WTO协定这一宏大的“国际贸易法典”的诞生，是GATT历史上“尊法派”对“传统派”的一次重大胜利，从而使国际贸易法乃至整个国际经济法的发展进入了一个新里程，并成为一种必然的发展趋势。实际上，WTO的成立，只是整个国际经济关系法制化进程中的一个缩影。从形式结构来看，国际经济关系的法制化，也就是构建国际经济法律秩序的过程。

本文拟采用学科交叉的方法，以国际关系理论研究国际经济法律秩序的构建问题，首先将介绍现行国际关系理论各主要流派（包括新现实主义学派、新自由主义学派、建构主义学派以及理想主义学派）关于国际经济法律秩序的基本理论。然后分析这些学派有关国际经济法律秩序创建、维持和变迁问题的主要机理。最后，在此基础上，进一步从国际经济法律制度与非法律国际经济制度关系的角度，探讨国际经济法律秩序的发展趋势。

一、以国际关系理论分析国际经济法律秩序：理论流派

无疑，国际经济法律秩序归根结底是由国际政治经济关系决定的，而且国际经济法律制度的“自主性”要远逊于国内法律制度。由此，欲求证国际经济法律秩序的内在机理，法律分析的方法容易陷入循环论证的逻辑困境，这就有必要借助“它山之石”——其他学科的交叉研究方法。

目前，国内的国际经济法著述在论证国际经济法律问题时，也使用国际经济学和国际关系学等方面的知识，但这只是用到其他学科的“知识”（所有法学学科的研究实际上也都如此）而已，而不是运用其他学科的研究方法，即不是严格意义上的“学科交叉”。就国际经济法学中研究方法的交叉，人们首先想到的应该是，其交叉的对象可选择“国际经济学”，因为这样就涵盖了“国际的”和“经济的”两个要素，再加上“法律的”分析，国际经济法学独特的交叉研究方法便具有了完整性。毋庸置疑，国际经济学是国际经济法学应当予以交叉的一个重要学科。然而，仅选择国际经济学作为国际经济法学科交叉的对象，实际上是不全面的。因当今的国际体系仍属于“无政府状态”，缺乏一个权位在各国之上的“世界政府”，故国家间的经济关系和法律关系等均深受国际政治关系的制约。例如，在 GATT 的发展史上，就有“权力导向”和“规则导向”之争；WTO 虽以规则为导向，但权力因素在现行的 WTO 法律体制内仍有相当大的存在空间。可见，对国际经济法律秩序的学科交叉研究，除了应包括反映国际经济关系的“国际经济学”之外，还应将反映国际政治关系的“国际关系理论”纳入其内，特别是其中探讨国际政治与国际经济互动关系的“国际政治经济学”，更可以成为研究国际经济法律问题的一种有效工具。

国际关系理论本身是一门新兴的学科，成熟于二战之后。但在战后相当长的一段时间里，国际关系理论与国际法学基本上处于相互分离的状态。传统上，国际法学者只以分析和阐释国家进行国际交往的法律规则为己任，而把有关这些法律规则的创建、维持和变迁等机理留给国际关系理论学者研究。晚

近，国际关系理论与国际法学出现了学科交叉的现象，以国际关系理论分析国际法的方法受到了西方学界的广泛重视。例如，在美国，近十多年来，此项交叉研究“已成为当代国际法学的一个新流派，也许是最令人振奋的一项学术发展”（美国国际法学会前任会长安娜－玛丽·斯洛特教授语）。而在西方以国际关系理论分析国际法的著述中，大量的又是与国际经济法律制度有关的研究。

从国际关系理论本身的研究方法来看，系整合政治学、社会学、经济学以及哲学等各相关学科知识和方法研究国际关系而形成的“工具箱”。相应地，经由国际关系理论这一“传输带”，可以更深维度的学科交叉方法探讨国际经济法的基本原理。

然而，值得注意的是，以国际关系理论研究国际经济法律制度，适用的一般只是国际关系理论中的原理部分，但国际关系理论中的原理普适于国际关系的整体，并非专门针对国际经济法律关系。由此，对国际经济法律制度的研究，在逻辑上应分为两个步骤：一是以法律分析的方法结合国际关系理论一般原理来分析“国际法律关系”的特点；其后，再按照前一步研究得出的结论，进一步探讨“国际经济法律关系”的特性。例如，“国际制度论”是国际关系理论的核心构成部分之一，但该理论研究的“国际制度”既包括国际法律制度，也包括非国际法律制度；既包括国际经济法律制度，也包括非法律国际经济制度。由此，如以“国际制度理论”研究国际经济法，先得厘清国际法律制度的“一级”特质，然后在此基础上继续甄别国际经济法律制度的“二级”特质。

秩序是法律制度的形式结构。① 目前，从国际经济关系的法制化程度来看，国际经济法律秩序虽已建立，但还远称不上健全和完善，在构成国际经济法律秩序的各要素上，都存在着不同程度的缺失，构建国际经济法律秩序仍然任重而道远。

第一，从完整性来看，战后迄今，因有世界贸易组织（WTO）、国际货币基金组织（IMF）和世界银行集团（WBG）等体制，国际贸易关系和国际金融关系的法制化似乎已经步入了成形的阶段；但在投资、竞争政策等重要领域，多边法律体制仍付诸阙如。WTO 坎昆会议已正式决定，作为“新加坡议

---

① 美国法学家博登海默认为，法律是秩序与正义的综合体。其中，秩序是法律制度的形式结构，而正义是法律制度的实质价值。详见［美］埃德加·博登海默：《法理学：法律哲学与法律方法》，邓正来译，中国政法大学出版社 2004 年修订版，第二部分“法律的性质与作用”。

题”的投资和竞争政策议题，都将无法列入 WTO 该新一轮回合的谈判。这就意味着要在这两大领域建立多边法律制度，可能已遥遥无期。

第二，从统一性来看，现行的多边经济法律制度为各国创设的权利义务标准并非完全一致。在 WTO 框架内，就普遍性义务对各成员方规定了相同的标准；但在货物或服务的市场准入上，对各成员方所作的承诺，并不一致。关于汇率和资本项目的开放问题，现行的 IMF 协定仍允许各国自由选择适用于自己的管理制度。在投资、竞争政策等领域，目前则仍为双边条约、区域性条约以及多边条约所控制，根本谈不上规则的统一性。

第三，从明确性来看，WTO 法律制度虽被许多人归为“硬法”，但其“硬度”实际上仍然有限。WTO 成立以来，与规则“形影相随”的例外机制不断被滥用以及困扰 WTO 各成员方的协定执行难等问题，本身就说明了规则的不明确性。就 IMF 体制而言，尽管在 1997 年亚洲金融危机之后，一时间要求强化国际货币金融制度的呼声四起，但因各国间货币金融关系的复杂性和多变性，在法律制度上，IMF 规则无论是过去、现在，还是将来，都不可能不保持相当程度的弹性。①

第四，从稳定性来看，即便是法制化程度最高的 WTO 多边贸易体制，也远非坚如磐石。西雅图会议和坎昆会议的无果而终，多哈回合谈判的险象环生，均暴露了 WTO 法律体制的潜在脆弱性。美国著名 GATT/WTO 学者杰克逊曾警示道，尽管现状还不至于击垮 WTO 体制，但危机已经显现；倘若 WTO 无法做到与时俱进，大国将会逐步抛弃这一多边体制，转向依靠诸边制度、区域性组织、双边措施乃至单边主义，从而导致 WTO 体制的式微。②

第五，从有效性来看，仍以执行最有制度保障的 WTO 协定为例，其实施实际上一直是 WTO 体制运作中的一大难题，主要是发达国家不愿兑现全部承诺，引起了广大发展中国家的强烈不满。在多哈回合发动前夕，发展中国家提出的有关 WTO 协定的执行问题就多达近百个。在国际经济法律领域，WTO 争端解决机制虽对国家之间的贸易争端实行强制性管辖，但其裁决的执行仍有赖于各国的“自力救济”。

国际经济法律秩序的这些先天性缺失，来自以民族国家为单位的现行国际体系的结构性特点。当代主流的国际关系理论学派无不承认现行国际体系的

---

① 详见拙文：《国际货币基金组织运行机制的主要特征及基本走向》，载《厦门大学学报》1999 年第 2 期。

② J. H. Jackson, *The WTO "Constitution" and Proposed Reforms: Seven "Mantras" Revisited*, *Journal of International Economic Law*, Vol. 4, 2001, p. 70.

"无政府状态"。有鉴于此，即便现在存在一种国际政治经济秩序，也只是一种"无政府状态下的秩序"。这种秩序的创制、维持和变迁，无不受到各国"私"权力对比状况（国际权力结构）的影响；反观国内社会，因处于"有政府的状态"，可以依靠中央政府的"公"权力来推行法治。总之，得到公权力维护的国内经济法律秩序之坚固性，是在"私"权力平衡状态下求得的国际经济法律秩序所无法比拟的。然而，对于国际经济法律秩序的具体分析，每一国际关系理论学派的观点则各不相同。

（一）新现实主义的秩序观

新现实主义学派认为，在国际社会，每个国家都具有相似的单位特征，均为自利理性的行为体，其行为受制于国际体系中的权力分配结构，因此，新现实主义又被称为"结构现实主义"。在"无政府状态"的国际结构中，各国对外交往的立足点是安全最大化。由于国家间的合作会造成相对收益上的差距而难以实现，国际秩序的建立与维持主要取决于大国间的权力平衡。由于在"无政府的"秩序原则下，国家只根据其在国际结构中所处的位置来确定自己的外交政策，于是，"自助"便成为国家求得自我生存的最可靠的国际关系手段。虽然大多数新现实主义者并不否认"无政府状态"下国际合作及国际制度（包括国际法）存在的必要性，但这些学者仍将权力视为决定国家行为及其结果的惟一变量，而国际制度充其量不过是内生于国际权力结构的附属物，只构成一种插入变量，实际上这就否定了国际制度的独立性。依此推断，新现实主义学派虽在一定程度上也承认国际法的作用，但始终认为权力结构可以主导国际法，在国际关系中，国际法所扮演的最多只是一个配角；同样，在国际经济领域，法制化也只能对权力产生有限的外在制约作用。

"霸权稳定论"被认为是新现实主义学派中关于国际制度最权威、最公认的一种理论。该理论发端于对国际经济秩序的分析，其要义是，在处于"无政府状态下"的国际社会，国际经济秩序的建立离不开一个合法的权威，只不过这个权威不可能是像国内社会那样的中央政府，而是一个在国际权力结构中居于支配地位的"霸权国"（准世界政府）。

首先，"霸权稳定论"主张，在"无政府状态"下，需要一个霸权国发挥"稳定器"的作用，否则各国间就会展开无序的竞争，以致造成国际经济秩序的混乱。正如该理论的创始人之一——美国学者吉尔平所指出的那样，"除非霸权存在，一种特殊类型的国际经济秩序，即自由经济秩序才能繁荣和充分发展”。① 为了维护国际经济秩序的稳定和平衡，霸权国除了依靠自己的威望之外，还应建立相应的国际经济制度（如开放的国际贸易体制和稳定的国际货币体制），并将这些制度作为“国际公共物品”提供给其他国家使用，并容忍这些国家的“免费搭车”行为，使之也可从中受益。

其次，霸权国对国际经济秩序的控制是以其经济上有“剩余”为基础的。然而，因为维持秩序的边际成本和边际收益总体上成反比，所以，霸权国将逐步耗尽自身的经济“剩余”。例如，为了维持自由贸易体系，霸权国不得不开放本国市场和向他国转让技术，从而导致自身经济和技术优势的不断丧失。除此之外，基于其他诸多的外部原因（如战争、过度扩张及残酷竞争等）和内部原因（如利益集团故步自封，生产率和创造力下降，社会精英成为食利者，政府和民众抵制变革，通货膨胀以及社会福利出超等），也将使霸权国国力逐步走向衰弱。② 在负担日益加重而“免费搭车者”越来越多的情况下，霸权国提供“国际公共物品”的能力和愿望将会丧失殆尽。一旦如此，国际经济制度的维持就难以为继，国际经济秩序将难逃由盛到衰的厄运。

显然，“霸权稳定论”的原理也适用于对国际经济法律秩序的分析。根据这些原理，主导国际经济法律秩序的因素是国家间的权力结构，尤其是霸权国“一国独大”的权力；然而，“成败皆由霸权国”，正因为极权和权力结构的不稳定性，国际经济法律秩序的大厦始终处于不断倾斜的状态，直至最终崩塌。

（二）新自由主义的秩序观

按照新自由主义的主张，权力不再是国家行为的惟一目标，全球相互依存、相互合作正逐步成为国际关系的主旋律。该学派虽不否认国家安全的重要性，但更加注重经济福利的目标。新现实主义学派最多只把经济分析用做其有关国家安全理论、观点和证实的来源和手段；而在新自由主义学派那里，经济问题成了国际关系理论研究越来越重要的主题之一。因此，较之新现实主义学派，新自由主义学派更加关注对国际经济法律制度的研究。

新自由主义的研究重心在于“国际制度论”，故该学派又被称为“新自由制度主义学派”。经常被该学派引用来解释国际合作以及在此基础上所生之国

---

① ［美］罗伯特·吉尔平：《国际关系的政治经济学》，杨宇光等译，经济科学出版社 1989 年版，第 88 页。

② ［美］查尔斯 P·金德尔伯格：《世界经济霸权 1500～1990》，高祖贵译，商务印书馆 2003 年版，第 352～363 页。金氏为“霸权稳定论”的创始人之一。

际制度的主要理论根据是理性主义和功能主义。理性主义理论认为，每个国家是理性、利己的主体，在国际关系中总是追求个体效用的最大化。然而，出于机会主义、信息不完全和不对称、外部环境的不确定性和复杂性、外部性的普遍存在和交易费用过高等诸如此类的原因，个体理性的简单综合未必就与集体理性一致，其间存在着“集体行动困境”等问题，当合作能给各国带来共同利益时，可能会因为无法协调它们的行动而无法达到目的，从而造成国际政治市场的“失灵”；而功能主义理论认为，国际制度具有的各种功能恰恰有助于克服国际合作中的这些障碍，促进各国共同利益的实现。正因为如此，对国际制度的需求便开始产生。概而言之，国际制度的功能包括：塑造结果预期并保持各行为体之间关系的稳定性和连续性；减少交易（谈判、监督和实施协议）环节的成本；鼓励国家为了未来的声誉而保持诚实；弥补“合同不完全”的缺漏；给予互惠的机会和可能，从而减弱不平等权力关系破坏稳定的可能性；使国家在不同事务领域互动联系，促成相互依赖，减少欺诈；可提供持续不断的、不偏不倚的信息，提高谈判各方的政策透明度，利于监督；促成资源的汇聚；为分散的各种行为聚焦要点；为消极的国家提供合作的动力（如技术、信息和专家等）；为解决或缓解冲突创造场所和模式（如引入中立的调解人）；通过国内制度加以实施（路径依赖），可改变行为体的偏好。有关国际制度的这种理性主义和功能主义理论同样也适用于对国际法的分析。①

晚近，新自由主义有关国际制度理论研究的另一项重要进展是，国际制度的形成是各国政府在国际和国内两大层面“双层博弈”的结果。从国内政治对国际制度的影响方面来看，国家在国际关系中的利益不是“外生”或“给定”的，因为国家只是国内社会中个人、团体的代理人，而这些个人、团体才是国际关系的主要行为体，正是它们之间利益互动的结果，推动了国家在国际关系中利益和偏好的形成，从而最终决定国家对国际制度创制、维持和变迁的立场与政策。同样，国际经济法律秩序的构建，也因循这种从“国内”到“国际”的“自下而上”的路径。②

与“霸权稳定论”不同，“国际制度论”虽既可适用于经济等领域的“低级国际政治”，也可适用于安全问题等“高级国际政治”，但这种理论最早始于对国际经济关系的分析。在全球化时代，各国经济相互依赖的程度达到了前

① W. J. Aceves, *Institutionalist Theory and International Legal Scholarship*, *American University Journal of International Law & Policy*, Vol. 12, 1997, pp. 227-266.

② Anne-Marie Slaughter, *Liberal International Relations Theory and International Economic Law*, *American University Journal of International Law & Policy*, Vol. 10, 1995, pp. 717-743.

所未有的水平，源于新制度经济学的“国际制度论”，更是大有用武之地，可直接成为研究国际经济法律秩序的分析工具。

（三）建构主义的秩序观

建构主义是现行国际关系理论中方兴未艾的一个学派。新现实主义学派及新自由主义学派均认为国际体系是一种“物质结构”（如国家之间权力或利益的分配），而建构主义学派主张国际体系主要是一种由“观念”建构的“社会结构”。这里的“观念”是指社会的共有知识，即所谓的“文化”，具体表现为规范、规则、制度、意识形态、组织等，当然也包括国际法（含国际经济法）在内，因为现行的国际体系不仅仅表现为由“各自为政”的国家组成的一个集合体，这些国家之间还存在着彼此认同的国际法律规则。概言之，新现实主义学派和新自由主义学派均强调权力和利益在国际关系中的重要性，两派的分歧主要是国际制度作用的大小；建构主义学派虽不否认权力和利益等概念，但更强调国际关系中的第三个因素——观念。该学派主张，权力和利益主要不是由物质条件决定的，而在很大程度上是由观念构建的。离开了各国的共有知识和预期，物质资源在很大程度上也就失去了目的和效用。例如，一旦“不得使用武力解决国际争端”这样的国际法原则得到建构，那么，在国际经济关系中，小国就不会视大国的武力构成对自己的实质性威胁。

那么，国际社会的“观念”（包括国际法）又是从哪里来的呢？新现实主义、新自由主义和建构主义三大学派都主张，国际结构的进化主要来自国家间的互动过程，但是，它们对这种互动过程性质的认识并不一致：新现实主义学派认为国家间的互动主要是适者生存的“自然选择”模式，这是对国际结构进化的一种“物质主义”解释；新自由主义学派和建构主义学派则均主张，国家间互动的主导逻辑是“文化选择”（主要是模仿和习得）。两大学派存有分歧之处在于，新自由主义学派奉行“理性主义”，认为能动者（主要是国家）是外生于社会进程的，它们的身份和利益是“给定的因素和常数”（如果有变化，也是发生在互动之前），模仿和习得只是从“因果关系”意义上影响国家行为。该学派重点讨论的是能动者对相互行为期望的因素；而当正常行为和非正常行为的相对期望效用发生变化时，国际结构也就发生了变化；建构主义学派则认为，国家是内生于社会进程的，国际社会结构与国家之间存在着双向的同构关系：一方面，在国家间的互动过程中，通过模仿和社会习得等途径，国家会形成认同（角色），认同决定其利益，以致形成国家间的共有知识。这种共有知识到达一定阶段又会固化为国际法；另一方面，国际社会结构（包括国际法）反过来又为国家间的互动提供社会环境，并对它们的认同和利益起到塑形的作用。当然，当国家间的互动进程发生变化时，就会再造国家的身份和利益，从而推动国际社会结构的变化，包括国际法的发展。①

建构主义理论通常也包含着对国际法的研究。美国学者温特是著名的建构主义学派代表人物之一。他根据国家不同的角色认同，从历史发展的角度，将“无政府状态”下的国际文化（社会）结构具体划分为三类，即以往的霍布斯式文化结构（国家之间互相视为“敌人”），现行的洛克式文化结构（国家之间互相视为竞争的“对手”）以及将来的康德式文化结构（国家之间互相视为“朋友”）。据此，温特进而认为，霍布斯式文化不可能产生真正意义上的国际法；洛克式文化则不同，在此类文化结构中，国际法是现代国际政治的深层结构的基本组成部分。虽然没有集中的执法机构，但是现在各国越来越承认国际法具有约束力（因之可以得到执行）。换言之，现代国家间的竞争受到国际法所承认的主权结构的限制，所以这种竞争的基础是法治。但是，在这种限制范畴内，竞争并不排除以暴力解决争端。正因为如此，现行的洛克式文化还不是一种完全的法治体系；而康德式文化结构的一个显著特征就是至少在实际上它是一个法治体系，这就限定了国家可以合法谋取自我利益的范围。虽然没有中央权力机关来执行这样的限定规则，但是，只要国家内化了这些限定规则，规则就会被视为对国家的合法约束，并可以集体的方式加以执行。②

（四）理想主义的秩序观

在近代史上，空前惨烈的一战粉碎了欧洲的百年和平局面。作为对战争灾难的反思，一些学者提出了“理想主义”国际关系理论，主张可对人性进行由恶到善的改造，国家也是如此，其政治行为同样可以改变，以致在国际关系中放弃强权政治，追求正义；建立集体安全，维护世界和平。与传统的“均势”理念不同，理想主义学派非常注重国际制度安排的维和力量，是故，该学派非常强调国际法的作用，认为国际秩序应体现正义，并建立在以自然法为基础的国际法之上。理想主义学派最重要的代表人物、美国第28届总统威尔逊曾明确指出：“和平与正义、国际法和国际组织，应当也可能是国际社会大家庭共同追求的一种目标和架构”；并相信“国际体系能够被改造成一种完全

① J. Brunnee & S. J. Toope, *International Law and Constructivism: Elements of an International Theory of International Law*, *Columbia Journal of Transnational Law*, Vol. 39, 2000, pp. 28-33.

② ［美］亚历山大·温特：《国际政治的社会理论》，秦亚青译，上海人民出版社2000年版，第342、352、383页。

和平和正义的世界秩序”。威尔逊倡导的理想主义国际关系理论实际上是“实定主义国际法”与“国际道德”相混合的产物，因此又被称为“法制—道德主义”国际关系理论。①

随着国际联盟的破产和二战的爆发以及战后世界很快进入冷战时代，理想主义被视为“乌托邦”的代名词，退出了西方国际关系理论的主流，新旧现实主义主张的“权力”、“权力结构”和新自由主义强调的“利益”等取代理想主义倡导的“正义”，成为国际关系理论中的核心概念。然而，在国际法学界，始终不乏有人主张，秩序作为国际法律制度的形式结构，其产生和发展不可能离开制度的实质价值——国际正义。尽管历史上理想正义主要是有关国际政治秩序的规范性理论，但也包括了有关贸易自由化等内容，其基本理念同样也适用于对当代国际经济法律秩序的分析。在经济全球化时代，资本自由和社会正义之间的矛盾不但没有缓和，反而更加突出。各国在构建国际经济法律秩序的过程中，不可能藐视国际正义的存在和影响。

总之，就“无政府状态下”国际经济法律秩序的特点而言，新现实主义的“霸权稳定论”认为，其属于霸权国凭借自身权力优势所“施加的秩序”；而在新自由主义的“国际制度论”看来，这是一种各国基于互利考虑而“商得的秩序”；根据建构主义的观点，则为各国在互动过程中依认同而形成的“自发的秩序”。② 如若按照理想主义的理论推理，其结论应当是，无论国际经济法律秩序属于哪一类秩序，都应符合国际正义的要求，否则就会出现“偏瘫”的症状。

二、以国际关系理论分析国际经济法律秩序：内在机理

如前所述，在秩序这一形式结构方面，国际经济法律制度与国内经济法律制度相比，存在着明显的局限性。国内社会比较成熟，并有中央政府负责立法、修法和执法；而国际社会仍属于“无政府状态”下比较原始的社会。缘此，总的来看，国际经济法律制度的创制和变迁不易，其实施效果（维持）可能也不及国内法，国际经济法律秩序的残缺性由此显现无遗。各种国际关系

---

① F. A. Boyle, *World Politics and International Law*, Duke University Press, 1985, pp. 51-52.

② 有关“施加的秩序”（imposed orders）、“商得的秩序”（negotiated orders）和“自发的秩序”（spontaneous orders）的分类，系借用美国著名国际关系理论学者奥兰·R·杨的概念。其中“自发的秩序”这一概念的最早使用者应为哈耶克。See Oran R. Young, *Regime Dynamics: The Rise and Fall of International Regimes*, in S. D. Krasner (ed.), *International Regimes*, Cornell University Press, 1983, pp. 98-101.

理论均在不同程度上说明了国际经济法律秩序创制、变迁和维持的这一特点。

（一）国际经济法律秩序的创制

在“无政府状态”下的国际社会，国际经济法律制度产生于国家间的互动过程，互动的结果能否产生国际经济法律制度还取决于权力的结构、利益的分配、观念的构建以及对正义的理解等因素。各种国际关系理论都在不同程度上表明，国际经济法律制度是一种稀缺的资源，创制国际经济法律秩序，并非易事。

其一，从表面上看，按照“霸权稳定论”，似乎只要霸权国有自己的利益和愿望，国际经济法律秩序的创制便可由其定于一尊。然而，事实并非如此。诚然，霸权国的存在对推动国际经济法律秩序的形成具有一定的作用，但绝不是国际经济法律秩序创制的一个必要条件，更谈不上是一个充分的条件了。① “霸权稳定论”主要指的是国际制度的“供给”问题，而在相当程度上忽略了国际制度的“需求”问题。实际上，对国际制度的需求来自各国对国际合作的共同利益。当今世界早已不是殖民主义时代，霸权国不可能随心所欲地以自己的利益塑造一个国际经济法律秩序，国际经济法律秩序建立的前提是各国必须具有共同利益，只有在其他国家也可从中受益的情形下，才可能接受和服从这种秩序。可见，在霸权体系中，国际制度的供给并不充裕，尤其是对国际法而言更是如此。因为按照主权原则，如无一国的明示或默示的同意，任何其他国家都不可能将一项具体的国际经济法律制度（条约或习惯）强加于该国。即便是一项国际经济法律制度能使各国共同受益（获得绝对收益），但是各国从中获益的程度（相对收益）往往大小不一，乃至差别甚大。在霸权国与其他国家之间的非对称合作中，很可能会出现这样的情形：一个“霸道的”而非“仁慈的”霸权国自己从一项国际法律制度中收获颇丰，但分给其他诸多国家的只是一些“残羹冷炙”。② 由此，“患不均”的结果，就有可能导致该项国际经济法律制度无法为各国所共同接受。

其二，从“国际制度论”来看，即使其肯定共同利益在创建国际制度中的驱动作用，但是，该理论所论证的仍然只是制度创设中的“需求”因素，而未能阐明制度创设中的“供给”问题。在创建国际制度的实践中，各国虽

---

① ［美］罗伯特·基欧汉：《霸权之后：世界政治经济中的合作与纷争》，苏长河等译，上海人民出版社 2001 年版，第 53 页。

② D. Snidal, *The Limits of Hegemonic Stability Theory*, *International Organization*, Vol. 39, 1985, pp. 580-590.

有合作的共同利益，但经常会受到合作过程中各种“二级变量”的困扰，其中最主要的同样是存在着“相对收益”的困境。① 具体而言，新自由主义认为，在国际政治领域，各国一般都计较己方可占有的相对收益，所以达成军控等协议的难度非常大；而在国际经济领域，各国更多关心的可能是绝对收益，因而寻求合作的机会就大。倘若如此，国际经济法律秩序的创制要易于国际政治法律秩序。然而，这种比较只有相对的意义，因为在国际经济关系中，各国不可能不在相当程度上关心本国可得的相对收益。因为本国与他国所得相对收益的差距，可能会导致自身在国际竞争中处于不利的地位；更为严重的是，一旦形成利益分配上的结构性不平等，进而会威胁到一些国家的长期利益。② 按照博弈论，即便在经济领域发生于各国之间的是“合作博弈”（如“捕鹿游戏”模式），而非“非合作博弈”（如“囚徒困境”模式），但是在复杂的协调型博弈中，由于存在如何在博弈各方之间分配利益的问题，从而往往使得合作性的解决方案很难达成；换言之，博弈各方虽然都认为有协议总比没有协议好，但是在具体形成怎样一个协议的问题上将会发生争议。由于一项国际经济法律制度的创制，将以法律的形式比较牢固地“锁定”各国间相对收益的分配规则，因而从中获益不多的一方对接受这种形式的国际制度，会持更加审慎的态度。例如，在坎昆会议上，发达国家想在“新加坡议题”等方面斩获重大利益，但只愿在农产品等议题上给发展中国家以“蝇头小利”。构筑此等不平衡之“双赢”局面的企图，理所当然要落空。

晚近，“国际制度论”的研究还表明，当今世界，国家与非国家行为体存在着“复合的相互依赖关系”，国内政治对国际制度创制的影响不容忽视。按照“公共选择理论”，西方国家政府因受国内各利益集团和选民的影响，即使一项国际经济法律制度的创制从整体上对本国而言利大弊小；但是，该国政府仍有可能因受国内反对集团的压力，无法作出顾全大局的决策。在全球化浪潮的冲击下，发达国家内部各阶层经济利益的分化更加严重，对政府自主参加国际经济立法活动所构成的制肘有增无减。

其三，在“国际观念论”者来看，既然国际法表现为各国在长期互动过程中所形成的共有知识，那么国际法律规则的供给速度必然有限。有鉴于此，

---

① A. Hasenclever, P. Mayer & V. Rittberger, *Theories of International Regimes*, Cambridge University Press, 1997, pp. 53-55.

② 参见［加拿大］斯蒂芬·麦克布莱德：《作为权力体制的国际经济协定》，载［加拿大］马乔里·格里芬·科恩、斯蒂芬·麦克布莱德编著：《全球化动荡》，段保良译，华夏出版社 2004 年版，第 31 页。

建构主义非常适合说明带有渐成式特点的国际习惯法的产生；而国际经济法律秩序主要建立在相关的国际经济条约之上，需要在一定期限内谈判达成这些具体的国际条约，对此，建构主义原理所能提供的解释显然“力不从心”。持该派观点的一些学者认为，建构主义所要证明的对象主要是那些能够建构国际社会基础的国际法原则（如主权原则、约定必须信守原则以及不使用武力原则等），即所谓的“构建性规则”，而不是众多的反映因果关系的“管理性规则”。① 然而，在实践中，建立国际经济法律秩序所依托的国际经济条约恰恰多由此类“管理性规则”构成。此外，该派的另一些学者还提出了“原则性信念”和“因果性信念”的概念。前者是指那些作为区分正确与错误、正义与非正义标准的规范性理念；而后者是指为个体如何达到具体目标提供指导的有关因果关系的理念。这两者均可对国际制度的形成发挥“路线图”的作用，但是，“原则性信念”事关各方进行合作的目标，而“因果性信念”影响的只是各方为实现目标所作的手段上的选择。在国际经济关系中，因各国尤其是南北国家之间对公平与正义的理解存在着深刻的分歧，在相当程度上缺乏“原则性信念”，这势必会阻碍有关国际经济法律制度的建构。②

其四，依“国际正义论”原理分析，哪怕新现实主义的“霸权稳定论”和新自由主义的“国际制度论”成立，然则，因一项国际经济法律制度的创制关涉各国相对收益如何分配的问题，如果一国从道义上感到利益分配对其不公，将会更加强化该国抵制此项国际经济法律制度的意愿。而建构主义的“国际观念论”也不是价值中立的学说，其世界观的基础是传统的理想主义。③ 如果各国在互动中无法就正义这一基本“观念”形成共识，那么，如上所述，“基础性文本”的模糊或“原则性信念”的欠缺，势必加大国际经济法律秩序建构的难度。

人类对正义的理解一直摇摆于自由和平等两端之间。在当代，“自由”的正义观虽然已被尊奉为西方国家主流的意识形态，但是，其无论如何也不可能成为独霸世界的一种“终结”话语；“平等”的正义观仍在顽强地坚守着自己的领地。表现在国际经济关系中就是，发达国家力主以资本自由为基础的

① A. C. Arend, *Legal Rules and International Society*, Oxford University Press, 1999, pp. 129-132, 137-148.

② A. Hasenclever, P. Mayer & V. Rittberger, *Theories of International Regimes*, Cambridge University Press, 1997, pp. 143-144.

③ [美] 亚历山大·温特：《国际政治的社会理论》，秦亚青译，上海人民出版社 2000 年版，第 3 页。

“形式正义”、“相称正义”和“交换正义”，而广大发展中国家所追求的是“实质正义”、“同等正义”和“分配正义”。例如，在多哈回合中，发展中国家提出的“特殊与差别待遇”的要求，就反映了此类“平等”的正义观。倘若这样的正义诉求得不到应有的满足，则国际经济立法活动将举步维艰。

值得注意的是，广义上的“国际正义”除了以国家为本体的“国家间正义”之外，还包括“全球正义”（世界正义）和“个人正义”（人类正义）。前者主张个人利益应服从跨国（全球）社会的整体利益，可归之为“社会正义”，如保护全球环境和维护公共健康等；后者是指赋予个人以权利义务的道义准则，如对劳工权利及知识产权等人权的保护。① 现在，无论是 WTO，还是 IMF，还是 WBG，都是在以自由市场理念为主色调的所谓“华盛顿共识”基础上运作的。然而，近年来，这样的国际经济法律体制，受到了以非政府组织（NGOs）为代表的国内和跨国市民社会的强烈挑战。事实证明，假如对市民社会所提出的有关“全球正义”和“个人正义”的诉求采取“临床隔离”的政策，国际经济立法活动就难以成功，1998 年经合组织《多边投资协定》谈判的流产和 1999 年 WTO 西雅图会议的失败，即为典型的例证。

（二）国际经济法律秩序的变迁

权力的结构、利益的分配、观念的构建以及对正义的理解等决定国际经济法律制度创制的上述因素，同样影响着国际经济法律制度的变迁。显然，在国际经济关系中，这些因素不是恒定的，始终处于或快或慢、或大或小的变化之中，但这并不意味着国际经济法律制度系建立在流沙之上。因为国际经济法律制度一经创设，将获得相当程度的自主性：首先，国际经济法律制度自此不会完全受到权力结构的摆布；在存续期间，国际经济法律制度也会形成自己的价值和功能；同时，在此类制度环境中互动，各国还会改变原来的利益和偏好，并培养其对制度本身价值的认同。此外，国际经济法律制度形成之后，基于秩序的维持有利于共同利益实现这样的事实，各国可能不会因更高标准的正义诉求得不到满足而任意主张破除既成的秩序。各种国际关系理论从不同的方面论证了国际经济法律秩序的持久特点。

“霸权稳定论”认为，随着霸权国的衰弱，国际经济法律秩序必然崩溃。但这一结论遭到了国际关系理论学界的普遍质疑，即使是同属新现实主义学派的诸多学者，也不同意“霸权稳定论”的这一论断。例如，“修正结构现实主

---

① ［英］赫德利·布尔：《无政府社会：世界政治秩序研究》，张小明译，世界知识出版社 2003 年版，第 62～68 页。

义”理论主张，在国际制度的创制过程中，国家权力至关重要，除非得到强国的支持；否则，国际制度将难以生成。然而，该理论强调，国际制度一旦建立，可在一定程度上脱离权力的桎梏，即在“后霸权”时代，国际制度仍然可以存续。出于对高昂的破坏代价和缺乏可替代性选择等因素的担忧，即使霸权国也不会轻易决定摒弃现行的国际制度，所以，既成的国际制度通常会产生存续的惯性，而且这些制度本身并不一定与构成其基础的国际权力结构的变化相同步。换言之，国家间权力分配状况与国际制度特征的非相合性决定了国际制度自主性的规范含义；而且，一定程度上的此类非相合性是可以接受的，甚至是有帮助的，因为它可使国际制度有足够的寿命和稳定性来产生对各方都有益的结果。① 无疑，国际经济法律创设之后，其与国际权力结构的非相合性将大于政治领域的国际法律制度，因而可获得更为持久的生命力。

新自由主义的“国际制度论”认为，在国际制度建立之后，各国的偏好在相当长时间内将保持基本稳定，即使其后国际制度赖以产生的利益模式发生变化，在一定条件下，国际制度往往仍然可以维持，其主要原因在于：第一，国际制度一旦形成，不可能从各国利益变化的角度时时对其加以评估。因为这样做需要付出很高的成本；而在制度建立付出高成本之后，就不可能在制度运行过程中连续不断地付出比较高的成本。第二，无疑，国际制度的存在可使决策成本下降，一旦国际制度因顾及国家短期利益的变化而遭到破坏，重建的代价将很高。第三，合理的国际制度通常并非从持续的国家利益中产生，而是源于制度本身所蕴藏的利益。正是由于国际制度的存在，改变了各国的动机和选择机会，从而使得各国不会在国家利益变化不大的情况下轻易主张推翻现行的国际制度。第四，虽然一项国际制度建立时的利益分布状况发生了变化，然而制度本身仍可存续。其中的缘由包括，一个国家可能会考虑，背离该国际制度虽可获得具体的利益，但同时将损害其在国际社会的声誉。第五，国际制度的建立是为了确保各国在改变决策标准时应进行相互协调和合作，从而促成一国在进行决策时，应同时考虑其他国家的利益。协调和合作的制度化，可以构成对单个行为者的限制，也使行为者认识到共同利益的重要性，从而不会轻易地以一己私利而破坏国际制度的延续性。② 因法律具有内在的稳定特性，故国际

---

① ［美］斯蒂芬·D·克莱斯勒：《结构冲突：第三世界对抗全球自由主义》，李少华译，浙江人民出版社 2001 年版，第 25 页。

② ［美］阿瑟·斯坦：《协调与合作：无政府世界中的制度》，载［美］大卫·A·鲍德温：《新现实主义与新自由主义》，肖容欢译，浙江人民出版社 2001 年版，第 50 ~ 52 页。

经济法律制度的维持能力较之一般的国际制度通常会更强，这一结论可通过从法律的角度分析以上有关国际制度存续的各项原因而得到佐证。

援用建构主义“国际观念论”进行论证，最能说明国际经济法律秩序的耐久性。因为整个国际法所属的国际文化结构通常具有抗变的能力。这种抗变能力来自文化的自我实现和自我加强的性质；详言之，一旦一种国际文化结构形成，这种文化结构中的行为体（国家）就会被这种文化结构所建构，文化话语中的内容和意义就会不断地通过行为体（国家）间的实践活动得到加强，从而造就“结构性稳定”，并形成强烈的“路径依赖”。作为一种文化形式的国际法要发生变更，必得先改变行为体（国家）的认同，舍此别无他途；而行为体（国家）认同的改变，需假以时日。总之，建构主义更适合用以说明“过去”和“静止”状态，而非“将来”和“变化”的情形。当然，建构主义强调观念的难以移转主要针对的是“构建性规则”或“原则性信念”，而“构建性规则”或“原则性信念”往往体现在国际制度的“原则”以及“准则”之中；如上所述，“原则”和“准则”不变，国际制度的性质也不会改变。例如，贸易自由化和非歧视待遇原则作为国际经济关系的基本理念，分别构成 GATT 的“原则”和“准则”。无疑，欲推翻这样的“原则”和“准则”，实属不易之事；而即使具体的“规则”和“决策程序”有变，但只要“道不变”，GATT 仍将是 GATT。

按照理想主义的“国际正义论”，正义构成秩序的基础，但在“无政府状态”下的国际社会，正义这一基础角色不应被无限制地夸大。罗尔斯认为，正义的主题即社会的基本结构，当代国际社会的基本结构系由秩序原则和权力分配状况两方面因素构成。以秩序原则观之，国际社会呈“无政府状态”；而以权力分配状况观之，富国拥有的权力要远大于穷国。在既无世界政府，穷国又缺乏足够的权力与富国抗衡的基本结构中，国际社会不可能实行“均贫富”，不可能实现资源从富国向穷国的大规模转移。① 由此，国家间的正义标准要低于国内社会。在各国对国际正义存有争议的情形下，只有以“起码正义”得不到伸张为由，方才主张“破旧立新”，摧毁现行的国际经济法律制度。正如罗尔斯在《万民法》一书中所指出的那样：“如果基于万民法的全球正义原则意味着要运用于我们的世界中极端的不正义、差强人意的贫穷和不平等，这样的诉求才可以理解。但是如果这意味着漫无目的地不断运用于——像

① 时殷弘：《国际政治——理论探究·历史概观·战略思考》，当代世界出版社 2002 年版，第 107~108 页。

人们说的，毫无目标——必将充满援助义务的假设世界，这一诉求就有了问题。”① 鉴于此，在国际经济关系中，一旦相应的法律秩序得以确立，哪怕存在着一定程度的“正义赤字”，仍能得以维持。

然而，需要指出的是，国际经济法律制度虽不易变迁，但并非永固。按照新现实主义的观点，当国家间权力分配状况与国际经济法律制度特征的非相合性超过可承受的极限时，此类制度便将崩溃。根据新自由主义理论，当各国从一项国际经济法律制度中获得的收益普遍地小于其支付的成本时，则该项制度便到了瓦解的时点。按照建构主义学说，在各国互动的过程中，认同改变的时间虽然漫长，但并非不可能，作为国际社会观念一种的国际法也总有更新嬗变之时；而对于国际经济法律制度中的具体“规则”（如 GATT 的关税税率）和“决策程序”（如 GATT 的协商一致原则），因只是一些“管理性规则”或“因果性信念”，其变化自在常理之中。以理想主义观之，一项建立在不同正义观基础之上的国际经济法律秩序，会因内部具体制度之间矛盾的不断加剧而逐步走向解体。无疑，一项被大多数国家认为所体现之正义不尽如人意的国际经济法律制度，将渐失其合法性，以致最终难逃衰亡的命运。

（三）国际经济法律秩序的维持

国际经济法律秩序的维持状况取决于国际经济法律制度的实施效果，即各国遵守国际经济法律制度的程度。从理论上分析，国际经济法律制度的实施效果应不及国内法律制度。通常而言，国际经济关系的法制化充其量不过是建立“以规则为导向”的法律秩序，还不可能达到国内法中的“法治”水平。

新现实主义强调国际经济关系中的权力因素，认为一国之所以遵守国际法是因为慑于违法会受到他国（尤其是大国）的惩处，由此观之，国际法可称之为“国际权力法”。② 在法理学上，依靠强制力推行法律制度的观点虽已受到越来越多的挑战，但制裁对法律实施的意义仍不可全盘否定。在国内社会，违法行为必受国家公权力的惩罚；而在“无政府状态下”的国际社会，对违反国际法的行为，各国只能采取“自助”手段，其对潜在违法者的阻却力显然不如国内社会。有鉴于此，一些法学家（如奥斯丁）就不认为国际法是法

---

① ［美］罗尔斯：《万民法》，张晓辉等译，吉林人民出版社 2001 年版，第 124～125 页。

② 英国著名国际法及国际经济法学者施瓦曾伯格曾从不同角度把国际法视为“国际权力法”、“国际互惠法”和“国际共同法”。参见［英］赫德利·布尔：《无政府社会：世界政治秩序研究》，张小明译，世界知识出版社 2003 年版，第 111 页。

律，而只是“有效用的国际道德”。对大国而言，虽然随着全球经济一体化进程的加快，各国间的相互依赖关系加强，小国通过运用“交叉报复”等手段对大国实行经济制裁的效果也在增强，但对大国破坏国际经济法律制度的侵害行为，小国的报复能力终归有限。尤其是在国际经济法律领域，一国违法受到国际社会武力制裁的可能性几乎没有，国际经济法律制度的实施与国际政治权力之间的联系就更为松弛。

新自由主义认为，各国遵守国际法的动力是为了换取其他国家也遵守国际法。基于这种相互受益考虑而维持的国际法，有时被称为“国际互惠法”。倘若各国遵守国际法系出于利己的动机，乃基于对结果的权衡而作出的自我利益选择，那么，按此推论，一国在认为守法的成本大于收益时，就会选择违约。对于国际经济法律制度来说，更是如此：首先，政治和社会领域的国际法可能关涉国际社会的基本秩序。一国违反这些国际法规则，往往会面临国际社会强大的集体压力。例如，一国无视国际人权法，可能会遭到西方国家的“人道主义干涉”。而国际经济法律制度体现的是各国具体经济利益的分配关系。各国以一己之利违反此类国际法的可能性较大，其受到的制裁压力通常也只限于受损害的国家。其次，各国在国际政治和社会领域的利益相对比较稳定，但在经济方面，其利益的可变性较大，特别是现代西方国家实行的是“内嵌的自由主义”，政府容易受到国内经济乃至政治、社会因素变化的影响而选择对外违反国际经济法律制度。例如，2002 年，布什政府为了获得美国钢铁业工人的选票，不惜违反 WTO 协定，动用其国内贸易法中的“201 条款”，采取单边主义的贸易保护措施，即属典型一例。通常而言，大国较之小国具有抵抗和吸收因违反国际法而带来的有形和无形成本的优势（如故意制造事件来转移其他国家的视线等），① 因而违法的频率可能会更高。

建构主义认为，对“权力”（强制）和“互惠”（利己）在国际法实施中的作用不能高估，二者只构成国际法被国家“内化”的第一、二个等级。在这两个等级上，国际法仅仅外在地影响到国家的行为；第三个等级是基于承认国际法规范的合法性而予以遵守（合法性）。只有在该等级上，国际法规范才涉及国家的身份和利益，行为体（主要是国家）才真正被“建构”。可见，按照建构主义的观点，一国遵守国际法可能被认为是其法治理念或更为广泛的价值观在起作用，从这个意义上讲，国际法是“国际共同体法”。美国哈佛大学教授科恩倡导的、具有重要影响的“跨国法律程序说”就是例证。该说主要

---

① O. Schachter, *International Law in Theory and Practice*, Martinus Nijhoff Publishers, 1991, p. 8.

运用建构主义理论，提出在复杂的互动过程中——国家及各种非国家行为体在国际、国内诉讼和仲裁活动中以及对立法机关的游说过程中，不断地重复运用国际法。由此，相关的国际法律规则就被内化为国内法律体制中的价值观念，从而使国际法得到各国的普遍遵守。① 分析法学派的一些学者有关国际法遵守的观点，与建构主义理论相通之处颇多。例如，英国法学家哈特认为，国际法的效力并非来自各国的武力制裁，而在于国际法与国内法一样也有一个“承认规则”；此类规则在另一位著名法学家凯尔森那里被称为“基本规范”，即“约定必须信守”，其构成国际法中其他规则的效力来源或依据。② 无可否认，法治观念在国际法的遵守中可起到一定的作用，但国际社会毕竟还不是法治很发达的成熟社会，因“法治观念淡薄”而违反国际经济法律规则的情形，仍为数不少。

建立在理想主义基础之上的自然法理论倾向于这样的一个立场，即一个完全或基本上丧失正义的规范，不配被称为“法律”。美国学者弗兰克认同康德式的理想主义理念，其提出的“合法性理论”是目前关于国际法遵守的主要学说之一。该说认为，“合法性”是国际法的力量源泉，只有国际法规则本身是公平的，才可能为各国所普遍遵守。但是，在此处，弗氏对“公平”的理解是狭隘的，将之等同于“程序正义”，而不是罗尔斯的“分配正义”。按照弗氏的解释，这种“程序正义”系建立在规则的确定性、有效性、一致性和依附性等各要素的集成之上。③ 显然，在有关国际法的遵守问题上，不但要维护“程序正义”，更应关注的是“实质正义”。现行的国际经济法律制度虽还谈不上丧失“起码正义”，但在发展中国家这方面看来，存在着“正义赤字”。而且，如果一项国际经济法律制度一开始在南北国家间的利益分配就是不公平的，那么，随着时间的推移，可能就会造成南北贫富差距越拉越大的“马太效应”，使得该项国际经济法律制度逐步丧失其合法性；而一项缺乏足够正义的法律制度不一定会马上被推翻，但其实施的效果必定大打折扣。

值得注意的是，对于各国遵守国际法包括维持国际经济法律制度的各种分析模式而言，通常不是“孰真孰假”的问题，而是各种模式能扮演“多大”

① H. H. Koh, *Why do Nations Obey International Law?*, *Yale Law Review*, Vol. 106, 1997, pp. 2641-2659.

② ［英］哈特：《法律的概念》，张文显等译，中国大百科全书出版社 1996 年版，第 229 页。

③ H. M. Franck, *The Power of Legitimacy among Nations*, Oxford University Press, 1990, pp. 18-19, 234-235.

角色的问题,① 即国际经济法律秩序的维持系由以上各种因素综合作用所致。在西方国际关系理论中，美国学者考克斯的“法律至上说”可谓独树一帜。考氏反对新现实主义所主张的国际体系结构以权力分配状况为特征的观点，认为国际法才是构成国际体系结构的基石；而能够成为国际体系结构基石的国际法实际上是指国际法的基本原则；而国际法的基本原则又可为具体之国际条约约束力的产生提供框架。例如，两个国家签订一项削减关税的协定，这一签约行为本身就默示地表明双方相互承认对方拥有主权（有权享受该协定项下之权利），并受有约必须信守原则的约束。据此，考氏进一步分析道，各国之所以愿意遵守这样的国际协定，当然受到其他国家报复权力威慑的影响（新现实主义的主张），但此类“外在”的作用是次要的；各国之所以守约，其“内在”的动力是主要的，而此类“内在”的动力又来自，一国若违反具体的国际协定，等于破坏了国际法中的国家主权和有约必须信守等原则，同时也将严重损害其自身的利益，如造成该国声誉的损失以及其他国家也可能会仿其道而行之等（新自由主义的主张）。此其一。其二，更为主要的是，各国自愿遵守国际协定乃根植于其对行为合法性的信念（建构主义的主张）。②

从上述对国际经济法律秩序的机理分析中可知：首先，国际经济法律秩序各要素之间是互相关联的。国际经济法律制度创制的艰难，直接造成了国际经济法律秩序在相当程度上缺乏“完整性”这一要素。同时，在创制国际经济法律制度的过程中，需要考虑各国间的权力对比和利益分配状况，并顾及各种不同的正义观，这就难以保证国际经济法律规则的普适性；相应地，国际经济法律秩序的“统一性”标准也将无法得到比较充分的满足。此外，为了求得各国对国际经济法律制度的接受，在对它们设定权利义务时，就要预留相当程度的弹性适用空间，这就为国际经济法律秩序中“明确性”之要素的获得设置了障碍；如规则缺乏明确性，必然会影响国际经济法律制度实施的“有效性”。进一步来看，在国际经济法律制度实施的效果得不到应有保障的情形下，对国际经济法律秩序“持久性”的维持，实际上就成了一种慢性病变、终至死亡的过程。

其次，国际经济法律秩序的创制、变迁和维持三者也是相互联系的。国际经济法律秩序创制不易，在一定程度上也强化了国际经济法律秩序变迁难的问

---

① A. Uuderdal, *Explaining Compliance and Defection: Three Models*, *European Journal of International Relations*, Vol. 4, 1998, pp. 5-30.

② S. A. Kocs, *Explaining the Strategic Behavior of States: International Law as System Structure*, *International Studies Quarterly*, Vol. 38, 1994, pp. 538-542.

题。因为一旦原有的国际经济制度被废弃，新的替代性制度又无以成就，则国际经济关系就会陷入无序的状态。另一方面，国际经济法律秩序变迁的迟滞，并不意味着国际经济法律制度在存续期间为各国所恪守，在国际经济法律制度实施效果不佳，又不得不进行维持的情况下，日积月累，一旦突发危机到来，往往将会导致既有国际经济法律秩序的突然崩溃。

三、以国际关系理论分析国际经济法律秩序：发展趋势

晚近，国际经济法律规范的数量不断膨胀，乌拉圭回合达成的 WTO“一揽子协议”就是此类国际法律规范“大爆炸”的表现。然而，这一现象是否意味着国际经济关系的法制化是人类社会发展的必然趋势呢？也就是说，有朝一日，国际经济法律制度会否完全取代那些非法律国际经济制度呢？以上本文所运用的只是国际关系理论中有关国际制度的一般原理。因为这些原理既适用于国际经济法律制度，也适用于非法律国际经济制度，所以仍未阐明国际经济法律制度和非法律国际经济制度孰优孰劣的问题。对于这样一个关键性的问题，尚需依国际关系理论以及法学理论交叉的研究方法作进一步的探讨。就此，总的一个分析结论是，随着经济全球化的进一步深化，各国间的相互依赖关系将愈加紧密，需要“供给”更多的国际经济法律规范加以维系；但这并不意味着国际经济法律制度必然优于非法律国际经济制度，两者既有替代性，又有互补性。

首先，在国际经济关系中，国际法作为国际制度的一个特殊种类，其区别于其他非法律国际制度的基本特征有哪些？

以往，受到国际关系理论学界广泛关注的是“国际制度”的概念，但对于“国际制度”的定义，始终存在着争议。其中较被普遍接受的是美国学者克莱斯勒的观点，即国际制度是指“在一定国际关系领域组织和协调国际关系的默示的或明示的原则、准则、规则和决策程序。”其中，“原则”（principles）指“关于事实、原因和公正的信念”，构成最高等级的规范；“准则”（norms）是“以权利、义务定义的行为标准”。可见，“准则”较之“原则”要更为具体；更加具体的是“规则”（rules），其为“对行为的具体令行禁止”，属于操作层面上的细则；而“决策程序”（decision-making procedures）是指“作出和贯彻集体决定的主导做法”。“决策程序”并不一定比“规则”更为具体，只是一种不同意义上的运作规程。对于这四类规范的地位和作用，克氏的基本分析为：“原则”和“准则”体现制度的基本特征，其变化是制度本身的变化，会导致制度性质的改变；同样的“原则”和“准则”可能会有许多与之相一致的“规则”和“决策程序”；而“规则”和“决策程序”的变化只是制度

内部的变化，不会导致制度性质的改变。①

对于克莱斯勒这个定义的批评主要集中在，其含义比较模糊，无法对以上国际制度构成四要素之间的关系作出明确的说明，尤其是“准则”的概念难以清晰地区别于“原则”和“规则”。简言之，该定义强调国际制度的机制化规范，而缺乏操作层面上的考虑。尽管如此，西方国际关系理论学界并不否认国际法存在于国际制度的范畴之内，且认为在国际制度的四大构成要素中，都包含了相应的国际法规范。例如，1944 年签订的《国际货币基金协定》确立了国际货币法律关系中的支付自由化“原则”。该制度的一个关键性“准则”有着这样的禁止性内容，即一国不能为了一己私利而采取单边的手段操控本国汇率，贻害他国。在战后相当长的一段时间里，这项“准则”主要是通过“钉住汇率”（“规则”）以及汇率发生变化时的磋商程序（“决策程序”）得以实现的。②

然而，国际法作为国际制度的一个特殊种类，其区别于其他形式国际制度的特征有哪些呢？近年来，国际关系理论学界普遍加强了对国际法在国际关系中特有价值的研究。美国国际关系学界跨学科研究国际法的一批有影响的学者曾在著名的国际关系学术刊物——《国际组织》的特刊（2000 年夏季号暨第 3 期）上以“法制化与世界政治”为题，撰写系列论文专门探讨制度主义下的国际关系法制化问题。他们提出了界定“国际法”的三要素：（1）“义务性”(obligation)，即规则应对行为体具有拘束力，而且这种法律上的拘束力并非来自强迫、互惠或道德的考虑；（2）“确定性”(precision)，指的是规则应以非模糊的方式设定命令性、授权性或禁止性行为规范。因在国际层面上往往缺乏有权解释的机构，故强调规则的确定性尤为重要；（3）“授权性”(delegation)，指独立的第三方（包括司法机关、仲裁机构及行政组织等）有权执行、解释或在争端解决过程中适用规则，以及可能有权进一步制定规则。从以上三要素的实质来看，它们都是围绕国际法的“强制性”特点展开的；详言之，“义务性”是从立法的内在方面强调了国际法规则所具有的强制性；而“确定性”是从立法的外在形式上保证国际法规则效力的顺利发挥；“授权性”则是从法律实施的层面上支持国际法律规则的强制力。

虽然对以该三要素甄别国际法规则的做法是否完全准确、完整的问题，似

---

① Stephen D. Krasner, *Structural Causes and Regimes Consequences: Regimes as Intervening Variable*, *International Organization*, Vol. 36, 1982, pp. 187-190.

② ［美］罗伯特·基欧汉：《霸权之后：世界政治经济中的合作与纷争》，苏长河等译，上海人民出版社 2001 年版，第 70 页。

仍可作进一步的探讨，但是其对国际法强制性特质的认同乃至强调，无疑是正确的。在认同上述三要素的基础上，这些美国学者提出，对一国际规则首先可运用“质”的分析方法（即三要素的有无），如得出的结论为，该国际规则不具有“义务性”、“确定性”和“授权性”的，则其不属于“国际法”的范畴（如各国间达成的“君子协定”等）；如该国际规则具备三要素而可归入“国际法”者，便可从“量”的方面（即三要素的强弱）对其进行分析，凡“义务性”、“确定性”和“授权性”均强的规则，构成国际法中理想的“硬法”，如 WTO《与贸易有关的知识产权协议》等；凡三要素中三项均为弱的，那么该国际法规则就属于典型的“软法”，如亚太经济合作组织发表的有关宣言等；如一国际法规则中的三要素中有一项或两项比较弱的，则可归入从“硬法”到“软法”过渡的不同中间等级。例如，《维也纳保护臭氧层公约》属于一要素（“义务性”）强，其他两要素（“确定性”和“授权性”）弱的国际公约；而《欧盟反倾销法》（《罗马公约》第 85、86 条）则属于有两要素（“义务性”和“授权性”）强，一要素（“确定性”）弱的情形，其相对于《维也纳保护臭氧层公约》而言，其国际法规则的硬度等级要高。① 以上有关国际法律制度和非法律国际制度的识别标准，当然也适用于区别国际经济法律制度和非法律国际经济制度。

其次，在国际经济关系中，国际法作为国际制度的一个特殊种类，其区别于其他非法律国际制度的特有价值是什么？

新现实主义者虽在一定程度上也承认国际法的作用，但始终认为权力结构可以主导国际法。因为“无政府状态下”的国际社会缺乏国际判决的执行机构，故所有的国际法都只能是“软法”，其所扮演的最多也只是一个“橱饰”的角色而已。据此，在国际经济领域，法制化只能对权力产生一定的外在制约作用，并非国际经济关系的必然发展趋势。例如，该学派中的“霸权稳定论”建议，霸权国为了延缓自身衰弱的进程，应减少自己所承担的义务。② 在这里，霸权国要减负的不仅仅是其承担义务的数量，而且包括其承担义务的力度，即霸权国倾向于摆脱硬性国际经济法律制度的过多约束，而更愿意接受那些软性的非国际经济法律义务，以便在是否为他国免费提供“国际公共物品”

---

① 有关国际法规则“三要素”特征的分析以及软硬等级的排列，详见 K. W. Abbott, Robert O. Keohane, Andrew Moravcsik, Anne-Marie Slaughter and Duncan Snidal, *The Concept of Legalization*, *International Organization*, Vol. 54, Issue3, Summer 2000, pp. 401-419.

② ［美］罗伯特·吉尔平：《世界政治中的战争与变革》，武军等译，中国人民大学出版社 1994 年版，第 185 页。

以及在何种程度上提供等问题上，为自己留有余地。

由于新自由主义较之新现实主义更强调国际合作，理所当然，以该学派观之，国际法在国际关系中的地位也得到了加强，其成为影响国家行为的一种主变量。新自由主义学者多从规范的功能角度分析国际法律制度和非法律国际制度的价值，所持的基本看法是：法制化是晚近国际关系发展的一个重要现象，但并不能由此得出结论说，这样的发展将构成今后一种必然的趋势；同时，也不能一般性地断言“硬法”优于“软制度”,① 因为二者各有优势，各国在不同情境中往往会有不同的选择。新自由主义的这一分析结论也适用于国际经济关系的法制化进程。就此，一些国际经济法学者对“硬法”和“软法”的分析及其得出的结论与新自由主义几近吻合。②

其一，新自由主义中的“国际制度论”认为，硬法和软制度均不应忽视。硬法在实施阶段成本较低，也能形成比较稳定的国际法律关系。但是，硬法制定的成本往往较高，对国际法律关系的适应性也较差；相反，软制度的制定成本比较低，并可适时加以修订，可以灵活应对国际关系发展的需要。具体而言：

从硬法的优势来看，第一，硬法更能保证各国承诺的可信度：一方面，硬法的高“确定性”和“授权性”可限制各国对其义务作出自行其是的解释；另一方面，硬法的高“义务性”可加大违法的成本，包括使违法者在国际社会中的声誉严重受损。第二，硬法因其规则本身比较明确，且实施更有保证，故更能降低依其所进行的交易的成本，尤其是减少达成补充协议的谈判成本。第三，硬法更能保证各种政治战略的实施。例如，实施资源和人才比较充裕的国家一般更倾向于采取硬法的方式实现自己的利益；又如，硬法的实施更难受到各国国内各种利益集团的干扰，从而提高实现国家利益的效率，并降低国内政治成本；再如，寻求尽量减少与其他国家发生政治冲突的国家，往往也看好硬法。第四，由于硬法可能具有“授权性”，即设立了规则解释和争端解决机制，因而可更为有效地处理“合同不完全”的问题。

反之，较之硬法，软制度也有其优势：第一，硬法虽然规则一般比较明确、具体，容易为各方所遵行，而且一国若要违约，将被诉诸相应的争端解决机制，这会对潜在的违约方产生威慑作用；但是，对于硬法的制定，各国通常均持慎重的态度，在谈判过程中需要咨询专家；有关部门对草案的审查和评估

① J. Goldstein, M. Kahler, R. O. Keohane & Anne-Marie Slaughter, *Introduction: Legalization and World Politics*, *International Organization*, Vol. 54, 2000, pp. 386-387.

② A. H. Qureshi, *International Economic Law*, Sweet & Maxwell, 1999, p. 24.

往往耗时许久；在有关条约签署之后，经常还须经过立法机关久拖不决的审议和批准；等等。显然，在这些环节，制定软制度的成本要低得多。第二，接受硬法本身意味着一国要对其他国家作出比较确定的妥协，形成对本国主权的一种限制；而软制度对各国的拘束力就要小得多，接受这样的制度一般不会付出太高的“主权成本”。由此，为了保持本国对外政策的灵活性，一些国家可能更青睐软制度。第三，对于那些刚刚形成或比较复杂的国际关系，因其具有不确定性，如贸然采用硬法，显有不妥。在这些情形下，可以软制度为先导，促成各国在不断“学习”和“模仿”的过程中，推动利益的磨合和互信的加强，不断地对制度本身作出调整和修正，最后可能会水到渠成，将软制度上升为硬法。第四，硬法有时虽可降低交易成本，但在一些情况下，因实难为一些国家所接受，从而使交易陷入僵局；而软制度一般具有相当的弹性，这就为各国进行讨价还价留下了空间，有利于在强弱或利益和价值观有异的国家之间，在不同时期的交易中达成妥协。①

其二，新自由主义的“全球治理”理论更是凸显了非法律国际制度的地位。该理论虽没有排斥国家的“统治”手段（包括国际法）在全球治理中的角色，但更强调的是多元主体共同参与、协商，以形成有序的、自治的和非正式制度化的调节机制，从历史发展的角度来看，其中包含着矫正目前存在的对硬法作用估价过高之倾向的意义。

随着全球化的发展，就法律规范和其他社会规范两者在社会治理中的重要性问题，在法理学上本身就存在着争议：以波斯纳为代表的一种观点认为，随着社会规模的扩大和社会生活的发展，仅靠非法律社会规范已难以奏效，需要进一步强化法律规范的地位；相反，以耶鲁大学艾里克森为代表的另一种观点主张，社会关系变得复杂的时候，政府就会缺乏能力获得和加工足够的信息，非法律社会规范能比法律规范发挥更好的作用。然而，更多的学者赞同，法律和非法律社会规范的执行机制不同，对信息结构的要求也不同，这就意味着它们可以在不同的层面上发挥作用，法律不可能消灭非法律社会规范。②

晚近，冷战的结束和全球化趋势的深化，潜伏多年的经济、安全、政治、生态和文化等危机渐次显露，面对这些日益严重的全球性问题，从全球治理理论开出的“药方”来看，其与未完全摆脱国家中心主义的“国际制度论”不

① K. W. Abbott & D. Snidal, *Hard and Soft Law in International Governance*, *International Organization*, Vol. 54, 2000, pp. 421-436.

② 张维迎：《法律与社会规范》，载吴敬琏主编：《比较》（第 11 辑），中信出版社 2004 年版，第 193 页。

同，强调的是民族国家体系的衰弱和全球市民社会的兴起。对传统上由国家及政府间组织垄断国际立法的合法性问题，全球治理理论提出了挑战。为了克服国际立法体制的这种“合法性危机”，该理论主张应加强各种非国家行为体（尤其是代表全球市民社会的非政府组织）对国际立法过程的参与，以使国际法能够更多地得到各方的自愿遵守；同时，该理论还强调各种非国家行为体应通过协调，在营造共识的基础上对全球事务实行调节性的管理，从而打破由国家及政府间组织依靠强制力进行“统治”的单一局面。例如，美国学者科格莱昂斯提出，应对全球性问题，需要有不同的国际制度形式，包括非国家行动、内部控制、相互承认、一致性规则、委托代理和放弃等六种。其中的“非国家行动”是指由非国家行为体来创建行为规范，实际上就是采取软制度或软法形式；“委托代理”是指各国政府将制定有关规则的权力让渡给一些国际组织。这些国际组织获得的代理权可以是宽松的（软性的），也可以是受严格约束的（刚性的）；而“一致性规则”则是指各国政府之间签订的硬性国际条约。“因为面对不同种类的全球性问题，并非所有的制度形式都同样有效”，所以“必须确认制度形式与需要解决的问题是否匹配”。① 因全球治理涉及的维度很广，既包括政治、社会及文化等问题，也涵盖经济领域，故该理论也可适用于对国际经济法律制度和非法律国际经济制度的比较分析。

其三，新自由主义的“自由理论”也相当重视软制度和软法在构建国际经济法律秩序中的作用。该理论的主要特点是强调国内政治对国际政治的影响，有的国际法学者运用该国际关系理论提出，作为国际立法活动结果的国际法规则，不可能在脱离国内法律体制的“真空”中形成，国际法律秩序的重构，应采取从“国内”到“国际”的路径。国际法的“自由理论”同样认为，在调整国内和跨国社会的个人、团体之间互动关系的国际法律渊源中，“自愿法”（主要是公司守则和新商人法等“软法”）是最重要，也是最有效的，因为它们无须经由任何中介就可直接作用于跨国关系的首要行为体；而在传统的国际法理论中，这些个人、团体的“自愿法”恰恰是被边缘化了的法律渊源。此外，国内和跨国社会的个人、团体之间的互动总是在政府制度的阴影下进行的，所以，调整这些互动关系的法律还有“跨国政府法”，这类法律既包括各国政府制定的“硬法”（涉外管制立法），也包括国际民间组织（如

① ［美］凯利·科格莱昂斯：《全球化与国际制度的设计》，载［美］约瑟夫·S·奈、［美］约翰·D·唐纳胡：《全球化世界的治理》，王勇等译，世界知识出版社 2003 年版，第 258、262 页。

巴塞尔委员会、证券委员会国际组织和国际保险监督官协会等）编纂的“软法”。①

较之新现实主义与新自由主义，建构主义是最重视国际法作用的一个国际关系理论学派。这与该学派的理想主义世界观密切相关。美国学者阿伦教授运用建构主义理论具体分析了国际法在建构国际社会中的特殊作用：第一，在构建国际体系方面，国际法的角色非同一般。诸如，国际法引入了国际关系的基石——国家主权原则；国际法为各种行为体确立了其在国际体系中的成员资格标准；国际法提供了决定其他法律规范效力的规则；国际法提供了外交语言；国际法为各种国际行为体提供了主张救济的法律依据，等等。第二，国际法在影响和改变国家的身份及利益方面确实发挥着作用：国家及各种非国家行为体都承认国际法的存在；各国对国际法的产生过程存在着普遍的共识；国际法律规则（尤其是国际条约）较之其他种类的国际规则更容易识别；相应地，因国际法规则引起的国家身份和利益的变化也比较易于确认；同时，在非单向度的相互构建关系中，国家利益和身份发生变化而导致国际法规则的发展也有明确的标准。尤其值得关注的是，阿氏提出并论证了这样一个观点——“有关国际法律体系性质的普遍原则”（如约定必须信守原则、主权平等原则和不干涉内政原则等）建构了现行国际体系的根本结构。②

建构主义虽然非常重视国际法的作用，但并不能说明在当代的国际经济关系中，国际法律制度将取代非国际法律制度。例如，按照温特的观点，国际法存在于目前仍然占主导地位的洛克式国际社会，但现行国际结构仍不是完整的法治体系，其他非法律国际制度仍有其存在的空间；只有到将来康德式文化成为主流国际结构时，国际社会才会真正实现法治的目标。然而，康德式的“世界大同”不能说是“乌托邦”，至少也只是一种遥远的理想。又如，阿伦的建构主义观点也只是笼统地强调国际法（尤其是其中的国际法基本原则）对建构国际社会的作用，对于具体的国际经济法律制度是否能发挥优于非法律国际经济制度的功能，并未作出明确的回答。

理想主义历来十分强调国际法的作用，但也并未排斥非法律国际制度的作用。从该学派的理论中可以推断，只要符合国际正义的要求，国际经济法律制度和非法律国际经济制度就可以并存。

---

① Anne-Marie Slaughter, *A Liberal Theory of International Law*, *The American Society of International Law Proceedings*, 2000, pp. 240-249.

② A. C. Arend, *Legal Rules and International Society*, Oxford University Press, 1999, pp. 129-132, 137-148.

如前所述，强制性是国际法律制度区别于非法律国际制度的主要标准，而强有力的争端解决机制是保证国际法律制度强制性的最终手段。在多边经济法律制度中，乃至整个国际法中的多边领域，WTO 争端解决机制首开先河，建立了对各成员方的强制管辖制度。许多学者认为，这是多边经济法律制度里程碑式的革命；但是，这种通过争端解决机制强制各国遵守国际法的做法，也遭到不少国际关系理论学者和国际法学者的反对。其中，一派学者提出了应将国际法遵守问题作为一种“管理过程”的理论，如美国学者阿伯伦·切尔斯和安通尼·罕德勒·切尔斯的“管理模式说”以及巴尼狄克特·金斯伯里的“管理程序说”等。这些学者主张，不应将国际法的遵守问题单纯看成是一种“执行模式”，或僵硬、简单地理解为“保持国家行为与法律规则的一致”，而应对其进行比较有“弹性”的全过程管理，包括建立公开和透明、报告和信息收集、确认和监督、劝解和争端解决、能力建设、审查和评估等制度，促使各国做到有必要、也有能力遵守国际法；而不是动辄就运用强制性的争端解决机制和施以报复的手段，因为这样不但会给受报复者和报复者均带来高成本，而且将引起国际法上严重的合法性危机问题。①

① G. W. Down, D. M. Rocke & P. N. Barsoom, *Is the Good News about Compliance Good News about Cooperation? International Organization*, Vol. 50, 1996, pp. 379-381; B. Kingsbury, *The Concept of Compliance as a Function of Competing Conceptions of International Law*, *Michigan Journal of International Law*, Vol. 19, 1998, pp. 345-372.

作者简介

左海聪

左海聪，1966年2月生，湖南郴州人。1984~1994年，在武汉大学法学院国际法系学习，获法学学士、硕士和博士学位。曾赴荷兰阿姆斯特丹大学国际法系、海牙国际法学院和罗马国际统一私法协会进行合作研究。现为武汉大学法学院国际法研究所教授、博士生导师、国际法研究所国际经济法研究室主任，兼任中国国际经济法学会常务理事、中国法学会世贸组织法研究会理事、湖北省珞珈律师事务所律师、武汉市中级人民法院专家咨询委员会委员和武汉仲裁委员会仲裁员。

主持国家社会科学基金青年项目“WTO法成案研究”、国际合作项目“欧盟外贸法研究”和教育部人文社会科学重点研究基地重大研究项目“外贸法比较研究”，参加国家级项目2项、省部级项目8项。著有《国际经济法的理论与实践》（独著，研究生教材）、《国际贸易法》（独著，21世纪法学规划教材），主编有《国际贸易法学》、《中国商事法》、《国际经济法案例评析》等3部著作，参编著作10部，在*Uniform Law Review*、《人民日报》（理论版）、《国际经济法论丛》、《中国国际私法与比较法年刊》、《国际法和比较法论丛》、《法学评论》、《法商研究》、《法学家》、《国际贸易问题》等学术刊物上发表中英文学术论文30余篇。多次向中宣部和商务部等中央和地方政府部门提交研究或咨询报告。研究成果中《论国际法部门的划分》（论文）2001年获湖北省社会科学优秀成果三等奖；《关于WTO幼稚产业保护条款的若干分析》（研究报告）2003年获司法部法学教材和法学优秀研究成果优秀奖，《WTO争端解决机制概论》2003年获司法部法学教材和法学优秀研究成果三等奖。主要研究领域为国际商法、WTO法、比较外贸法和国际经济法基本理论。

国际商法的产生、发展和未来

——兼谈和平崛起中的中国的对策

左海聪

目　　次：

（二）顺应国际商法全球化的趋势，积极加入国际公约和采纳国际惯例

（三）顺应国际商法非国内化的趋势，重新定位国际商事惯例的适用顺位

（四）尊重国际商事仲裁的自治性，加强对国际商事仲裁的支持

（五）确认国际商法的独立学科地位

21世纪，和平崛起中的中国在促进全球经济发展方面将发挥更为重要、更加积极和更富建设性的作用，我国企业将更为全面和深入地从事各种国际商事交易，开展国际竞争。这种涉外经济发展态势对国际商法的实践和理论提出了新的要求。我国政府和企业需要更为积极有效地参与和处理国际商事法律事务，我国国际法学界也需要更加深入地研究国际商法的各种宏观和微观问题。

客观而言，迄今为止我国法学界对国际商法没有给予足够的重视。国际商法一直没有被作为一个独立或相对独立的研究领域来对待，国际商法的宏观和整体研究成果十分匮乏，甚至对国际商法的概念也没有明确一致的认识。本文从国际商法的定义入手，首先分析国际商法的产生，进而从宏观的角度检视国际商法在20世纪的发展，最后探讨国际商法在21世纪的发展趋势和我国的相应对策，以期对我国的国际商事法律实践和国际商法学研究有所裨益。

一、国际商法及其产生

（一）国际商法的概念

我国学者对国际商法（International Commercial Law, International Business Law or International Trade Law）概念的理解很不一致。有学者认为，国际商法是调整国际商事交易和国际商事组织的各种法律规范的总称，其渊源包括国际条约、国际惯例和国内法，其范围主要包括代理法、合伙企业法、公司法、外商投资企业法、合同法、买卖法、产品责任法、票据法和国际商事仲裁法。①也有学者认为，国际商法是调整国际商事关系的法律规范的总称，其渊源包括国际商事条约、国际商事惯例和国内法，其范围主要包括合同法、代理法、买卖法、产品责任法、海上货物运输法、海上保险法、票据法、商事组织法、工

① 沈四宝、王军、焦津洪编著：《国际商法》，对外经济贸易大学出版社2002年版，第1~4页及目录。

业产权法和国际商事争端解决程序法。① 上述两种定义基本相同，而且都将国内法作为国际商法的渊源之一，只是在范围上有所不同。

本文从实在法和统一法的观念出发，主张国际商法是调整国际商事关系的统一实体规范和争端解决程序规范的总称。第一，国际商法是实在法，是以国际公约和国际惯例为主要渊源形式并为法院和仲裁机构解决国际商事争议时所适用的法律；它不是存在于理论形态的比较法。第二，国际商法是统一私法，是独立于国内民商法、专门而且统一适用于国际商事关系的法律；国内民商法、国内经济法和国际经济法不属于国际商法的范围。第三，从范围上看，国际商法包括国际商事代理法、国际商事合同通则、国际货物买卖法、国际货物运输法、国际货物运输保险法、国际支付法、国际借贷法、国际融资租赁法、国际投资合同法、国际担保法、国际知识产权保护法、国际知识产权交易法和国际民事诉讼和国际商事仲裁法，因为在这些领域存在统一的国际商事惯例或公约；而在公司法等领域，由于不存在统一的国际商事惯例或公约，因而不属于国际商法的范畴。

国际商法，作为一个法律部门，具有以下特征：

1. 国际商法调整的社会关系是一种商事关系

"商事关系"，指平等商事主体之间的财产关系。平等主体指自然人、法人和非法人企业，财产关系包括商事代理关系、物权关系、知识产权关系和债权关系。婚姻家庭、收养和继承等民事关系不属于国际商法所调整的商事关系的范围。

《联合国国际贸易法委员会国际商事仲裁示范法》对"商事"一词的注释说明是："商事"一词应作广义的理解，以便包括产生于所有具有商事性质关系的事项，无论这种关系是否为合同关系。具有商事性质关系的事项包括但不限于下列交易：任何提供或交换货物或服务的贸易交易；买卖合同；商事代表或代理；保付代理；租赁；咨询；设计；许可；投资；融资；银行；保险；开发协议或特许；合资经营和其他形式的工业或商业合作；客货的航空、海上、铁路或公路运输。我国《仲裁法》第 2 条规定，平等主体的公民、法人和其他组织之间发生的合同纠纷和其他财产权益纠纷，可以仲裁。另外我国在加入 1958 年《承认和执行外国仲裁裁决公约》时对商事争议作了保留，在保留声明中提到，"契约性和非契约性商事法律关系"具体是指：由于合同、侵权或者根据有关法律规定而产生的经济上的权利义务关系，例如货物买卖，财产租赁，工程承包，加工承揽，技术转让，合资经营，合作经营，勘探开发自然资

① 陶凯元主编：《国际商法》，暨南大学出版社 1999 年版，第 1、5 ~ 7 页及目录。

源，保险，信贷，劳务，代理，咨询服务和海上、民用航空、铁路、公路的客货运输以及产品责任，环境污染，海上事故和所有权等，但不包括外国投资者与东道国政府之间的争端。

2. 国际商法调整的社会关系是一种具有国际因素的商事关系

国际商法调整的商事关系具有国际因素。即商事关系的主体、客体或内容至少有一项具有国际因素。商事交易的主体，如果一方、双方或多方具有不同国籍，或其住所、营业所位于不同的国家，即为主体具有国际因素；主体不具有国际因素，但商事关系所指向的标的位于另一国家或产生、变更或消灭商事关系的法律事实发生在另一国家，也可认为具有国际因素。

以上是从广泛意义上来理解国际商事关系的国际性的。这种理解为国际商事仲裁、我国司法实践所认同。1985 年《联合国国际贸易法委员会国际商事仲裁示范法》第 1 条第 3 款规定，国际仲裁包括：1. 营业地在不同国家的当事人之间的争议的仲裁；2. 仲裁地和当事人的营业地位于不同国家的仲裁；3. 主要义务履行地和当事人的营业地位于不同国家的仲裁；4. 与争议标的关系最密切的地点和当事人的营业地位于不同国家的仲裁；5. 当事各方明确同意仲裁标的与一个以上国家有关的仲裁。我国民事诉讼法和仲裁法均未对“国际”或“涉外”作出规定，最高人民法院 1992 年《关于适用〈中华人民共和国民事诉讼法〉若干问题的意见》第 304 条规定，当事人一方或双方是外国人、无国籍人、外国企业或组织，或者当事人之间民事法律关系的设立、变更、终止的法律事实发生在外国，或者诉讼标的物在外国的民事案件，为涉外民事案件。这一解释也可以适用于涉外仲裁。可见，《联合国国际贸易法委员会国际商事仲裁示范法》和我国法律都是从广泛意义上来理解“国际”或“涉外”之含义的。

3. 国际商法仅指调整国际商事关系的统一实体规范和争端解决程序规范，不包括冲突规范，也不包括国内民商法

依据冲突规范确定适用于国际商事关系的国内法，是调整国际商事关系的传统方法。这被称为间接调整方法。国际商法是直接适用于国际商事关系的实体法，它直接规定国际商事主体在国际商事关系中的权利义务，所运用的是一种直接调整方法。国际商法有别于冲突规范，也不同于各国民商法。

（二）国际商法的产生

1. 国际商法于何时产生？

国际商法于何时产生？以何种事件或法律文件的产生为标志？这是一个尚无定论的问题。施米托夫教授将国际商法的发展分为三个阶段：中世纪商人法时期（11～17世纪）；商人法被纳入国内法时期（18～19世纪）；新商人法时期（当代）。而且，即使在第二阶段，商人法也没有完全丧失其国际性，而且其作为商人间的习惯仍然在发挥着作用。① 遗憾的是，他没有具体讨论新商人法时期到底始于何时。

我国国际私法学者在研究统一实体法（与本文所主张的国际商法中的实体法部分基本重合）产生时，一般认为最早的统一实体法产生于19世纪末，并援引当时的知识产权公约作为实例。② 但没有进一步分析产生的标志和产生的原因。

本文认为，国际商法，作为一个独立的法律部门，产生于19世纪末20世纪初，其标志为1919年国际商会的成立。从19世纪末开始，直接规定国际商事交易关系中当事人权利义务的条约和习惯应运而生并逐渐发展。国际商事统一公约首先在知识产权领域产生，具体成果为1883年的《保护工业产权巴黎公约》和1886年的《保护文学艺术作品伯尔尼公约》。1896年国际海事委员会（COMITE MARTIME INTERNATIONAL，CMI）成立，总部设于比利时的安特卫普，由各会员国的国内海事委员会和一些个人会员组成，致力于海事私法的统一。此外，国际法协会（International Law Association，ILA）也把制定统一私法作为其宗旨之一。1919年，第一次世界大战结束后一年，国际商会（International Chamber of Commerce，ICC）成立。该组织总部设在巴黎，由国际商业组织和企业组成，并在众多国家成立分会，主要从事贸易与银行惯例的编纂和研究工作。国际商法在这一时期大量出现，反映了世界市场得以形成这一客观现实的需要。伴随着资本主义进入帝国主义阶段，主要资本主义国家将世界市场瓜分完毕。国际货物买卖、国际直接投资、国际借贷交易空前频繁，这使得运用冲突法解决法律纠纷方法的弊端充分显现，也促使了国际意识的复归。一方面，商人们推动各自的政府制定统一公约进行协调，另一方面，商人们也注意有意识地通过自己的机构来编纂自发形成的惯例。国际商会的成立是商人们国际意识复归和商人们要求国际商事统一法的集中体现。

2. 谁需要国际商法？为什么需要国际商法？

谁需要国际商法？从前面的分析已经清楚，是商人，从事国际商业的商人。这与国际经济法的产生动力是一样的。但国际经济法是经由国际法的途径、通过消除贸易壁垒的方法来实现商人们扩展交易的愿望的。

---

① ［英］施米托夫：《国际贸易法文选》，赵秀文译，中国大百科全书出版社1993年版，第4～24页。

② 韩德培主编：《国际私法新论》，武汉大学出版社1997年版，第10页。

为什么需要国际商法？答案是：商人们希望能像从事国内商业一样，有一套统一的规则，摆脱因适用不同国家的民商法而给国际商业带来的障碍。

传统的通过冲突规范确定适用于国际商事关系的国内法的方法，使商人在从事国际商业时需要面对从事国内商业时所没有的法律障碍，即商人需要同时面对本国和外国民商法。事实上，商人不熟悉外国的民商法，也不可能熟悉多个外国的民商法；他不愿选择他不熟悉的外国民商法；他不知道他的商业行为将受何种法律调整；他担心外国法院处理争议时对本国当事人会有偏袒。因此，由于要面对不同国家的民商法，法律本应有的可预见性和一致性不复存在。法律成了国际商业的障碍。

理想的解决方法当然是创设一套独立于各国民商法的统一适用于国际商业的法律，使商人在从事国际商业时能获得从事国内商业时同样的法律环境：面对一套而不是多套法律制度。正如《联合国国际货物销售合同公约》序言所述及的：采用照顾到不同的社会、经济和法律制度的国际货物销售合同统一规则，将有助于减少国际贸易的法律障碍，促进国际贸易的发展。

如何创设一套独立于各国民商法的统一适用于国际商业的法律呢？由各国制定条约，最后形成全球合同法乃至全球商法，这是一种方法。由商人们借助于法律专业人士的帮助编纂自发形成的规则，也是一种方法。事实上，在商人们的推动下，两种方法都得到了运用。遗憾的是，一个多世纪过去了，今天人类还远没有实现这一目标。

二、国际商法在20世纪的发展

百年沧桑，国际商法在20世纪获得了巨大的发展，国际商法立法机构相继设立，拟定了众多的国际公约、示范法和国际商事惯例；国际商事仲裁备受欢迎，成为解决国际商事纠纷的主要途径；各国法院在审理国际商事案件时也越来越多地适用国际商法，并日益尊重国际商事仲裁。

（一）国际商事立法机构相继成立，民族国家和国际商业组织积极参与国际商事立法活动

在20世纪之前，从事国际商法制定的机构主要有成立于1896年的国际海事委员会（CMI）。进入20世纪，历史见证了多个重要国际商事立法机构的陆续成立。继国际商会成立后，1926年由国际联盟支持，在罗马设立了国际统一私法协会（UNIDROIT），作为一个政府间的国际组织，其宗旨是对协调国

家间私法（尤其是商法）的现实需要和各种方法进行研究，起草各种法律文件。① 可以说其主要任务即是制定统一的国际商法。1945年成立的联合国欧洲经济委员会曾编纂过一些关于特定交易的格式合同。1966年，联合国第21届大会决定成立联合国国际贸易法委员会（UNCITRAL），该组织于1968年正式开始工作，是联合国专门从事统一国际商事立法的机构。此外，一些由商人组成的行业协会，如谷物与饲料贸易协会、国际羊毛织品机构、波罗的海国际航运公会等，也对特定交易制定格式合同。

上述政府间组织和民间组织及其立法工作有以下特点：1. 组织本身都获得了巨大发展，具备了广泛的代表性。这种发展，主要是缘于二战后一大批发展中国家获得独立，其政府加入到上述政府间国际机构，其私人企业加盟民间机构和行业协会。2. 发达国家，尤其是欧洲国家及其商人主导了上述机构的立法活动。如同国际公法曾是欧洲公法一样，国际商法首先也是在欧洲发展起来，逐渐扩展到世界其他地区的；兼之发达国家具有法治传统，立法经验丰富、研究积累深厚、法律专家充足，其占据主导实为不可避免。发达国家中，德、法、意等大陆法系国家以比较法和法律编纂方面的技能见长，而英、美由于其商业实践对世界影响最大也优势明显。3. 立法的方法主要有：起草公约供外交会议通过，制定示范法供各国立法采用，编纂国际商事惯例供商人选择使用。其中，国际商会主要从事惯例的编纂，基本上不从事公约和示范法的起草。UNIDROIT 和 UNCITRAL 都是具有普遍性的国际商法制定机构，并且都运用各种统一法的方法，两者的职能和宗旨是重合的，因而在一定程度上存在相互竞争。但由于两者沟通较好，在立法项目上相互重复的情况并不多见。

20世纪国际商事立法机构的成立为国际商法的发展奠定了制度基础，估计这些制度架构在21世纪不会有大的变化。

（二）国际商事实体法已蔚然大观，初步形成体系

20世纪，国际商事实体法获得了巨大的发展，以国际商事公约、国际商事惯例、普遍性格式合同和示范法为渊源形式的国际商事实体法已形成体系，涵盖了国际商事交易的许多重要领域。1. 国际公约。UNIDROIT、UNCITRAL 和 CMI 制定了关于国际代理、国际货物买卖、国际货物运输、国际支付、国

---

① UNIDROIT, *An Introduction to the UNIDROIT*, 16 September 2002.

际融资租赁的一系列公约。① 2. 国际惯例。ICC、UNIDROIT 和其他机构制定了多种国际惯例，涵盖贸易术语、托收、信用证、国际商事合同的一般规则、海上保险条款、国际保理、国际特许经营等领域。② 关于国际特许经营的惯例，有 UNIDROIT 1998 年制定的《国际特许经营指南》。3. 示范法。在电子商务方面，有 UNCITRAL 1996 年制定的《电子商务示范法》。

上述立法活动有以下特色：1. 国际商事立法机构总是首先在国际商法中选择那些发展成熟的特定领域作为其立法议题，例如，早期在传统议题（如货物买卖、海上运输、贸易术语、票据、信用证等）方面的立法就是如此；同时对于新出现的国际商业交易形式，国际商事立法机构往往也总能作出及时反应。在多式联运、电子商务、国际保理等方面的立法则属此列。2. 从 ICC、UNIDROIT 和 UNCITRAL 所运用的立法方法来看，如前所述 ICC 方法单一，只从事惯例的编纂。UNIDROIT 和 UNCITRAL 在 20 世纪 80 年代中期之前，只进

① 关于国际代理的公约，有 UNIDROIT 1983 年《国际货物销售代理公约》（尚未生效）。关于国际货物买卖的公约有 UNIDROIT 1964 年《国际货物买卖统一法公约》、UNIDROIT 1964 年《国际货物买卖合同成立统一法公约》、UNCITRAL 1980 年《联合国国际货物销售合同公约》（CISG）和 UNCITRAL《联合国国际货物销售时效期限公约》。关于国际货物运输的公约，有 CMI 1924 年《统一提单的若干法律规则的国际公约》（海牙规则）、1968 年《有关修改统一提单若干法律规则的国际公约的议定书》（维斯比规则）、UNCITRAL 1978 年《联合国海上货物运输公约》（汉堡规则）、1929 年《统一国际航空运输某些规则的公约》（华沙公约）、1955 年《修改华沙公约的议定书》（海牙议定书）、1961 年《统一非缔约承运人所办国际航空运输某些规则以补充华沙公约的公约》（瓜达拉哈拉公约）、1952 年《国际铁路货物联运协定》（国际货协）、1961 年《关于铁路货物运输的国际公约》（国际货约）、1980 年 UNCITRAL《联合国国际货物多式联运公约》（尚未生效）。关于国际支付的公约，有 1930 年《汇票、本票统一法公约》、1930 年《统一支票法公约》、UNCITRAL 1988 年《联合国国际汇票与国际本票公约》（尚未生效）和 1988 年《UNIDROIT 国际保理公约》。关于融资租赁的公约，有 1988 年《UNIDROIT 国际融资租赁公约》。

② 关于国际商事合同的一般规则，有《UNIDROIT 国际商事合同通则》（1994 年）。关于国际货物买卖的惯例，有 ICC 1936 年制定的《国际贸易术语解释通则》（INCOTERMS，现行文本为 2000 年文本）、联合国欧洲经济委员会制定的格式合同、各种国际贸易协会制定的格式合同。关于国际货物运输及保险的惯例，有波罗的海国际航运公会制定的《统一杂货租船合同》、《贸发会议/国际商会多式联运单证规则》、伦敦保险协会 1912 年制定的《协会货物条款》（现行文本为 1982 年修订本）。关于国际支付的惯例，有 ICC 1967 年制定的《托收统一规则》（现行文本为 1995 年修订本）、ICC 1933 年制定的《跟单信用证统一惯例》（UCP，现行文本为 1993 年修订本）、国际保理商联合会 1988 年制定的《国际保理惯例守则》（现行文本为 1997 年修订本）。关于国际特许经营的惯例，有 UNIDROIT 1998 年制定的《国际特许经营指南》。

行国际公约的制定，但此后，都开始重视惯例或示范法等软法的制定，UNIDROIT 制定了《UNIDROIT 国际商事合同通则》，使其声名大振。UNCITRAL 也制定了很有影响的《电子商务示范法》。这表明了国际商事立法机构在立法方式上的一种重大转变。3. 上述公约和惯例中，以 INCOTERMS、UCP、CISG、《海牙规则》和《UNIDROIT 国际商事合同通则》影响最为深远。UCP 规定了银行处理跟单信用证业务的详尽规则，现已为世界各国银行采用，可以说已由国际惯例变成了国际商事习惯。INCOTERMS 对买卖双方在交货、风险转移等方面的义务分 13 种情形作了明确的规定，除北美外，世界其他各国的商人已普遍将其用于国际货物买卖合同的谈判和履行。CISG 统一了关于国际货物买卖合同的订立和双方权利义务的规定，已为世界上 50 多个国家所接受，其中包括除英国和日本之外的所有贸易大国。《海牙规则》为海上承运人规定了强制性义务，为绝大多数海运国家所接受。《UNIDROIT 国际商事合同通则》试图创设一套专门规范国际商事合同的规则体系。4. 国际商事立法出现了一种“非国内化”趋势。例如，《联合国国际货物销售合同公约》第 9 条就规定，合同当事人应被视为已默示同意：普遍接受的国际惯例适用于他们之间的合同。这意味着，国际惯例应优先于公约本身和国内法的适用。依据《UNIDROIT 国际商事合同通则》的规定，通则在两种情形下可作为国际商事合同所适用的法律。一是当事人明示选择时。① 另一种情形是当事人选择“一般法律原则”、“国际商事惯例和习惯”或“商人法”作为合同所适用的法律时。② 这开辟了一条使国际商事合同真正摆脱国内法的道路。如果它能像 UCP 那样获得全球认同，就能成为调整各类国际商事合同的全球统一法。从其公布以来在学术界、商业界、法院和仲裁庭所引起的积极反应来看，这种前景是有

---

① 通则认为，通则代表一种合同法规则体系，这些规则为各国现存法律体系所普遍采用，或者最能适应国际商事交易的特殊要求，因此，当事人有理由明确选择通则作为其合同的适用法，以替代选择某一国内法。通则建议当事人在明示选择通则时，最好与仲裁条款一同使用。因为在仲裁中，如果当事人授权仲裁员根据“公平及善意原则”裁决，仲裁员当然可以依据当事人所选择的通则作为适用的法律；即便没有此一授权，允许仲裁员依据国内法之外的法律规则作出裁决也是一种发展趋势。但如果由法院审理，法院可能不认可这一选择。

② 通则认为，在这种情况下，为避免或尽量减少此类模糊概念给确定合同内容带来的不确定性，最好是求助于一套系统和界定明确的规则，如通则。

可能实现的。①

（三）国际商事争端解决富有成效

国际商法的自治性要求争端解决的自治性，因此商人们更愿意选择自治性争端解决途径——国际商事仲裁，当他们不得不运用国际诉讼时，他们又希望各国法院能够尊重和适用国际商事规则，而不是适用国内法。

1. 国际商事仲裁成为解决国际商事纠纷的主要途径。20 世纪，苏黎士机构商会仲裁院、瑞典斯德哥尔摩商会仲裁院、国际商会仲裁院、美国仲裁协会、中国国际经济贸易仲裁委员会相继于 1911 年、1917 年、1923 年、1926 年和 1956 年成立。这些仲裁机构，加上 1892 年成立的伦敦仲裁院等机构，构成了当今世界主要的仲裁机构。它们每年受理国际商事案件 4000 件左右；②此外，还有更多的国际商事案件通过临时仲裁解决。国际商事仲裁成为解决国际商事纠纷的主要途径。

2. 各国均确认仲裁协议之排除法院管辖的效力，同时承认仲裁条款的独立性和仲裁庭对自身管辖权的裁定权。大陆法系国家，在 19 世纪就确认仲裁协议排除法院管辖。英美法系国家则长期坚持“法院管辖权不容剥夺”的原则。1925 年美国《联邦仲裁法》规定，法院有义务应当事人依据仲裁协议提出的中止诉讼的请求而中止诉讼，从而改变了奉行已久的原则。英国 1979 年《仲裁法》也确认了仲裁协议排除法院管辖的效力。1923 年日内瓦《仲裁条款议定书》和 1958 年《承认和执行外国仲裁裁决公约》（简称 1958 年《纽约公

---

① 通则的广泛影响体现在：1. 对学术界的影响。围绕通则，已有不胜枚举的国际学术会议召开，发表了大量的学术论文和专著，而且通则已进入了很多国家大学法学院的课堂。2. 作为示范法的影响。荷兰新民法典的制定、加拿大魁北克新民法典的制定、德国债法的修订、俄罗斯民法典的制定、爱沙尼亚新债法的起草、立陶宛民法典的制定、捷克民法典的制定、美国统一商法典买卖编的修订、中国合同法的制定、阿根廷新民法典的制定都借鉴或参考了通则的有关规定。3. 对商业界的影响。根据 UNIDROIT 的一项调查，在对调查作出回答的被调查者中，近 2/3 的被调查者在合同谈判中使用了通则的条款；1/4 的被调查者选择通则作为合同的准据法；合同类型涉及买卖、商事代理和经销、建筑工程、运输和保险等。4. 在仲裁和诉讼中的运用。根据 UNIDROIT 的一项调查，至 1997 年，当事人、法官或仲裁员已在数百件案件中使用了通则的规定，以某种方式适用了通则规定的法院判决和仲裁裁决超过了 50 件。本脚注上述内容转引自 Michael J. Bonell, *An International Restatement of Contract Law: the UNIDROIT Principles of International Commercial Contracts*, 2nd, ed. Transnational Publishers Inc. 1997, pp. 231-254.

② 赵健：《国际商事仲裁的司法监督》，法律出版社 2000 年版，第 61 页，脚注 31。

约》）均确认仲裁协议排除法院管辖的效力。

3. 1958 年《纽约公约》缔结后，先后有一百多个国家参加，其中包括所有在仲裁和国际经济交往中的重要国家。这些参加国的法院均有义务承认和执行另一参加国仲裁庭的裁决，这使得国际商事仲裁在执行力上拥有了法院诉讼无法比拟的优势。

4. 各国法院一般均对国际商事仲裁进行各种必要的支持，如协助当事人指定仲裁员，协助当事人或仲裁庭取证，采取财产保全措施，等等。

5. 1976 年，《UNCITRAL 仲裁规则》问世，其后为许多仲裁中心和仲裁机构所采用。1985 年《UNCITRAL 国际商事仲裁示范法》通过，该示范法反映了国际商事仲裁领域的最新发展，吸收了国内和国际仲裁立法的先进成果，较好地平衡了当事人意思自治和法院的司法监督，对各国制定和改进其仲裁立法产生了深远影响。1958 年《纽约公约》、1976 年《UNCITRAL 仲裁规则》和 1985 年《UNCITRAL 国际商事仲裁示范法》使国际商事仲裁法趋于统一。

（四）国际商法学在欧美成为一门独立的法律学科

20 世纪国际商法的巨大发展给法学研究也带来了显著的变化。一部分商法学者和国际法学者专注于国际商事条约和惯例的各种专题和综合研究，成为一个新的法学职业研究群体——国际商法学者，而他们所研究的国际商法也成了一门新的学科。欧美法学院和商学院普遍开设了国际商法的课程，在教材方面则出现了以“国际商法”、“国际贸易法”、“国际商事交易”、“出口贸易”为名称的新教科书。教材中，最早的是施米托夫教授的《出口贸易：国际贸易的法律与实务》（1948 年），20 世纪 60 年代，在法国、苏联和美国也出现了同样类型的教科书，如法国教授 Philippe Kahn 所著《国际商业买卖》（1961 年），苏联学者 D. M. Genkin 的教材《苏联对外贸易和法律调整》（1961 年），美国 W. S. Surrey 和 C. Shaw 合著的《国际商事交易法律指南》（1963 年）。①

学者们在国际商法的研究中，还逐渐形成了不同的学术流派。其中以施米托夫的“新商人法理论”和法国学者古德曼（Goldman）的“商人自治法理论”影响最大。值得一提的是，学者们的学术研究对国际商法的发展也产生了推动作用。例如，联合国国际贸易法委员会就是在施米托夫等学者的大力推动下成立的，国际统一私法协会的《国际商事合同通则》的制定和修订也是在学者的支持和参与下完成的。

---

① ［英］施米托夫：《国际贸易法文选》，赵秀文译，中国大百科全书出版社 1993 年版，第 30 页。

三、国际商法在21世纪的发展趋势

（一）受经济全球化的推动国际商法仍将获得巨大发展

国际商法的产生，是商事交易国际化达到一定程度的结果，国际商法的发展，取决于国际商事交易在广度和深度上的拓展。20世纪最后20年左右开始的经济全球化使得国际商事交易空前活跃，极大地促进了国际商法的发展。但20世纪只是经济全球化的初级阶段，在21世纪，经济全球化进程由于各种合力将持续推进，进而实现全球经济的高度一体化，促进世界经济的巨大增长。首先，新兴市场的成长将为世界经济的发展开辟广阔的前景。中国经济在21世纪上半期可能成为世界第一大经济，印度的经济规模在21世纪将空前膨胀，在东南亚、拉丁美洲，也会孕育出若干较大的新兴市场（如印度尼西亚、巴西），这将从根本上改变世界经济地理景观，空前增加世界经济的总量。① 这一进程必然伴随着国际商事交易的极大拓展。其次，科技进步将为世界经济的发展奠定坚实的技术基础。在21世纪，新技术革命的浪潮将一浪高过一浪，生生不息。生物技术的发展将促进农业的发展，新材料的采用、新资源的开发将为制造业提供无尽的原料，信息技术的发展和普及将提高所有产业的效益。总之，科技进步将确保新兴市场的成长和壮大，为人类创造无穷的物质财富。最后，全球和区域贸易体制的有效运转将促进国际贸易的扩大和世界经济的增长。从1948年到1994年，GATT的成功运作大大削减了各种贸易壁垒，扩大了世界贸易。WTO自1995年运转以来，积极致力于实现农产品贸易自由化、扩大服务贸易和解决成员间的争议，取得了明显的实效。相信WTO在21世纪会持续稳定地推动国际贸易自由化。在区域贸易一体化方面，各主要经济体的发展势头都很强劲。欧盟迅速东扩，按照2000年12月签订的《尼斯条约》，到2010年欧盟的成员将扩大到27个，至2004年5月1日欧盟成员已扩大到25国。美国计划建立一个包括所有美洲国家的美洲自由贸易区。中国政府2001年表示，将在10年内建立中国—东盟自由贸易区。这预示着在21世纪全球和区域贸易自由化程度将不断提高，从而为世界经济增长提供动力。

---

① 按照世界银行的一项预测，按照购买力平价计算到2020年世界排名前十五位的经济体依次是：中国、美国、日本、印度、印度尼西亚、德国、韩国、泰国、法国、中国台湾地区、巴西、意大利、俄罗斯、英国和墨西哥。本脚注上述内容转引自：Charles W. Kegley and Eugene R. Wittkopf, *World Politics: Trend and Transformation*, 7th edition, Worth Publishers, 1999, at 99.

世界经济的巨大增长必然伴随着国际商事交易数量上的增多、密度上的增强和方式上的增加。与此相适应，为国际商事交易确立统一规则并提供可预见性的国际商法也将获得大的发展。首先，尽管国际商法在20世纪已获得巨大发展，初步形成体系，但由于一些国家对发展国际商法的重要性认识不够或者参与不充分，一些重要领域（如国际借贷、国际证券交易等）的法律还没有制定出来，一些国际公约（如《联合国国际汇票与国际本票公约》、《国际货物销售代理公约》等）一直未能生效，这就需要制定或修订有关公约并积极使其生效，或制定相应的国际惯例。其次，随着国际商事交易的数量增多、密度增强，原来立法要求不迫切的领域现在变得迫切了，这也需要制定新的公约或惯例。再次，随着新的商业交易形式的出现和发展，同样需要制定新的公约和惯例。

施米托夫教授认为，国际商法的出现和发展是20世纪最重要的法律发展之一。① 20世纪末和21世纪初的形势使我们有理由相信在21世纪国际商法仍会有巨大发展，并成为人类法律实践中最为活跃的领域之一。

（二）国际商法的“非国内化”和“全球化”趋势将日益显著

国际商法，是作为冲突法的对立面产生的，其目的是要确立一套专门适用于国际商事交易的规则，并统一适用于全球范围内的国际商事交易，从而消除因各国民商法的差异而给国际商业造成的障碍。因此，国际商法从产生那一天起，就内在地要求通过全球化而在世界范围内获得普遍适用性，通过非国内化而成为一套不同于国内民商法的独立规则体系。

确立一套不同于国内民商法的、专门适用于国际商事交易的独立规则体系，即国际商法，是一个艰苦而漫长的过程。各国的民商法都凝练了本国的民族传统和习惯，并深深地影响着各国的法律职业人士。现在需要由这些带着本国民商法烙印的法律职业人士，通过比较研究，通过体认国际商业实践的需要，创设一套不同于各国民商法、又能为各国所接受并在各国的国际商事交易中适用的规则体系，其所付出的艰辛可想而知！还有，如何保证各国仲裁员和法官统一适用国际商法也是一个大难题。各国仲裁员和法官在处理案件时，很容易以本国法的概念和逻辑来解释国际统一法，这将使国际统一立法的效果大打折扣。由于不存在统一的解释机构，目前避免上述司法不协调现象的方法只能是在仲裁员和法官之间就如何一致地解释和适用国际商法进行尽可能广泛的

① ［英］施米托夫：《国际贸易法文选》，赵秀文译，中国大百科全书出版社1993年版，第2页。

交流。

20世纪国际商法初成体系，使国际商法的非国内化进程也清晰可辨。但是，初成体系与完整体系的建立，尚有较大距离；而且如何实现各国在适用国际商法上的一致性，更需要制度创新和漫长积累。这都是历史交给21世纪的使命。

已制定出来的国际商法要在世界范围内获得普遍适用性，也是一个艰苦而漫长的过程。国际商法，目前是由数以十计的国际公约和国际惯例构成的，每一个公约或惯例都要独立地获得自己的普遍适用性，其总和才构成国际商法的整体普适性。20世纪的经验表明，一项公约或惯例要想获得普遍接受是很不容易的，往往是漫长而艰难的。CISG，作为最成功的公约之一，迄今仍有包括英国和日本在内的许多国家尚未加入。在21世纪，随着经济全球化进程的进一步推进，各国将会更认同国际商法的作用，从而在加入国际商事公约或接受国际惯例上持更为积极的态度。因此，可以预期，20世纪的重要国际商事立法将被广泛接受。例如，更多的国家，不排除英国和日本，将加入CISG；《UNIDROIT国际商事合同通则》将有可能被世界各国的商人所接受，并被法院和仲裁庭视为国际惯例，乃至国际习惯。同样，21世纪新的国际商事立法也将较容易获得广泛接受。

（三）国际商事立法的方法仍为实证和推理两种，但以实证的方法为主

在法律制定的方法上，始终存在推理方法和实证方法的分野。① 推理的方法认为，立法过程必须是推理的，必须以理性为依据；立法者依据理性来决定现有规则的存废，立法者也可以依据理性制定其认为合理的新规则；制定出来的法律应是清晰并符合逻辑的规则体系。实证的方法则认为，立法只是把现有的调整人类社会关系的法律规则整合为一体，即将经验世界中存在的实在法编纂成简明、易懂和更容易为当事人接受的体系。尽管在现实中，推理的方法也要考虑实在法，实证的方法也需运用推理，但两者的根本取向是明显不同的。国内立法中，法国、德国的民商法典是推理方法的典范，美国《统一商法典》则是实证方法的实例。在20世纪的国际商事立法中，ICC的INCOTERMS和UCP、《UNIDROIT国际商事合同通则》和《海牙规则》显然是运用实证方法的结果，CISG的制定主要也是运用实证的方法，而《汉堡规则》则是推理方法的产物。

---

① ［英］施米托夫：《国际贸易法文选》，赵秀文译，中国大百科全书出版社1993年版，第280~282页。

从被接受的程度或态势来看，INCOTERMS、UCP 和《海牙规则》获得了广泛的接受，《UNIDROIT 国际商事合同通则》自 1994 年公布以来颇受欢迎，呈现出很好的态势，而旨在取代《海牙规则》的 1978 年《汉堡规则》迄今仍未能获得广泛接受。这表明了推理方法的失败和实证方法的相对成功。背后的原因是：国际商法是私法，当事人意思自治是首要原则；法律源于商人的商业实践，源于法官、仲裁员对商业惯例的解释和适用，同时经编纂的法律又要由商人认可和接受；只有反映商业实践真实面貌和需要的法律才会被接受；符合理性（事实上往往是内国民商法的法律理性）但背离商业实践的立法将会成为一纸空文。

因此，可以认为，在 21 世纪实证的方法将占主导，但推理在特定情形下仍将发挥作用。

（四）国际商事立法的形式仍将体现为公约和惯例两大类，但惯例的作用将更为突出

如前所述，在 20 世纪 80 年代以前，国际公约是国际商法的主要形式，但自那以来，国际惯例日益成为国际商事立法的主要形式。这种趋势在 21 世纪还将持续下去。如果说，20 世纪是国际商事公约的世纪，那么，21 世纪将是国际商事惯例的世纪。

国际商事公约作为国际商法的渊源，有利有弊。其优点在于对缔约国具有确定的法律约束力，缔约国往往还通过并入或转化的方法使其成为国内法的一部分，从而由本国法院或仲裁庭在具体的案件中适用。但其弊端也颇多。一是谈判艰难且统一程度有限，各国在谈判时需要对各国民商法的相应规定做取舍、妥协和调和，各国都希望本国的法律概念、原则和规则得到更多的体现和尊重，这使得谈判经常是艰难异常；即使能达成一致，通常也是一个各国法律的公分母，或者是一个充满模糊性条款的协议；① 二是其生效较难，许多经过艰苦谈判、耗费大量人力物力的公约由于批准国有限而未能生效；三是缔约国的数量往往有限，仅仅在缔约国之间实现法律的统一；四是修改困难，有时不能适应国际商事实践发展的需要；五是即便进行修改，又同样面临生效难、参加国有限的问题，即便生效，也会由于一部分其前身条约的参加国参加新公

---

① Loukas Mistelis, "*Is Harmonization a Necessary Evil?: the Future of Harmonization and New Sources of International Trade Law*", (Ian Fletcher, Loukas Mistelis and Marise Cremona eds), *Foundations and Perspectives of International Trade Law*, London: Sweet &Maxwell, 2001, at 22.

约，另一部分则选择留在前身条约，而导致该法律领域出现支离破碎的情形。

国际商事惯例作为国际商法的渊源，则具有明显的优点。首先，国际商事惯例主要是运用实证方法的结果，其内容能反映和满足现实国际商业实践的特定需要，具备公平合理性和明确性。其次，国际商事惯例由商人接受而产生约束力，不需要繁杂的批准和生效过程。再次，可以通过各国商人的认同和接受，获得普遍性。最后，国际商事惯例可随国际商业的变化由国际商事立法机构定期修改，从而维持其先进性。

基于以上理由，可以相信，在21世纪，国际商事惯例将成为国际商法的主流。

（五）国际商事立法的协调性、均衡性将会加强

在20世纪60年代成立的UNCITRAL曾与其他在此之前已经存在的机构（如CMI、UNIDROIT）在工作主题上出现重复，并有取代后者的倾向。例如，UNCITRAL制定《汉堡规则》，准备以之取代CMI主拟的《海牙规则》；UNCITRAL制定《联合国国际货物销售合同公约》以取代UNIDROIT制定的两个《海牙公约》。但是，其他机构在后来的实践中证明了自身的存在价值。ICC继续在编纂商业惯例方面发挥重要作用，UNIDROIT通过制定《国际商事合同通则》以及保理、融资租赁等公约巩固了自己作为一般性国际商事立法机构的地位，CMI也仍然在海商立法方面发挥积极作用。而且这些机构在制定法律文件时，都注意与其他机构已制定的立法保持协调，并在选择立法主题上尽量避免与其他机构重复。在21世纪，多个国际商事立法机构仍将长期并存，立法机构的相互协调问题将更加突出。因为，一方面随着立法活动的深入，各立法机构的专业界限渐趋模糊，重复选题的可能性日趋增大；另一方面，各立法机构为获得更多的资源，加强自己的地位，都会竞相选择最热门、最富价值的领域作为自己的工作议题，也会人为地造成重复。因此，加强立法机构的相互协调，以避免不必要的资源浪费和不同立法之间的冲突，在21世纪势在必行。

在20世纪的国际商事立法中，各种力量的影响很不平衡。发达国家，尤其是欧洲和美国，主导了国际商事立法，发展中国家的影响十分微弱。这在一定程度上也使得已制定的某些法律具有某些方面的不平衡性，在发达国家企业的利益与发展中国家企业的利益出现冲突时，国际商事立法会更多地顾及发达国家企业的利益。在21世纪，随着中国、印度和其他发展中国家的兴起，随着其企业影响力的增强、法制的完备、法学的发达和法律专业人士水平的跃升，它们对国际商事立法的影响将逐渐增大。大陆法系、普通法系、中华法

系、日本法系、印度法系、伊斯兰法系均将对国际商事立法产生实质影响，国际商事立法的过程和结果将更为平衡。

（六）国际商法的领域将扩广，将新订和修订一大批国际商事法律文件

1. 一般分析

20世纪国际商事立法成果，尚未完全覆盖所有的商事交易领域，新的国际商事交易方式也会不断出现，当这些交易活动足够复杂和成熟，需要有法律规则来调整、或需要进行系统性编纂时，就应制定新的国际商法。例如，电子商务的法律问题，随着电子商务在全球的日益推广和技术上的成熟，制定更为全面的立法将变得迫切。又如，随着资本市场的日益发展，跨国证券交易活动越来越频繁，制定相应的法律规则也势在必行。

现有的国际公约和惯例，有的已经过时或部分过时，需要废除，或以新法律来取代。例如，海牙规则自1924年制定以来，一直是调整国际海上货物运输的主要公约，但是近80年的形势变化，已使得该公约所确立的承运人责任制度需要加以变革。可以预期，在汉堡规则难以获得普遍接受的既成事实下，国际社会将会制定一部新的公约。①

有的公约和惯例，随着时间的推移和形势的变化，也需要不断进行修订。例如，ICC的INCOTERMS和UCP，在20世纪最后20多年里，基本上是以10年为期进行修订，如果这种趋势得以维持，在21世纪，上述两个重要惯例也将进行10次左右的修订。

2. 近期立法课题

在UNCITRAL，6个工作组正在积极从事有关立法工作。其中，私人融资基础设施工程工作组正制定关于私人融资的基础设施工程的示范法，该示范法制定出来后，将对UNCITRAL 2001年的《UNCITRAL私人融资基础设施工程法律指南》起补充作用。国际仲裁和调解工作组2002年完成了《UNCITRAL国际商事调解示范法》，现正制定关于临时保护措施和书面仲裁协议构成要件的文件。运输法工作组正在起草一份关于国际货物运输的法律文件。电子商务工作组在2001年完成《UNCITRAL电子签名示范法》后，正在考虑在国际票据领域发展电子商务的法律障碍问题。破产法工作组正在准备一项破产法立法指南。担保权益工作组则正在准备关于担保权益的立法指南。

---

① Francesco Berlingieri, *A New Convention on the Carriage of Goods by Sea: Port-to-Port or Door-to-Door?* 1-2 *Uniform Law Review* (2003), at 265; Zuo Haicong, *A Call for the Restoration of Contractual Freedom in Cargo Shipping*, 1-2 *Uniform Law Review* (2003), at 309-318.

UNIDROIT 的成员国大会于 2001 年 12 月的第 55 次会议上通过了 2002～2004 年度的工作计划。依据该计划，UNIDROIT 近期的立法重点有 5 个方面。一是移动设备的国际利益。UNIDORIT 已于 2001 年制定了《移动设备国际利益公约》和《关于航空设备具体事项的议定书》并已获通过。UNIDROIT 现正对海运、公路运输等其他运输方式所涉及的运输工具制定议定书。二是《UNIDROIT 国际商事合同通则》的修订。该修订工作已经在 2004 年完成。三是关于特许经营的示范法。自 1998 年公布《国际特许经营指南》以来，特许经营研究组一直准备一项关于特许经营披露的示范法。该示范法的草案已经起草完毕，并于 2002 年 9 月提交执行理事会审查。四是相互联结的跨国资本市场的交易。该立法将特别关注下列问题：为证券的取得确立清晰和一致的规则，尤其是针对通过经纪人在多层控股公司间接持有证券；创造一个标准化的全球股票（global shares）；发展能够促进新兴市场证券交易的规则；发展适用于所谓“非当地化”交易的协调或统一规则；考察对世界范围的收购要约制定规则的需要性和可行性。研究组已于 2002 年 9 月举行了第一次会议。五是跨国民事诉讼的原则和规则。该项工作预计在 2004 年完成。①

UNCITRAL 和 UNIDROIT 的上述工作计划基本决定了在未来 20 年左右国际商法的立法重点，各国政府、实务界和学术界可围绕上述课题进行研究，未雨绸缪。

（七）国际商事纠纷解决的非国内化趋势和自治趋势将更为显著，国际商事诉讼制度可能获得突破性发展

在 21 世纪，随着国际商法向全球化和非国内化方向发展，国际商事纠纷解决的非国内化趋势和自治趋势将更为显著。一方面，国际商事仲裁将会向普遍适用国际商法而不是国内法的方向发展，同时还会得到国内法院更多的司法协助。另一方面，各国法院也会基于促进本国对外经济贸易的需要和对国际商事纠纷的国际性和独特性的体认，普遍适用国际商法而不是国内法来解决国际商事纠纷。

21 世纪国际商事诉讼制度可能获得突破性发展。目前已有两种建立世界性商事诉讼制度的方案在准备之中。第一种方案由海牙国际私法协会制定，旨在制定世界范围内关于管辖权和民商事领域外国判决的承认与执行的公约，但谈判国对此存在根本性的分歧。第二种方案是由美国法学会和国际统一私法协会发起的计划，准备制定一项《跨国民事诉讼原则和规则》，这一立法旨在为

① UNIDROIT, *An Introduction to the UNIDROIT*, 16 September 2002.

有效审理跨国民事诉讼案件确立坚实基础（该立法仅限于审理阶段，即管辖权问题已经解决但判决的承认与执行尚未开始之间的阶段），并确保具有不同国籍、位于不同住所地和居所地的所有当事人获得公正待遇。这两种方案是相互补充和支持的，第一种方案的实现显然要困难一些，第二种方案相对而言较容易完成。但无论如何，只要有一种方案得以完成，并获得国际社会的广泛采纳，都将是国际商事诉讼制度的重大突破，且将有力地促进国际商法的发展。

（八）一般性结论

如同任何其他预测一样，对国际商法的发展趋势会有乐观和悲观两种预测，而且与对世界和平及发展的前景预测相关联。悲观主义者从“新帝国”理论、文明冲突理论的出笼，从纽约世贸大厦的倒塌及阿富汗、中东的硝烟，或许会认为21世纪将是一个充满冲突、动荡和战争的世纪，世界经济不会有大的发展，国际商法的前景也将是一片暗淡；或者纯粹从法律的角度看，认为由于国际社会和国际商业社会无法形成共识，由于缺乏强有力的国际立法机构，加上人们对国际商事立法方法和工具的种种不同认识，21世纪国际商法的前景也不容乐观。乐观主义者则会认为，全球政治均衡和多极化将会逐步确立并得以维持，经济全球化趋势不可逆转，世界经济将得到前所未有的发展，国际商法必将获得大的发展并趋向完善。

笔者同意第二种对世界和平和发展前景的预测，对国际商法的前景持一种审慎乐观的态度。从法律层面看，由于20世纪国际商法的大发展已经为国际商法的进一步发展奠定了较为坚实的制度架构，积累了丰富的经验，留下了有益的借鉴或教训，国际商法可以，也应该获得更大的发展。我们有理由相信，在21世纪，人们会更多地运用编纂的方法，更多地采用国际惯例等软法的形式来制定国际商法，以更好地体现国际商法的自治性；国际商法，作为一套与各国民商法相区别的独立规则体系，将为世界各国商人普遍采用；法官和仲裁员将更趋向于以非国内化的方式统一解释和适用非国内化和全球化的国际商法。

四、中国在理论与实务上的对策

自改革开放以来，我国在国际商事立法和司法方面的实践情况大致如下：

1. 国际商事立法。我国主要由国务院外经贸主管部门所属条法司参加在UNIDROIT和UNCITRAL的活动，我国是UNIDROIT 59个成员之一，并且是理事会成员。我国也是UNCITRAL 36个成员之一。我国积极参加了上述机构的主要立法活动，包括（但不限于）《联合国国际货物销售合同公约》、《联合国国际货物多式联运公约》、《联合国国际汇票与国际本票公约》、《UNIDROIT 国际保理公约》、《UNIDROIT 国际融资租赁公约》、《UNIDROIT 国际商事合同通则》等重要公约和惯例的制定。我国也是国际商会的国家会员国之一，并成立了国际商会中国国家委员会，该委员会在国际商会修订 UCP 和 INCOTERMS 的过程中提出了自己的建议。我国在上述立法活动中，致力于维护发展中国家的利益，致力于达成使当事人利益趋于平衡的规则，为国际商法的发展作出了自己的贡献。2. 国际商事公约的加入。我国加入了《联合国国际货物销售合同公约》、《国际海上避碰规则公约》、《统一国际航空运输某些规则的公约》等国际公约，依据我国《民法通则》的规定，在上述国际条约的规定与国内民商法的规定不相同时，我国法院应优先适用国际公约的规定。3. 国际商事惯例的采纳和确立。我国贸易公司、运输公司、保险公司、银行在商业实践中广泛采用一些具有普遍性的国际惯例，如 INCOTERMS、UCP 等；同时，也通过制定自己的格式合同、格式提单、格式保险条款，确立自己的商业惯例。4. 国内涉外商事立法。我国民事基本法《民法通则》不仅规定了我国参加或缔结的国际商事条约的优先地位，同时也规定，在国际公约和国内法没有规定的情况下，可以适用国际商事惯例，从而确立了国际商事惯例的辅助渊源地位。我国《海商法》、《票据法》和《合同法》的制定也较为充分地参照了国际公约和国际惯例。例如，我国《海商法》关于海上货物运输合同承运人责任的规定，就借鉴了海牙规则、维斯比规则和汉堡规则的相关规定；我国《合同法》第 402 条和第 403 条就借鉴了《UNIDROIT 国际货物销售代理公约》的相关规定。① 5. 涉外商事诉讼和国际商事仲裁。我国很早就将涉外商事审判与国内民商事审判分别对待，并建立了较为独立的海事审判体系。我国法院受理和审结了大量的涉外商事案件，为国际商事交易的顺利进行提供了有力的法律保障。我国涉外仲裁机构也仲裁了大量的涉外商事案件，成为世界上受理案件数量最多的国际商事仲裁机构之一。

但是，与欧美发达国家成熟和占主流的实践相比，再考量 21 世纪国际商法的发展趋势，我国的国际商事立法和司法实践还有相当的差距要弥补，还有诸多的问题要解决。

---

① 参见左海聪：《国际经济法的理论与实践》，武汉大学出版社 2003 年版，第 241 ~ 247 页。

（一）顺应国际商事立法过程均衡性加强的趋势，重视和加强对国际商事立法活动的参与

如前所述，在21世纪，在国际商事立法过程中，中国、印度和其他发展中国家对国际商事立法的影响将逐渐增大，各大法系均将对国际商事立法产生实质影响，国际商事立法的过程和结果将更为平衡。我国作为发展中国家中人口最多、经济规模最大、法律制度自成一体的国家，应该也能够在国际商事立法中逐渐发挥建设性作用。为此，我国可以考虑采取以下措施：1. 建立我国立法、行政、司法机关协调参加国际商事立法活动的机制。现行体制下，我国立法和司法机关基本不参与国际商事立法机构的活动。但是，我国加入的国际商事公约是我国法院直接适用的法律，国际商事惯例是我国法院可以适用的辅助法律渊源，一些国际商事公约、惯例、示范法对我国立法机关制定相应的国内法具有直接的影响或重要的参考价值，因此，立法和司法机关参与国际商事立法活动，并与行政机关协调行动，对制定符合我国利益的国际商事公约、惯例、示范法以及批准国际商事公约和在我国适用有关公约和惯例，是十分有益和必要的。立法、行政、司法机关协调参与国际商事立法活动，应有制度化的机制，该机制应明确上述机构在准备提案、参与起草谈判、参与外交会议的职权范围和合作方式及内容。此外，这一协调机制还应适当考虑企业界和学术界的参与问题。2. 加大我国参与国际商事立法活动的力度。目前，我国对国际商事立法进程的影响有限，这与我国投入的人力和物力不足有一定关系。我国目前参与国际商事立法机构活动的人员主要限于商务部条法司的法律官员，人数十分有限，而国际立法机构在同一时间内准备的国际商事公约、惯例、示范法通常在十件以上，这使得我国很难有效地参与所有的国际商事立法活动。建立立法、司法、行政机关协调参与的机制能解决部分问题。重要的是加大人力和物力的投入，确保我国能实质性地参与所有国际商事公约、惯例和示范法的准备、谈判和通过。3. 推动和加强对拟议中的国际商事公约、惯例和示范法的研究。国际商事公约、惯例、示范法的制定是专业性极强的工作，每项公约、惯例、示范法的起草、谈判和通过都需要比较各国的相关立法、判例和学说，提炼和反映国际商业实践的一般做法。如果没有充分的研究，在提出合理的议案、反驳或支持他国的议案、达成一致意见方面，就难以有所作为。因此，必须加强和推动相关的研究工作。不仅我国立法、司法、行政机关的相关工作人员要加强有针对性的研究，上述机构还可以委托我国高校和研究所进行专项研究或进行合作研究，国家社会科学基金和各部委研究基金也可以对相关课题的研究进行倾斜。

（二）顺应国际商法全球化的趋势，积极加入国际公约和采纳国际惯例

全球化的经济要求全球化的国际商法，国际商法必将成为各国商人广泛采用的全球规则。① 我国不仅要积极参与国际商法的制定，更要积极加入国际公约和采纳国际惯例，推动国际商法全球化进程。1. 对于已经缔结或生效的国际商事公约，我国要加强研究加入的利弊。如果在研究后认为利大于弊，则应适时加入。对于那些已为大多数国家接受的公约，更要加快研究和批准的进程。例如，UNIDROIT 关于国际保理和国际融资租赁的公约，现已生效，其内容是对若干容易引起冲突的法律问题的协调，且与我国的民商立法并无明显冲突，我国可以考虑在研究后适时加入。又如，如果一项新的国际海上货物运输公约缔结，且反映了我国的意愿和利益，我国可以积极促成公约的生效，并加入公约。2. 对于那些公平合理、被普遍接受的国际惯例，我国企业应该尽早接受。例如，《UNIDROIT 国际商事合同通则》，是对国际商事合同惯例的成功编纂，正获得越来越多国家的接受，我国企业在国际商事合同实践中也可以更多地将该通则选为合同适用的法律。又如，在海上运输保险领域，各国保险业多采用伦敦保险业协会的 1982 年协会货物条款，我国有的保险公司仍使用 1963 年的协会货物条款，似可吐故纳新。3. 对于那些成熟的示范法，我国在制定相关法律时也应适当借鉴。例如，电子商务本身就要求全球统一或协调的法律规则，UNCITRAL 已制定了关于电子商务、电子签名和国际贷记划拨方面的示范法，我国如果制定相应法律，应充分借鉴这些示范法。

（三）顺应国际商法非国内化的趋势，重新定位国际商事惯例的适用顺位

目前世界各国关于国际商事惯例适用顺位的做法主要有两种，一种将国际商事惯例作为解决国际商事纠纷的辅助法律渊源，只有在国内法没有规定的情况下才适用国际商事惯例。另一种将国际商事惯例作为解决国际商事纠纷的主要法律渊源之一，可以优先于国内民商法的相应规定而适用。前一种做法为瑞士、泰国的民法典所规定，后一种做法为法国、奥地利晚近的判例所支持，也被 CISG 和 UNIDROIT 国际商事合同通则所确认。笔者认为，后一种做法能够体现国际商法的自治性，符合商人的合理期待，反映了国际商法非国内化的趋

---

① 关于经济全球化是否导致法律全球化的问题，学界存在诸多争议。本文作者认为，一般来说，经济全球化不会导致法律全球化，比如，宪法、刑法、民法就不会因为经济全球化而全球化。但国际商法是一个例外。全球化是国际商法的内在要求，经济全球化必然极大地促进和最终成就国际商法的全球化。

势，代表着未来的发展方向，是可取的。

如前所述，我国《民法通则》采取了前一做法，这与国际商法非国内化的趋势是不相适应的。笔者建议，我国在新的《民法典》中应确立国际商事惯例相对于国内法的优先适用顺位。

还需指出的是，目前我国涉外商事审判中，仍然存在部分法官不重视、不了解甚至漠视国际商法的现象，其结果是在本应适用国际商法的情形下不适当地适用了国内法，从而使国际商事主体的合理期待落空。最高人民法院可以考虑通过举办培训班、研讨会和加强涉外商事审判指导等方式逐步解决上述问题。

（四）尊重国际商事仲裁的自治性，加强对国际商事仲裁的支持

我国现行《民事诉讼法》和《仲裁法》总体上是尊重国际商事仲裁的自治性和支持国际商事仲裁的，这符合国际通行做法。我国多数法院在司法实践中，也是本着支持仲裁的原则和态度，尊重当事人的仲裁选择，正确处理涉外或外国仲裁裁决的撤销、承认与执行的。但现行立法和司法实践中也存在一些问题。

在仲裁协议所应具备的内容上，我国《仲裁法》第 16 条和第 18 条否定临时仲裁，否定对仲裁机构约定不明确的仲裁条款的效力。这种过于严格和僵硬的规定，违背了当事人意思自治原则，与国际通行做法不相符合，有必要及时予以修订。对于上述第 16 条和第 18 条的规定，最高人民法院和一些地方法院通过进行较为宽松的解释，已尽量赋予一些内容不明确的仲裁协议以法律效力。但也有一些法院，由于认识上的原因，仍然对上述规定作严格解释，否定了不少内容不明确的仲裁协议的法律效力。

在涉外或外国仲裁裁决的撤销、承认与执行问题上，我国一些法院存在着下列问题：在办案程序上有法不依或者违反法律规定；错误地解释和适用相关法律规定；过于苛严地解释和适用相关法律规定。① 其结果是否定了许多本应予以承认和执行的仲裁裁决的效力，侵害了当事人的合法权益，并在一定程度上损害了我国的国际信誉。这些问题与实体法适用方面的问题一脉相承，也可以采用同样的方法加以逐步解决。

（五）确认国际商法的独立学科地位

目前我国法学界的一般做法是将国际商法作为广义国际经济法的一部分或

---

① 赵健：《国际商事仲裁的司法监督》，法律出版社 2000 年版，第 262～273 页。

作为大国际私法的一部分。但是，这两种做法都有一定的局限性。大国际私法将直接和间接调整国际民商事关系的法律置于一体，可以获得对调整国际商事关系法律的整体认识，但目前还很难逾越各国学者长期以来将国际私法主要视为冲突法这一约定俗成的做法所导致的障碍。广义国际经济法将公法和私法融于一体，可以较为全面地把握企业从事国际商业所面临的各种跨国法律问题，但无法成立一个和谐贯通的学科体系。

如前所述，大致在20世纪60年代，西方国家就基本确立了国际商法学的独立法学部门地位。可以认为，在这些国家，独立法学部门的确定对国际商法的学术积累、人才培养和实务指导都起到了积极作用，这也部分地解释了为什么这些国家能够在世界国际商法学术研究和实务中处于领先地位。我国在和平崛起的过程中，要想在国际商法的制定和实施方面发挥更大的作用，必须加强国际商法的研究，必须尽早确立国际商法学的独立法学部门地位。

笔者在1996年就曾经提出国际法四部门说，认为：除国际公法和国际私法这两个传统的法学部门外，广义国际经济法可以再进一步分为国际经济法和国际商法两个部门。① 可惜至今未引起足够重视。笔者至今仍然认为这种做法在理论上是一种较为科学的划分方法，符合国际学术界的既定做法，应考虑加快实施。

如果暂时无法实施，也还有一种变通的做法，就是继续维持广义国际经济法作为第三国际法学科的地位，但在广义国际经济法中，可以将调整国家间经济关系的狭义国际经济法（也称国际经济管理法，regulatory international economic law）和调整国际商事关系的国际商法（也可以称为国际经济交易法，transactional international economic law）作为两个相对独立的体系来阐述。② 具体地说，国际经济管理法作为上编，讨论WTO法、国际货币基金组织法、世界银行体制、区域贸易协定、巴塞尔协议、双边贸易、投资和税收协定；将国际商法（国际经济交易法）作为下编，阐述和研究国际商事条约和惯例。上编和下编各有自己的总论和分论，各有自己的实体法和争端解决程序法。与现有的广义国际经济法教材相比，这种做法能够使学生更加清晰地把握两个相互联系但又有显著区别的法律领域，也将有助于我国国际经济法和国际商法研究在各自领域的细化和积累。

---

① 左海聪：《论国际法部门的划分》，载《中国国际私法与比较法年刊》1998年卷。

② 将国际经济法分为 transactional international economic law 和 regulatory international economic law 是美国著名国际经济法学家 John H. Jackson 教授的提法。See John H. Jackson, *Global Economics and International Economic Law*, *Journal of International Economic Law* (1998), Vol. 1, pp. 8-9.